CHECKS
for VETS

**A Guidebook
to Help Wartime Service Veterans
and Their Surviving Spouses
Receive VA Pensions
to Pay for Long-Term Care**

★

*Contains samples of all the forms you need
and tips for successfully filing a claim
for an Aid and Attendance or Housebound pension*

★

JOSEPH SCOTT MCCARTHY

D1472189

PENNSYLVANIA

Jourda Publishing
511 Towne Square Way
Pittsburgh, PA 15227
http://www.checksforvets.com

The opinions and ideas expressed in this book are those of the author and do not represent the views of the Department of Veterans Affairs, any other governmental agency, or any other party.

This book is designed as a guide to provide information and is sold with the understanding that the publisher and author are not engaged in rendering legal or other professional services. If legal or other expert assistance is required, a competent professional should be consulted.

Every effort has been made to make this book as accurate as possible; however, this book should be used only as a general guide and not the sole source of information. The information contained within should always be verified and is current only up to the printing date.

The author and publisher shall have neither liability nor responsibility to any person or entity with respect to any loss or damage caused or alleged to have been caused, directly or indirectly, by the information contained in this book. The author and publisher are not responsible for pension benefit denials.

Publisher's Cataloging-in-Publication Data

McCarthy, Joseph Scott.
    Checks for vets : a guidebook to help wartime service veterans and their surviving spouses receive VA pensions to pay for long-term care / Joseph Scott McCarthy.
        p. cm.
    Includes index.
    LCCN 2009922568
    ISBN-13: 978-0-9820351-2-2
    ISBN-10: 0-9820351-2-8
    1. Veterans—Services for—United States—Handbooks, manuals, etc. 2. Veterans' families—Services for—United States—Handbooks, manuals, etc. 3. Military pensions—United States—Handbooks, manuals, etc. 4. United States—Armed Forces—Pay, allowances, etc.—Handbooks, manuals, etc.   I. Title.
    UB357.M33 2009   362.86'0973
                    QBI09-600065
First Edition

Cover photograph provided courtesy of
National Archives and Records Administration
Signal Corps Photo October 1949

Concept by History Link 101

For my father's memory
and to all veterans who served.

For Joanne, the love
and inspiration of my life.

TABLE OF CONTENTS

List of Illustrations vii

Preface ix

Acknowledgments xiii

Introduction xv

Chapter 1: VA Pensions and Benefits:
Past, Present, and Future 1

Chapter 2: Aid and Attendance and Housebound Pensions:
Overview of Eligibility 7

Chapter 3: Aid and Attendance and Housebound Pensions:
The Nuts and Bolts of Eligibility. 11

Chapter 4: Understanding Pension Rates:
How Much Money Can You Expect to Get? 25

Chapter 5: Starting the Application Process:
Steps to Submit a Claim. 29

Chapter 6: Filing an Informal Claim:
Avoid Delays and Save Thousands of Dollars. 33

Chapter 7: Discharge Record:
How to Identify and Locate This Document 39

Chapter 8: Aid and Attendance and Housebound Pensions: Sample Application Forms and Tips on Completing the Forms 51

Chapter 9: Pharmacy and Other Health Benefits: Free Healthcare for Aid and Attendance and Housebound Pension Recipients 99

Epilogue 105

Appendix 1: Veterans Service Organizations and VA Facilities 107

American Legion 108

National Association of County Veteran Service Officers 115

Disabled American Veterans 116

Veterans of Foreign Wars of the United States 125

VA Facilities 132

Appendix 2: Additional VA Benefits and Services 187

Aid and Attendance Benefits for the Spouse of a Veteran Receiving Service-Connected Disability Compensation . . 188

Pharmacy Benefits for All Eligible Veterans: Discounted Prescription Medications 189

Requesting Replacement Medals, Awards, and Decorations 190

Notes 197

Glossary 201

Index 207

About the Author 217

LIST OF ILLUSTRATIONS

Figures

6.1   Sample Form 21-4138: Statement in Support of Claim
(informal claim for a veteran) 35

6.2   Sample Form 21-4138: Statement in Support of Claim
(informal claim for a surviving spouse) 36

6.3   Sample Form 21-22: Appointment of Veterans Service
Organization as Claimant's Representative 37

7.1   Sample discharge record 40

7.2   Sample Standard Form 180 (SF 180):
Request Pertaining to Military Records. 46–47

7.3   Sample Letter to the NPRC
requesting a discharge record 48

8.1   Sample Form 21-2680: Examination for Housebound
Status or Permanent Need for Regular Aid
and Attendance 56–57

8.2   Sample Form 21-4138: Statement in Support of Claim. 59

8.3   Sample Letter from Provider 60

8.4   Sample Form 21-526: Veteran's Application
          for Compensation and/or Pension .65–78

8.5   Sample Form 21-534: Application for Dependency and
          Indemnity Compensation, Death Pension and Accrued
          Benefits by a Surviving Spouse or Child 83–90

8.6   Sample Form 21-8416: Medical Expense Report 92–93

8.7   Sample Form 21-22: Appointment of Veterans Service
          Organization as Claimant's Representative 96

9.1   Sample Form 10-10EZ: Application
          for Health Benefits 101–103

A.1   Sample Standard Form 180 (SF 180): Request
          Pertaining to Military Records 192

Tables
A.1   Disability compensation rates for 2009 188

PREFACE

For more than eight years I have helped thousands of eligible wartime service veterans and their surviving spouses obtain Aid and Attendance and Housebound pensions to help pay for long-term care. Many veterans, their surviving spouses, and professionals who work with them have told me that they were frustrated because information from the VA explaining how to apply for these pensions was confusing and located in many different reference sources. They have asked for a comprehensive guidebook that explains these pensions, helps them determine their eligibility, lets them know where to locate the records they will need, explains how to obtain the right application forms, and shows how to complete the forms. Therefore, this book focuses on how to qualify for and file for Aid and Attendance and Housebound pensions.

Imagine that you have just made the agonizing decision to move your eighty-one-year-old father into an assisted living facility because he can no longer care for himself due to being disabled. He is an honorably discharged veteran of World War II who has no dependents. Care in an assisted living facility will cost approximately $3,000 per month. Your father has a total income of $1,400 per month from Social Security and interest. He has assets of $60,000 from savings and certificates of deposit (CDs), and he has no debts; his net worth is $60,000. How will you be able to afford the cost of the assisted living facility? The answer is an Aid and Attendance pension. Because your father is a veteran of World War II who was honorably discharged, has caregiver needs due to his disability, has a net worth of less than $80,000, and meets the income requirements, he is eligible to receive a pension check for $1,644 per month from the Department of Veterans Affairs (VA) Aid and Attendance pension. Combining the $1,400 per month income from Social Security and interest with the $1,644 per month from the VA pension, he will be able to pay the $3,000 monthly cost for care in an assisted living facility. After your father starts to receive the Aid and Attendance pension, he will also be eligible to receive free medications from a VA mail-order pharmacy.

Surviving spouses of wartime service veterans are also eligible for this pension; however, they are not eligible for free medications.

For example, your eighty-two-year-old mother is a surviving spouse of a veteran of the Korean War who was honorably discharged. Your mother never remarried and has no dependents. She is now in need of a caregiver who will come to her home to help bathe, dress, and prepare meals for her due to her disability. This service will cost $2,000 per month. Your mother has $40,000 in assets from CDs and savings. Her combined income from Social Security, interest, and a pension from her late husband's former employer is $1,100. Since her deceased husband was an honorably discharged veteran, she has caregiver needs due to her disability, she has a low net worth, and she meets the income requirements, she is eligible to receive an Aid and Attendance pension check for $1,056 monthly. Combining the VA money with her Social Security, interest, and late husband's work pension, she has a total income of $2,156 per month. This amount would pay for the home-care service. Since she needs to use her savings to pay other bills such as pharmacy, food, and property taxes, the availability of the VA pension is the "difference maker" in terms of her ability to remain in her own home.

Another type of pension provided by the VA is the Housebound pension. It is available to veterans and their surviving spouses who have low income, low net worth, and are confined to their homes due to a permanent disability.

To receive Aid and Attendance and Housebound pensions, you must be a wartime service veteran or the surviving spouse or surviving dependent child of a wartime service veteran. Unlike other VA programs for which, to receive benefits, you must prove you were war wounded or injured in an accident while in uniform, the Aid and Attendance and Housebound pensions do not require that a veteran served in combat. You could have served stateside during World War II, for example, and still qualify.

Many wartime service vets and their surviving spouses live alone and do not eat well because they have difficulty cooking for themselves. In my work with veterans as an admissions and marketing director for assisted living facilities, I have met many who are living in less-than-optimal conditions. Many need help with activities of daily living (ADL), like bathing, dressing, and remembering to take medications that are critically important to their health, such as blood thinning and blood pressure medications; they frequently need to be hospitalized because of inconsistent self-administration of medications. Many are confined to their homes because of a permanent disability and need transportation services. Aid and Attendance and Housebound pensions help pay for the ADL care and transportation services that they need.

A veteran service officer for the American Legion once said that most people operate on minutes and hours; the VA operates on months. In other words, if you make even a trivial mistake on your application, it may be returned to you for corrective action, and you may lose a month or more in the claim process. If you submit a claim that is complete and error free and you are eligible for a pension, the VA can approve your claim faster; this means that you may save thousands of dollars in out-of-pocket costs for medical expenses, such as assisted living and nonmedical home care, because you will receive your pension check sooner. This book will help you understand the pension eligibility requirements and how to file your claim accurately.

While submitting an error-free claim can shorten your claim process, there will still be a waiting period before your claim can be approved. The waiting period for pension approval is different in each state and is dependent on a number of factors, including the retirement of significant numbers of VA regional office employees; the number of responsibilities placed on the regional office, such as processing foreign country claims; and whether the regional office sends its claims to other offices for processing. The waiting period also varies according to the backlog of claims the VA is processing. However, once the VA determines that you are eligible to receive a pension, the check you receive will contain a lump sum amount retroactive to the first of the month after your application date.

The best way to honor our heroic veterans is to put checks in their pockets, or in the pockets of their surviving spouses, to enable them to lead a dignified retirement life. The Aid and Attendance and Housebound pensions are one such way to honor veterans and their surviving spouses.

The information contained in *Checks for Vets* was obtained from my personal experience, VA pamphlets and Web sites, VA and veterans service organization personnel, and countless veterans and their families.

ACKNOWLEDGMENTS

I wish to thank the friends at the American Legion, local County Veteran Service Offices, National Personnel Records Center, and Department of Veterans Affairs. Without their gracious assistance, this book would not be possible. Of special note, this book has been reviewed by the American Legion National in Washington, DC.

I owe a huge debt of gratitude to my wife, Joanne, because this book would not be possible without her tremendous effort. She took my very rough, disorganized first draft and, as my developmental editor, turned it into a workable manuscript. She also graced this endeavor with her enthusiastic support, thorough research of reference sources, and countless editing revisions.

Additionally, I would like to thank my son, David, and daughter, Laura, who provided ideas and support. I also extend many thanks to Barbara Flanagan for her initial review of the content for clarity.

Special thanks go to my team of literary professionals headed by Sharon Goldinger, editor and consultant. Thank you for your guidance, expertise, and support. Peri Poloni-Gabriel provided the cover design, and Sue Knopf was responsible for interior design. Both did a wonderful job of crafting an attractive guidebook.

I also acknowledge the invaluable mentoring provided by David Laman, M.D. and the professional assistance of Ellen Spain, Ph.D. and the members of Pennwriters' Pittsburgh East Writers Group.

INTRODUCTION

When most people think of VA benefits, they think of the GI Bill, which helps with college tuition reimbursement, or the VA Home Loan program, which helps finance a home. Most people are aware of the VA health system for veteran healthcare needs, and it would be unthinkable to bury a veteran without a cemetery marker because the VA can provide one at no cost. However, veterans and family members are often unaware that the VA offers Aid and Attendance and Housebound pensions, which help pay for care in an assisted living facility, caregivers in the home, and transportation services.

Aid and Attendance and Housebound pensions are *non-service-connected pensions*, which are for veterans whose disability or death was not caused by or aggravated in the line of duty in the active military. These pensions are not to be confused with VA service-connected disability compensation payments, which are for veterans whose disability was caused by an illness or combat-related injury while in the line of duty in the active military; the compensation paid is proportional to the degree of disability. A veteran may not receive a non-service-connected pension and a service-connected disability compensation payment at the same time. If a veteran believes he or she meets the eligibility requirements for both a pension and disability compensation, the veteran should apply for both. If the VA determines that the veteran is qualified for only one of these benefits, the VA will pay the appropriate benefit. If the VA determines that the veteran is qualified for both benefits, the VA will pay the higher-rate benefit. Note: VA terminology can be confusing at times, but this book explains VA terms so that they are easier to understand. Be sure to consult the glossary if you are unsure of a term.

Aid and Attendance and Housebound pensions are available to wartime service vets, their surviving spouses, and their surviving dependent children who meet the eligibility rules. This book, however, *addresses only eligible wartime service vets and their surviving spouses,* as in my experience they are the main recipients of these pensions. In general, wartime service vets and their surviving spouses who are disabled, have a low net income, and who have a net worth of less than $80,000 meet the eligibility criteria for either an Aid and Attendance pension or a Housebound pension. Chapter 3 provides a detailed explanation of net income and net worth. In my years of experience working with wartime service vets and their surviving spouses, I have found that a great majority qualify for these pensions and never knew these programs existed.

Checks for Vets provides a historical perspective of VA pensions and benefits, discusses eligibility, describes the care-needs qualifications of these pensions, explains wartime service, and lists special circumstances related to eligibility. It presents information on pension rates so you know how much money you can expect to receive and summarizes the pension application process. You will find step-by-step instructions on how to file for pension benefits and how to file an informal claim if you do not yet have all the information and documents necessary to make a formal application. You will learn how to identify and locate discharge records which you'll need in order to file a claim. In addition, sample forms and tips for successful completion of forms are provided to help minimize errors. Please note that the forms and URLs included in this book were correct at the time of publication and that the forms may be revised at any time. Readers should check the VA Web site or with the agencies mentioned to obtain the most recent version of the forms.

Veterans and their surviving spouses have different eligibility requirements and pension rates, and they need different information to complete some forms. You will find an explanation of these differences and how they apply to either the veteran's or surviving spouse's claim.

Veterans receiving Aid and Attendance and Housebound pensions are eligible to receive free pharmacy and other health benefits. The cost of prescription medications is often as much of a concern as paying for caregivers. In chapter 9, you will find information explaining the application procedure for receiving pharmacy and other health benefits.

Appendix 1 provides contact information for VA facilities and veterans service organizations. This information was current at the time of publication; readers should check with the agencies mentioned to verify the contact information. Personnel at these offices will help you apply for pension benefits. Veterans service organization personnel will also check all your forms before you file your application with the VA to make sure they are error free, which will help to expedite your claim process.

Through my work with veterans, I have come across many who were not eligible to receive Aid and Attendance and Housebound pensions but were eligible to receive discounted VA prescription medications. Information about these additional pharmacy benefits can be found in appendix 2.

When helping veterans obtain pensions, I enjoy hearing firsthand accounts of heroic service, which often resulted in the vets' earning of medals and citations. Many veterans mention that they have lost their decorations and wish they had them. Therefore, appendix 2 also includes information on how to apply for replacement medals and decorations.

Maximizing the potential of these benefit programs can be accomplished only by educating healthcare, legal, and financial professionals—and the public at large. Key people who can benefit from this information are admissions directors at assisted living facilities; nonmedical home-care provider administrators; independent living administrators; elder law attorneys advising clients on estate planning; social workers discharging hospital patients; financial planners providing options on how to pay for long-term care; people with power of attorney; guardians; and, of course, wartime service veterans, their surviving spouses, and family members assisting them.

The more that veterans and their surviving spouses know about these pensions, the easier it will be for them to receive the money that they deserve. By using the tips, examples, and resources provided in *Checks for Vets,* qualified persons will be able to receive their benefits in a timely manner.

1

VA Pensions and Benefits:
Past, Present, and Future

Many veterans and their surviving spouses ask if they can count on pensions from the Department of Veterans Affairs (VA) being available in the years to come. While there are certainly no guarantees, you can reason that Congress would face much backlash if it decided to rescind veteran pension benefits.

Pensions can be traced back to the birth of the country when the Pilgrims authorized legislation that provided support for any soldier injured in the defense of the colony. The first law in the colonies on pensions, enacted in 1636 by Plymouth, provided money to those disabled in the colony's defense against Indians. Other colonies followed Plymouth's example.[1]

During the Revolutionary War, the 1776 Continental Congress encouraged enlistments by instituting pensions for its disabled soldiers. It granted half pay for life in cases of serious disability. Because the Continental Congress lacked the authority and the money to make the pension payments, the payments were made by the individual states. In 1789, with the ratification of the U.S. Constitution, the first Congress assumed the burden of paying veterans' benefits. The first federal pension legislation was passed in 1789.

By 1816, pensioners numbered 2,200. In that year the growing cost of living and a surplus in the U.S. Treasury led Congress to raise allowances for all disabled veterans and to grant half-pay pensions for five years to widows and orphans of soldiers of the War of 1812. A new principle for veterans' benefits, providing pensions on the basis of need rather than on disability, was introduced in the 1818 Service Pension Law. The law provided that every person who had served in the War for Independence and was in need of assistance would receive a fixed pension for life. The rate was $20 per month for officers and $8 per month for enlisted men. In 1858 Congress authorized half-pay pensions to veterans' widows and to their orphaned children up to the age of sixteen.

The General Pension Act of 1862 provided disability payments based on rank and degree of disability and liberalized benefits for veterans' widows, children, and dependent relatives. The law covered military service in time of peace as well as during the Civil War. In President Lincoln's second inaugural address in 1865, he called upon Congress "to care for him who shall have borne the battle and for his widow and his orphan." This quote was later adopted as the VA's motto.

The Consolidation Act in 1873 revised pension legislation, with payments based only on a veteran's degree of disability. The act also began the Aid and Attendance program, in which a disabled veteran could receive payments to hire a nurse or housekeeper.

The first important pension law in the twentieth century was the Sherwood Act of 1912. Under this act, veterans of the Mexican War and Union veterans of the Civil War could receive pensions automatically at age sixty-two, regardless of whether they were sick or disabled. As a result, the record shows that of the 429,354 Civil War veterans receiving pensions in 1914, only 52,572 were disabled.

After December 24, 1919, all payments to veterans arising from disability or death from World War I were regarded as compensation rather than pensions. From 1924 to 1932 an expansion and liberalization of benefits for veterans resulted in a 62 percent increase in expenditures for veterans. In March 1933, all payments to veterans were again regarded as pensions. It was not until World War II that the distinction between compensation and pension again was made.

During the Great Depression, the lack of jobs and savings made survival for veterans perilous. On May 19, 1924, Congress intervened by passing the World War Adjustment Compensation Act. The act provided a bonus to

World War I veterans based on the length and location of their service: $1 for each day served in the United States and $1.25 for each day served overseas. However, the catch was that veterans who were authorized bonuses of more than $50, were not paid immediately. Instead, they were issued adjusted service certificates from the Veterans' Bureau. These certificates were a form of endowment policy payable twenty years from the date of issue and generally had a face value of $1,500. As the Depression worsened, veterans began calling for immediate payment of the "bonuses," as the certificates came to be called. In March 1932, a small group of desperate veterans from Oregon began marching to Washington, DC. Word of the march spread and unemployed veterans from across the country descended on the nation's capital. In June, with an estimated 15,000 to 40,000 veterans and their families camped out in Washington, DC, health officials grew concerned about the threat of disease. In response, on June 11, 1932, the newly created Veterans Administration (VA) established an emergency hospital at Fort Hunt, Virginia, to treat the marchers. On June 17, a large group of marchers laid siege to the U.S. Capitol, where the Senate was considering a bill proposing immediate payment of the bonuses. The bill was overwhelmingly defeated, and frustrations mounted as the summer wore on. A riot ensued in July when city police officers and government agents tried to evict some of the marchers. President Hoover eventually ordered the army to forcibly remove from the city about 3,500 veterans, many with their wives and children, who refused to leave. Although the marchers failed to get immediate results, in 1936 Congress authorized early payment of the bonuses.

The bonus march of 1932 revealed serious shortcomings in how America cared for its defenders as they made the transition from military to civilian life. The march set the stage for Congress to address the problem in the future. In 1944, Congress addressed World War II veterans returning to civilian life by passing one of the most significant pieces of legislation ever produced by the federal government: the Servicemen's Readjustment Act, commonly known as the GI Bill of Rights. This legislation provided up to four years of education, federally guaranteed home or business loans, and unemployment compensation. Assistance acts were subsequently passed for the benefit of veterans from the Korean War, the Vietnam War, the Persian Gulf War, and the All-Volunteer Force.

In the early 1950s, the Korean War created new veterans on top of the millions who came home from World War II; each month 2.5 million veterans and dependents received $125 million in compensation and pensions. Following a study of pensions, the VA in 1959 introduced a sliding scale of pension payments based on a recipient's income, rather than a flat-rate pension. The Veterans' Pension Act of 1959 also specified that anyone already on the pension rolls as of June 30, 1960, could elect to remain under the old law.

The Vietnam War resulted in more than 7 million Vietnam-era veterans. A major difference between Vietnam-era veterans and veterans of earlier wars was the larger percentage of disabled. One of the ways Congress assisted the disabled was to provide the 1971 Veterans' Mortgage Life Insurance program.

The number of veterans eligible for pensions grew rapidly between 1960 and 1978. World War II veterans were reaching age sixty-five, when veterans could be classified as totally disabled by virtue of their age alone. To address the escalating cost of pensions, Congress in 1978 passed the Veterans' and Survivors' Pension Improvement Act. Earlier law excluded from consideration the earned income of a veteran's spouse. The 1978 law mandated that all family and retirement income be counted in determining a veteran's eligibility for pensions and the amount paid. Under the new law, most World War II veterans would not be entitled to pensions because all family income had to be counted. The change resulted in a large reduction in the number of veterans qualifying for pensions.

The 1980s saw some streamlining of benefits by Congress. A minimum service requirement was introduced. Veterans who had enlisted after September 7, 1980, and officers who were commissioned or who entered active military service after October 16, 1981, must have completed two years of duty or the full period of their initial service obligation to be eligible for most VA benefits.

In the late 1980s, proponents seeking cabinet-level status for the VA pointed out that the VA was the largest independent federal agency in terms of budget. Because one-third of the U.S. population was eligible for veterans' benefits, proponents argued, the agency responsible for veterans should be represented by a cabinet secretary having direct access to the president. In response, President Reagan signed legislation in 1988 to elevate the VA to cabinet status, and on March 15, 1989, the Veterans Administration became the Department of Veterans Affairs.

The Omnibus Budget Reconciliation Act of 1990 limited eligibility for disability pensions. Previously, low-income wartime veterans over age sixty-five had been automatically classified as disabled. The new law, applying to claims filed after October 1990, required that to be classified as totally disabled, a veteran of any age had to be considered unemployable as a result of a disability that was reasonably certain to continue throughout the life of the disabled person seeking the pension.

In 1991, Congress passed the Persian Gulf Conflict Supplemental Authorization and Personnel Benefits Act, which considered the conflict a war in terms of determining a veteran's eligibility for wartime-only pensions.

In response to the increased number of female veterans, the VA informed these women that they were equally entitled to veterans' benefits. The Veterans Health Care Act of 1992 provided gender-specific services and programs to care for female veterans.

In 1994, the Center for Minority Veterans was authorized by Congress. The center not only promotes the use of existing programs by minority veterans but also proposes new benefits and services to meet the specific needs of minority veterans.

Of the 23.8 million veterans alive at the beginning of 2008, most served during a period of war. There were also 37 million dependents of living veterans and survivors of deceased veterans, representing 20 percent of the population. In 2007, the VA provided compensation and pension benefits to over 3.7 million veterans and beneficiaries. The VA paid average annual amounts of $8,509 in pension benefits to veterans and $3,829 in death pension benefits to survivors of deceased veterans.[2]

2

AID AND ATTENDANCE AND HOUSEBOUND PENSIONS: OVERVIEW OF ELIGIBILITY

Before you fill out any claim forms and apply for benefits, you should be aware of the eligibility requirements that you must meet to receive a pension. The VA has three levels of pensions for veterans and their surviving spouses, ranging from basic pensions at the lowest level, Housebound pensions at the next level, and Aid and Attendance pensions at the highest level. Aid and Attendance and Housebound pensions are benefits paid in addition to the basic pension; you cannot get the higher levels of pension benefits without meeting the basic pension eligibility criteria. The Aid and Attendance and Housebound pension eligibility criteria for wartime service veterans and their surviving spouses, outlined in this chapter, incorporate the basic pension eligibility criteria.

ELIGIBILITY CRITERIA FOR WARTIME SERVICE VETERANS

If you are a wartime service veteran, you may be entitled to receive an Aid and Attendance pension or a Housebound pension if you meet the following eligibility requirements:

1. Annual family net income (income minus expenses) is below a yearly limit set by law. Effective December 1, 2008, the annual net income limits are as follows (see chapter 3 for further explanation of net income):

   a. Aid and Attendance pension
      i. Wartime service veteran with no dependents: below $19,736
      ii. Wartime service veteran with one dependent: below $23,396

   b. Housebound pension
      i. Wartime service veteran with no dependents: below $14,457
      ii. Wartime service veteran with one dependent: below $18,120

   Note: A veteran with one dependent is usually a veteran living with a spouse.

2. No set limit has been established on how much net worth (assets minus debts) a wartime service veteran and his or her dependents can have, but net worth cannot be excessive. Generally, net worth must be less than $80,000. (Assets do not include one's primary home and first car.) The decision as to whether net worth is excessive depends on the facts of each individual case. (See chapter 3 for further explanation of net worth.)

3. A wartime service veteran must be permanently and totally disabled. For VA pension purposes, *permanent and total disability* means that with reasonable certainty the veteran will not be able to maintain a substantially gainful job due to his or her disability. The disability must be non-service-connected and not due to willful misconduct. *Non-service-connected* means that the disability must not have been caused or aggravated by military service.

4. The veteran must have care-needs requirements. To meet these requirements, a veteran typically receives care in an assisted living facility or receives nonmedical home-care services. A physician must

document the need for these caregiver services. (See chapter 3 for further explanation of care-needs qualifications.)

5. The veteran must have had ninety days or more of active military service, at least one day of which was served during official wartime. To have served during wartime, the veteran did not need to see combat. For example, the veteran may have served in Alaska and still be eligible. (See chapter 3 for details of wartime service.)

   Note: Veterans who entered active duty after September 7, 1980, generally must have served twenty-four months or the full period for which called or ordered to active duty. There are exceptions to this rule; check with a veteran service officer (VSO) for details.

6. The veteran's discharge must be honorable or general and not be due to willful misconduct.[1]

ELIGIBILITY CRITERIA FOR SURVIVING SPOUSES OF WARTIME SERVICE VETERANS

If you are a surviving spouse of a deceased wartime service veteran, you may be entitled to receive an Aid and Attendance pension or a Housebound pension if you meet the following eligibility requirements:

1. Annual family net income (income minus expenses) is below a yearly limit set by law. Effective December 1, 2008, the annual net income limits are as follows (see chapter 3 for further explanation of net income):

   a. Aid and Attendance pension—Surviving spouse of a wartime service vet with no dependents: below $12,681

   b. Housebound pension—Surviving spouse of a wartime service vet with no dependents: below $9,696

   Note: A surviving spouse does not usually have any dependents.

2. No set limit has been established on how much net worth (assets minus debts) a surviving spouse of a wartime service veteran can have, but net worth cannot be excessive. Generally, net worth must be less than $80,000. (Assets do not include one's primary home and first car.) The decision as to whether net worth is excessive depends on the facts of each individual case. (See chapter 3 for further explanation of net worth.)

3. The surviving spouse of a wartime service veteran must be permanently and totally disabled. For VA pension purposes, *permanent and total disability* means that with reasonable certainty the surviving spouse will not be able to maintain a substantially gainful job due to his or her disability.

4. The surviving spouse must have care-needs requirements. To meet these requirements, a surviving spouse typically receives care in an assisted living facility or receives nonmedical home-care services. A physician must document the need for these caregiver services. (See chapter 3 for further explanation of care-needs qualifications.)

5. The spouse must have been married to the wartime service veteran for at least one year before the veteran's death (unless they had a child). *A person who has divorced a wartime service veteran is not considered a surviving spouse of a wartime service veteran and cannot claim benefits.*

6. The deceased wartime service veteran also must have met the following requirements:

    a. The vet must have had ninety days or more of active military service, at least one day of which was served during official wartime. To have served during wartime, the veteran did not need to see combat. For example, the veteran may have served in Alaska and still be eligible. (See chapter 3 for details of wartime service.)

        Note: Veterans who entered active duty on or after September 7, 1980, generally must have served twenty-four months or the full period for which called or ordered to active duty. There are exceptions to this rule; check with a VSO for details.

    b. The veteran's discharge must have been honorable or general and not have been due to willful misconduct.

    c. The veteran's death must not have been due to a disability from the veteran's active military service. A disability not due to active military service is called a *non-service-connected disability*.[2]

Aid and Attendance and Housebound Pensions: The Nuts and Bolts of Eligibility

Now that you have an overview of who is eligible to receive a pension, the next step is to learn the details of the eligibility qualifications.

NET INCOME

An important part of eligibility is meeting the net income requirements. Countable income minus eligible expenses equals net income. The following definitions and examples explain how the VA determines your net income.

Income (Often Referred to as Countable Income by the VA)

VA pensions are for wartime service veterans and their surviving spouses with limited income. It is important to understand what the VA considers countable income. Generally speaking, countable income is income that is regular, irregular, or nonrecurring (received on a one-time basis) and does not meet an income exclusion. *When completing an application form, be sure to report all income.* The VA will determine which income to include and which income to exclude when processing your request for benefits. Once a pension is granted, the VA will send an annual letter to the wartime service veteran or the surviving spouse, checking whether any of the income has changed since the claim was filed. The VA can also check reported income claimed on the annual IRS tax return of the wartime service veteran or the surviving spouse.

Common Sources of Countable Income

Examples of income that the VA includes in countable income are as follows:

- ▶ Salary (the gross amount of wages before any deductions are made for taxes, Social Security, insurance, etc.).

- ▶ Dividends and interest.

- ▶ Income from property that has a recorded deed. If the property is owned jointly, the income of the various owners is determined in proportion to shares of ownership of the property.

- ▶ Installment income. Installment income is determined according to the amount received or anticipated during a twelve-month annualized period.

- ▶ Social Security and U.S. Railroad Retirement Board income.

- ▶ Military retirement pay.

- ▶ Incomes of a dependent spouse and children.

- ▶ Insurance dividends.

- ▶ Jury duty pay.

- ▶ Black lung benefits.

- ▶ Income from workers' compensation and unemployment compensation programs.[1]

Common Exclusions from Countable Income

Examples of income that you should report but the VA excludes from countable income are as follows:

- ▶ Welfare.

- ▶ Supplemental Security Income (SSI) from Social Security.

- ▶ VA pension benefits.

- ▶ Reimbursement for a casualty loss.

- ▶ Profit from the sale of property.

► Cash surrender value of life insurance.

► Wages earned by dependent children that do not exceed the sum of (1) the lowest amount of gross income for which a federal income tax return must be filed and (2) the amount paid by the children for postsecondary educational expenses.[2]

Note: The above are not all-inclusive lists of countable income and exclusions from countable income. Check with a VSO if you have questions regarding countable income.

Expenses Deducted from Income

When completing an application form, be sure to report all appropriate expenses as they reduce net income. Types of expenses to report are as follows:

► Medical expenses *not reimbursed by another payer.* Be sure to include unreimbursed money you paid to an assisted living or nonmedical home-care provider because of impaired health.

► Expenses related to last illnesses, burials, and just debts. (Contact a VSO for details of these expenses.)[3]

Typically, eligible expenses are unreimbursed medical expenses. However, only a portion of unreimbursed medical expenses will be deducted from your income. (To be deducted, unreimbursed medical expenses must exceed 5 percent of the maximum annual pension rate [MAPR]; the VA will calculate the appropriate amount of medical expenses to deduct from your income.)

Net income, not gross income, is the deciding factor for pension eligibility. If the wartime service veteran or the surviving spouse has a net income that is zero or negative, then he or she is entitled to the full pension rate. If the wartime service veteran or the surviving spouse has a positive net income (more countable income than allowable expenses), then he or she will receive a reduced pension rate. The pension will be reduced dollar for dollar by the amount of positive net income. (See chapter 4 for Aid and Attendance and Housebound pension annual rates.)

Unreimbursed medical expenses (such as those you pay for assisted living, nonmedical home care, health insurance, medications, or transportation services) will offset income, and these costs should be listed in their entirety.

Many people have not gotten the full pension because they did not list *all of their unreimbursed medical expenses*, such as the full cost of assisted living.

Examples of How the VA Calculates Net Income

This section includes three examples of how the VA might calculate your net income.

Example 1 (based on 2009 pension rates):

You are a widowed wartime service veteran without dependents, are disabled, and have caregiver needs. You have a net worth of $20,000; a monthly income from Social Security, a work pension, and interest equal to $2,000; and combined out-of-pocket monthly medical expenses from assisted living, health insurance premiums, and medications equal to $3,000. After the VA subtracts 5 percent of the MAPR, your deductible medical expenses equal $2,950, so your approximate net monthly income for VA purposes is negative $950. Because you are disabled, have a low net worth, and have a negative net income, the Aid and Attendance maximum rate of $1,644 will be paid monthly to you. Note: VA calculations of net monthly income may vary slightly from those in this example due to rounding. (This example was used to fill in sample Forms 21-526 and 21-8416 in chapter 8.)

Example 2 (based on 2009 pension rates):

You are a wartime service veteran without dependents, are disabled, and have caregiver needs. You have a net worth of $55,000; a monthly income from Social Security, a work pension, and interest equal to $2,000; but only $1,500 in out-of-pocket monthly medical expenses. After the VA subtracts 5 percent of the MAPR, your deductible medical expenses equal $1,450, so your approximate net monthly income is positive $550. Because you are disabled, have a low net worth, and have a net monthly income below the income limit, you are still entitled to a pension, but it will not be the maximum amount. Since you have a positive net income, the pension will be reduced by the amount over zero net income. In this case, you would get approximately $1,094 monthly from the VA ($1,644 Aid and Attendance pension minus $550 net income). Note: VA calculations of net monthly income may vary slightly from those in this example due to rounding.

Example 3 (based on 2009 pension rates):

You are a surviving spouse of a wartime service veteran without dependents, are disabled, and have caregiver needs. You have a net worth of $20,000; a monthly income from Social Security and interest equal to $1,200; and combined out-of-pocket monthly medical expenses from nonmedical home care, health insurance premiums, and medications equal to $1,371. After the VA subtracts 5 percent of the MAPR, your deductible medical expenses equal $1,337, so your approximate net monthly income for VA purposes is negative $137. Because you are disabled, have a low net worth, and a negative net income, the Aid and Attendance maximum rate of $1,056 will be paid monthly to you. Note: VA calculations of net monthly income may vary slightly from those in this example due to rounding. (This example was used to fill in sample Form 21-534 in chapter 8.)

NET WORTH

Meeting the net worth threshold is another eligibility requirement. The following definitions and examples explain how the VA determines your net worth.

The VA defines *net worth* as the market value of all real and personal property less mortgages or other claims against the property: the value of assets minus the value of debts. Net worth does not include the house you live in or a reasonable area of land it sits on.[4] Net worth also does not include the value of personal items you use every day, like your clothing, furniture, and vehicle. (You are allowed to exclude only one car when reporting net worth.) When reporting net worth, be sure to subtract the amount owed for any asset. For example, if you own a second car, subtract from the resale value what is owed to get the net worth of the second car.

> **Example:**
> You are a veteran who owns a home and a car, has two certificates of deposit (CDs) worth $30,000 each, and has $15,000 in a savings account. Your home and car are not counted when figuring your net worth. For VA pension purposes, your net worth equals $75,000, the value of your two CDs and savings account.

The net worth of the wartime service veteran or the surviving spouse cannot be excessive. The decision as to whether a claimant's net worth is excessive depends on the facts of each individual case. The VA's needs-based programs are not intended to protect substantial assets or build up an estate for the benefit of heirs.[5] Generally, the net worth threshold is $80,000. However, in 2006, the VA introduced a life-expectancy calculation into the pension approval process related to net worth. Using life-expectancy tables, the VA may approve a pension for a wartime service veteran or the surviving spouse with a net worth that is higher than $80,000; the VA may also deny a pension when the net worth is less than $80,000. In my experience of working with wartime service veterans and their surviving spouses, most have a net worth that is under the VA-determined threshold.

Unlike some other government programs, the VA does not look back three to five years or more when determining net worth eligibility for Aid and Attendance and Housebound pensions. You may want to get advice from an elder law attorney or financial planner about how to meet the net worth threshold.

Wartime service veterans or their surviving spouses with a net worth greater than the threshold determined by the VA are asked to spend down to the threshold before being granted a pension. The VA allows you to spend down assets during the approval process. A common way of spending down to the threshold is withdrawing from one's assets to pay for assisted living or nonmedical home-care costs. The net worth that you have at the time of approval is what counts, not the net worth that you had at the time of application. For questions about net worth eligibility, contact a VSO.

If the net worth of the wartime service veteran or the surviving spouse exceeds the threshold when the pension is awarded, the pension will be forfeited until the person's net worth falls below the threshold.

Examples of assets that contribute toward net worth are as follows:

- ► Stocks and bonds
- ► Mutual funds
- ► CDs
- ► Individual retirement accounts (IRAs) and 401(k) accounts
- ► Savings accounts
- ► Coin and stamp collections
- ► Second car
- ► Real estate other than your primary home and the reasonable area of land that it sits on
- ► Vacation homes, including timeshare properties
- ► Cash, including bank accounts[6]

Note: The preceding is not an all-inclusive list of assets. Check with a VSO if you have questions regarding assets.

CARE-NEEDS QUALIFICATIONS

Another eligibility criterion is that you must have care needs. Typically, a disabled veteran or surviving spouse meets the care-needs qualification by receiving care in an assisted living facility or by receiving nonmedical home-care services. The following definitions and examples explain how to meet the care-needs qualification.

Aid and Attendance Pension

To meet the care-needs qualification for an Aid and Attendance pension, one of the following conditions must exist:

► The claimant needs the aid of another person to perform personal functions required in activities of daily living (ADL), such as bathing, eating, dressing, remembering to take medication, toileting, adjusting prosthetic devices, or protecting himself or herself from the hazards of his or her daily environment.

► The claimant is bedridden in that his or her disability (or disabilities) requires that he or she remain in bed apart from any prescribed course of convalescence or treatment.

► The claimant is a patient in a nursing home due to mental or physical incapacity.

► The claimant is blind or so nearly blind as to have a corrected visual acuity of 5/200 or less in both eyes or concentric contraction of the visual field of five degrees or less.[7]

Example:
Your sister, a veteran of World War II, is a resident in an assisted living facility and is paying out of pocket for the assisted living costs. She has a permanent disability that renders her unable to perform ADLs, so caregivers at the assisted living facility provide her ADL care such as bathing and medication management. The care she receives at the assisted living facility satisfies the care-needs qualification for Aid and Attendance benefits.

Housebound Pension

To meet the care-needs qualification for a Housebound pension, the claimant must be substantially confined to his or her immediate premises because of a permanent disability.[8]

> **Example:**
> Your sister, a veteran of the Korean War, is a widow, is confined to her home due to a permanent disability, but is able to provide her own ADL care. Because of her disability, she requires oxygen therapy, has difficulty walking for which she uses a wheeled walker, and her physician ordered her driver's license taken away. She is paying out of pocket for transportation services in order to go food shopping and to keep doctors' appointments. Since her disability caused her to lose her driver's license, and she now needs transportation services to leave her home, she satisfies the care-needs qualification for Housebound benefits.

Qualifying for either of these pensions is based on the need for care. You cannot file for Aid and Attendance benefits or Housebound benefits without medical necessity as documented by a physician. A personal physician or a house physician at an assisted living facility will suffice; a VA doctor is not necessary for this documentation. Form 21-2680 is used to document the need for care. (See sample Form 21-2680 in chapter 8.)

WARTIME SERVICE

One of the eligibility requirements for obtaining Aid and Attendance and Housebound benefits is wartime service. This section provides lists of the eligible war periods and special groups that are recognized by the VA as providing active military service.

Wartime Periods

The following are considered official wartime periods:

- ► Mexican Border Period: May 9, 1916, through April 5, 1917, for veterans who served in Mexico, on its borders or in adjacent waters.

- ► World War I: April 6, 1917, through November 11, 1918; for veterans who served with the U.S. in Russia, the ending date is April 1, 1920. Service after November 11, 1918, and before July 2, 1921, is considered World War I service if the veteran was in active service after April 5, 1917, and before November 12, 1918.

▶ World War II: December 7, 1941, through December 31, 1946. If the veteran was in service on December 31, 1946, continuous service before July 26, 1947, is considered World War II service.

▶ Korean War: June 27, 1950, through January 31, 1955.

▶ Vietnam War: February 28, 1961, through May 7, 1975, for veterans who served in the Republic of Vietnam during that period; August 5, 1964, through May 7, 1975, in all other cases.

▶ Persian Gulf War: August 2, 1990, through a date to be set by law or presidential proclamation.[9]

World War Service by Special Groups

A number of groups that have provided military-related service to the United States can receive VA benefits. To qualify, a discharge by the Secretary of Defense is needed. Service in the following groups has been certified as active military service for benefit purposes:

▶ Women's Air Force Service Pilots (WASPs)

▶ World War I Signal Corps Female Telephone Operators Unit

▶ World War I Engineer Field Clerks

▶ Women's Army Auxiliary Corps (WAAC)

▶ Quartermaster Corps female clerical employees serving with the American Expeditionary Forces in World War I

▶ Civilian employees of Pacific naval air bases who actively participated in the defense of Wake Island during World War II

▶ Reconstruction aides and dietitians in World War I

▶ Male civilian ferry pilots

▶ Wake Island defenders from Guam

▶ Civilian personnel assigned to Office of Strategic Services (OSS) secret intelligence

▶ Guam Combat Patrol

- ▶ Quartermaster Corps members of the *Keswick* crew on Corregidor during World War II

- ▶ U.S. civilians who participated in the defense of Bataan

- ▶ U.S. merchant seamen who served on block ships in support of Operation Mulberry in the World War II invasion of Normandy

- ▶ American merchant marines in oceangoing service during World War II

- ▶ Civilian Navy Identification Friend or Foe (IFF) radar technicians who served in combat areas of the Pacific during World War II

- ▶ U.S. civilians of the American Field Service who served overseas in World War I

- ▶ U.S. civilians of the American Field Service who served overseas under U.S. armies and U.S. army groups in World War II

- ▶ U.S. civilian employees of American Airlines who served overseas in a contract with the Air Transport Command between December 14, 1941, and August 14, 1945

- ▶ Civilian crewmen of U.S. Coast and Geodetic Survey vessels who served in areas of immediate military hazard while conducting cooperative operations with and for the U.S. Armed Forces between December 7, 1941, and August 15, 1945; qualifying vessels are the *Derickson, Explorer, Gilbert, Hilgard, E. Lester Jones, Lydonia Patton, Surveyor, Wainwright, Westdahl, Oceanographer, Hydrographer,* and *Pathfinder*

- ▶ Members of the American Volunteer Group (Flying Tigers) who served between December 7, 1941, and July 18, 1942

- ▶ U.S. civilian flight crew and aviation ground support employees of United Air Lines who served overseas in a contract with the Air Transport Command between December 14, 1941, and August 14, 1945

- ▶ U.S. civilian flight crew and aviation ground support employees of Transcontinental and Western Air, Inc. (TWA), who served overseas in a contract with the Air Transport Command between December 14, 1941, and August 14, 1945

► U.S. civilian flight crew and aviation ground support employees of Consolidated Vultee Aircraft Corp. who served overseas in a contract with the Air Transport Command between December 14, 1941, and August 14, 1945

► U.S. civilian flight crew and aviation ground support employees of Pan American World Airways and its subsidiaries and affiliates who served overseas in a contract with the Air Transport Command and Naval Air Transport Service between December 14, 1941, and August 14, 1945

► Honorably discharged members of the American Volunteer Guard, Eritrea Service Command, between June 21, 1942, and March 31, 1943

► U.S. civilian flight crew and aviation ground support employees of Northwest Airlines who served overseas under the airline's contract with the Air Transport Command between December 14, 1941, and August 14, 1945

► U.S. civilian female employees of the U.S. Army Nurse Corps who served in the defense of Bataan and Corregidor during the period January 2, 1942, to February 3, 1945

► U.S. flight crew and aviation ground support employees of Northeast Airlines Atlantic Division who served overseas as a result of Northeast Airlines' contract with the Air Transport Command during the period December 7, 1941, through August 14, 1945

► U.S. civilian flight crew and aviation ground support employees of Braniff Airways who served overseas in the North Atlantic or under the jurisdiction of the North Atlantic Wing, Air Transport Command, as a result of a contract with the Air Transport Command during the period February 26, 1942, through August 14, 1945

► Chamorro and Carolina former native police who received military training in the Donnal area of central Saipan and were placed under the command of Lt. Casino of the 6th Provisional Military Police Battalion to accompany U.S. Marines on active combat patrol from August 19, 1945, to September 2, 1945

- The Operational Analysis Group of the Office of Scientific Research and Development, Office of Emergency Management, which served overseas with the U.S. Army Air Corps from December 7, 1941, through August 15, 1945

- Members of the Alaska Territorial Guard during World War II who were honorably discharged under section 8147 of the Department of Defense Appropriations Act of 2001[10]

Allied Veterans with Service during World War I or World War II

Certain VA benefits are available for former Czechoslovakian or Polish service members who served during World War I or World War II in armed conflict against an enemy of the United States if they have been U.S. citizens for at least ten years.[11]

Filipino Veterans with Service during World War II

Certain VA benefits are available for members of the following groups:

- Old Philippine Scouts

- Commonwealth Army Veterans, including certain Filipino guerrilla forces and New Philippine Scouts who reside in the United States and who are citizens or lawfully admitted for permanent residence.[12]

Note: The above are not all-inclusive lists of wartime service veterans groups. Check with a VSO if you have questions regarding wartime service.

SPECIAL CIRCUMSTANCES

In addition to the eligibility qualifications previously covered, the VA recognizes certain special circumstances when awarding Aid and Attendance and Housebound pensions. If you believe that any of the following special circumstances may apply to you, contact a VSO for details on your eligibility.

- If you are a wartime service veteran receiving service-connected disability compensation checks from the VA for a combat or accident-related injury and have a disability rating of 30 percent or greater, then your spouse may be entitled to receive Aid and Attendance benefits if he or she is disabled, has care needs, and meets the net income and net worth eligibility criteria.[13] (See appendix 2 for further explanation of service-connected disability compensation.)

► If you are a disabled wartime service veteran with low income and a low net worth and your spouse is personally performing your activities of daily living (bathing, dressing, etc.), you may qualify to receive Aid and Attendance benefits. A physician must document your need for care on Form 21-2680.[14]

► If a wartime service veteran or surviving spouse dies while awaiting a decision on granting pension benefits, the VA may still release the money. This situation is referred to as accrued benefits. An application for accrued benefits must be filed within one year of the date of death.[15]

► If you are the surviving spouse of a wartime service veteran and you remarried a nonveteran on or after January 1, 1971, and the nonveteran died or the remarriage ended in divorce prior to November 1, 1990, then your eligibility for VA pension benefits as a surviving spouse may be restored.[16]

► If you are a wartime service veteran or surviving spouse and are a resident in a nursing home and not eligible for Medicare or Medicaid, you may be eligible to receive an Aid and Attendance pension. Nursing home care not covered by Medicare or Medicaid may be an eligible expense that can be reported when applying for pension benefits.[17]

► If a wartime service veteran or surviving spouse is incarcerated in a local, state, or federal prison, he or she is ineligible for a pension, effective on the sixty-first day of imprisonment. The VA will inform the veteran or surviving spouse of the conditions under which the pension payments may be resumed upon release from incarceration.[18]

Understanding Pension Rates: How Much Money Can You Expect to Get?

At this point, you may be wondering how much money you can expect to receive from the VA to help pay for long-term care. The money you receive as a wartime service veteran or surviving spouse from an Aid and Attendance pension or Housebound pension can have a life-changing impact in that it can enable you to afford caregivers in your home or in an assisted living facility. A wartime service veteran or surviving spouse can receive either an Aid and Attendance pension or a Housebound pension, not both. The VA determines which pension you are eligible to receive.

The current maximum pension rates for 2009 begin on page 26. The pensions provide tax-free money paid directly to wartime service veterans or their surviving spouses that does not have to be repaid.

In my experience, most wartime service veterans and their surviving spouses needing long-term care receive the maximum rate because their net worth is low and they have zero or negative net income. Most wartime service veterans and their surviving spouses receive about $900 to $1,000 a month in income from Social Security and maybe a few hundred dollars per month from a work pension and interest. Their biggest unreimbursed expense is often the monthly cost for an assisted living facility or nonmedical home care, and 100 percent of this cost can be counted as a medical expense, as long as medical necessity is documented by a physician on Form 21-2680. (See chapter 8 for sample Form 21-2680.) The monthly cost of a private room in an assisted living facility can easily equal $3,000 or more; this expense alone can make net income zero or negative. Few wartime service veterans and their surviving spouses have positive net income or excessive net worth if they live in assisted living facilities or receive nonmedical home care.

PENSION RATES

Aid and Attendance and Housebound pension rates for wartime service veterans are listed under the VA category of "improved disability pension rates"; Aid and Attendance and Housebound pension rates for surviving spouses of wartime service veterans are listed under the VA category of "improved death pension rates."

1. The 2009 improved disability pension rates effective December 1, 2008, are as follows:

    a. Aid and Attendance pension

        i. Veteran needing regular aid and attendance, no dependents: $19,736 ($1,644 per month)

        ii. Veteran needing regular aid and attendance, one dependent: $23,396 ($1,949 per month)

    b. Housebound pension

        i. Veteran permanently housebound, no dependents: $14,457 ($1,204 per month)

        ii. Veteran permanently housebound, one dependent: $18,120 ($1,510 per month)[1]

Note: A veteran with one dependent is usually a veteran living with a spouse.

Dependents generally include spouses and unmarried biological children, adopted children, and stepchildren under the age of eighteen. If a child is older than eighteen, then to be considered a dependent, he or she must have become permanently incapable of self-support before turning eighteen years of age or must be in an approved school and under age twenty-three.[2]

2. The 2009 improved death pension rates effective December 1, 2008, are as follows:

   a. Aid and Attendance pension—Widowed spouse of a veteran needing aid and attendance, no dependents: $12,681 ($1056 per month)

   b. Housebound pension—Widowed spouse of a veteran, permanently housebound, no dependents: $9,696 ($808 per month)[3]

   Note: A surviving spouse does not usually have any dependents.

Note: The above rates are adjusted annually each December according to the consumer price index to match inflation. The most current rates can be located at the VA Web site.

Use the following steps to find the current pension rates for veterans:

1. Go to http://www.va.gov.

2. On the left-hand side of the screen, highlight "Benefits" and click on "Compensation & Pension."

3. On the left-hand side of the screen, click on "Rate Tables."

4. On the left-hand side of the screen, click on "Pension Rate Tables."

5. On the left-hand side of the screen, click on "Improved Disability Pension (Veterans)."

6. Find the rate that applies to either Housebound or Aid and Attendance (A&A) benefits.

Use the following steps to find the current pension rates for surviving spouses of veterans:

1. Go to http://www.va.gov.

2. On the left-hand side of the screen, highlight "Benefits" and click on "Compensation & Pension."

3. On the left-hand side of the screen, click on "Rate Tables."

4. On the left-hand side of the screen, click on "Pension Rate Tables."

5. On the left-hand side of the screen, click on "Improved Death Pension (Widows and Children)."

6. Find the rate that applies to either Housebound or Aid and Attendance (A&A) benefits.

LONG-TERM CARE INSURANCE AND VA PENSIONS

As you can tell from the Aid and Attendance and Housebound pension rates, eligible wartime service veterans or their surviving spouses may receive significant amounts of money to help pay for long-term care. Purchasing a long-term care insurance policy is also an option to help pay for long-term care. In my experience, though, many long-term care insurance salespersons are unaware that Aid and Attendance and Housebound pensions are available to wartime service vets and their surviving spouses; therefore, these pensions may not be factored in when quotes are provided for long-term care insurance.

Some people may question whether these VA pensions will still be offered to wartime service veterans and their surviving spouses years from now. Aid and Attendance benefits have been available since 1873, and you can reason that politicians would face unfavorable consequences if they proposed to slash a pension funding long-term care for wartime service veterans and their surviving spouses. If you are comfortable with this reasoning, then incorporate the Aid and Attendance and Housebound pensions into your retirement plans.

Remember, it is important to consider all the options available to help pay for long-term care. You may want to consult with a VSO, financial planner, or elder law attorney to help you make an informed decision about planning for long-term care needs.

5

STARTING THE APPLICATION PROCESS: STEPS TO SUBMIT A CLAIM

Now that you have determined that you are probably eligible for a pension and know how much money you can expect to receive from the VA, the next step is to submit a claim for benefits. The VA will determine whether you receive the Aid and Attendance pension or the Housebound pension. The following list summarizes the claim process:

1. File an informal claim, if necessary. An informal claim is filed if you do not yet have all the necessary information to make a formal application; it can save the veteran or surviving spouse thousands of dollars. (See chapter 6 for tips, sample informal claim forms, and how an informal claim saves money.)

2. Locate the veteran's discharge record (see chapter 7 for detailed information on locating the discharge record) from the following sources:

   a. Your home or bank

   b. County courthouse (county VSOs can help locate a discharge record in the county courthouse)

   c. National Personnel Records Center (NPRC)

3. Obtain all forms needed for the application (see chapter 8) using the following sources:

    a. The VA Web site

    b. Veterans service organizations

    c. VA regional offices

4. Complete the following forms (as applicable) using the discharge record as a reference. Note: The forms are listed in the order of priority to complete them. Forms 21-2680 and 21-4138 are listed first because of the time needed for a doctor to complete the form and a care provider to write a letter substantiating the care you receive.

    a. Forms for a wartime service veteran:
        i. 21-2680 (physician examination)
        ii. 21-4138 (statement to support your claim, with a letter from care provider attached)
        iii. 21-526 (main application form for veterans)
        iv. 21-8416 (unreimbursed medical expenses)
        v. 21-22 (authorization for a VSO to be your representative to the VA)

    b. Forms for the surviving spouse of a wartime service veteran:
        i. 21-2680 (physician examination)
        ii. 21-4138 (statement to support your claim, with a letter from care provider attached)
        iii. 21-534 (main application form for surviving spouses)
        iv. 21-8416 (unreimbursed medical expenses)
        v. 21-22 (authorization for a VSO to be your representative to the VA)

When filling in forms, print legibly. Many applications have been returned for a simple error like an illegible word or a box left empty. Remember, make a careless error and you may delay the approval process by a month or more.

5. Attach copies of supporting documents to your forms.

6. Make a copy of all forms and supporting documents before you submit them, and keep the copy for your files.

7. Apply for your pension benefits. Note: You cannot file for pension benefits in any other state except the veteran's or surviving spouse's state of residency. If you try to file using a VSO outside your home state, the VA will turn the file over to the resident's home state, which will delay the processing of your pension application.

   If possible, hand-deliver your application forms (with attached supporting documentation) to a VSO. Since applications have been known to be lost in the mail or lost before being routed to a VSO, hand-delivery is the safest way to deliver your forms. If you have not yet obtained a certified copy of the original discharge record, the VSO can make the certified copy at the same time that you hand-deliver your application. VSOs can also double check forms for any errors before submitting your claim.

8. Follow up with the VSO in about one or two months. Do not take for granted that all is well and that all information has been received by the VA. The VSO can look up the status of your application on a computer or contact the VA for your application status and give you an update.

9. Promptly reply to all letters from the VA requesting additional information. Some requests require you to check a box and return that portion of the letter to the VA. If you receive such a letter from the VA, contact a VSO for assistance.

10. Periodically check your bank account for direct deposit of pension payments.

6

FILING AN INFORMAL CLAIM: AVOID DELAYS AND SAVE THOUSANDS OF DOLLARS

Veterans or their surviving spouses who want to file for Aid and Attendance pensions or Housebound pensions but do not yet have the information necessary to complete all the application forms and cannot yet provide all the supporting documents should file an informal claim for these benefits.[1]

To file an informal claim,

1. Complete Form 21-4138, Statement in Support of Claim. (See the sample completed forms for a veteran [figure 6.1] and for a surviving spouse [figure 6.2] in this chapter.)

2. If you have the veteran's discharge record, make a photocopy and attach it to Form 21-4138. For an informal claim, you do not need a certified copy of the discharge record. A certified copy of the discharge record (as opposed to a photocopy) will be required when you file your formal claim.

3. If possible, hand-deliver your informal claim form to a VSO. You may also mail your informal claim form to your regional VA office.

   a. If you hand-deliver your claim form to a VSO, also complete Form 21-22 as this form authorizes the VSO to represent you to the VA and assist you with your claim. (See the sample form [figure 6.3] in this chapter.)

b. If you mail your claim form to the VA, mark the envelope "Attention: Triage Center" and send it via certified mail with a return receipt requested.

4. Make a copy of your informal claim for your records.

The VA or VSO will stamp the form as received, and this stamp will serve as the official date of application. Benefit payments will be made retroactive to the first of the month following the application date. (For example, if you apply on February 27, payments will be made retroactive to March 1; if you apply on March 3, payments will be made retroactive to April 1.) If you wait until all the paperwork is complete and you have all the supporting documentation (a certified copy of the discharge record, proof of out-of-pocket medical expenses, etc.) you may lose a month or more, which can mean thousands of dollars in delayed pension money.

Note: Formal claims for Aid and Attendance and Housebound pensions must be filed within one year of submitting your informal claim.[2] When you file the formal application, attach a copy of your informal claim.

Contact a VSO if you have questions about filing an informal claim.

Figure 6.1 Sample completed Form 21-4138: Statement in Support of Claim (informal claim for a veteran).

<table>
<tr><td colspan="3"></td><td>OMB Approved No. 2900-0075
Respondent Burden: 15 minutes</td></tr>
</table>

VA Department of Veterans Affairs	**STATEMENT IN SUPPORT OF CLAIM**

PRIVACY ACT INFORMATION: The VA will not disclose information collected on this form to any source other than what has been authorized under the Privacy Act of 1974 or Title 38, Code of Federal Regulations 1.576 for routine uses (i.e., civil or criminal law enforcement, congressional communications, epidemiological or research studies, the collection of money owed to the United States, litigation in which the United States is a party or has an interest, the administration of VA Programs and delivery of VA benefits, verification of identity and status, and personnel administration) as identified in the VA system of records, 58VA21/22, Compensation, Pension, Education and Rehabilitation Records - VA, published in the Federal Register. Your obligation to respond is required to obtain or retain benefits. VA uses your SSN to identify your claim file. Providing your SSN will help ensure that your records are properly associated with your claim file. Giving us your SSN account information is voluntary. Refusal to provide your SSN by itself will not result in the denial of benefits. The VA will not deny an individual benefits for refusing to provide his or her SSN unless the disclosure of the SSN is required by Federal Statute of law in effect prior to January 1, 1975, and still in effect. The requested information is considered relevant and necessary to determine maximum benefits under the law. The responses you submit are considered confidential (38 U.S.C. 5701). Information submitted is subject to verification through computer matching programs with other agencies.

RESPONDENT BURDEN: We need this information to obtain evidence in support of your claim for benefits (38 U.S.C. 501(a) and (b)). Title 38, United States Code, allows us to ask for this information. We estimate that you will need an average of 15 minutes to review the instructions, find the information, and complete this form. VA cannot conduct or sponsor a collection of information unless a valid OMB control number is displayed. You are not required to respond to a collection of information if this number is not displayed. Valid OMB control numbers can be located on the OMB Internet Page at www.whitehouse.gov/omb/library/OMBINV.html#VA. If desired, you can call 1-800-827-1000 to get information on where to send comments or suggestions about this form.

FIRST NAME - MIDDLE NAME - LAST NAME OF VETERAN *(Type or print)*	SOCIAL SECURITY NO.	VA FILE NO.
John Joseph Smith	000-00-0000	C/CSS -

The following statement is made in connection with a claim for benefits in the case of the above-named veteran:

This is an informal claim for a non-service-connected veteran pension. I am requesting Aid and Attendance pension benefits. Attached is a photocopy of my discharge record. I will file a formal claim ASAP and will attach a copy of this informal claim to my formal claim.

I CERTIFY THAT the statements on this form are true and correct to the best of my knowledge and belief.

SIGNATURE	DATE SIGNED
John Joseph Smith	01-05-2009

ADDRESS	TELEPHONE NUMBERS *(Include Area Code)*	
714 Happy Lane Anytown PA 11111	DAYTIME 412-555-1212	EVENING ——

PENALTY: The law provides severe penalties which include fine or imprisonment, or both, for the willful submission of any statement or evidence of a material fact, knowing it to be false.

VA FORM AUG 2004	**21-4138**	EXISTING STOCKS OF VA FORM 21-4138, JUN 2000, WILL BE USED	CONTINUE ON REVERSE

(A blank copy of this form was obtained from the VA Web site, http://www.vba.va.gov/pubs/forms/VBA-21-4138-ARE.pdf.)

Figure 6.2 Sample completed Form 21-4138: Statement in Support of Claim (informal claim for a surviving spouse). In the boxes at the top of the form, fill in the veteran's name and Social Security number.

OMB Approved No. 2900-0075
Respondent Burden: 15 minutes

Department of Veterans Affairs | **STATEMENT IN SUPPORT OF CLAIM**

PRIVACY ACT INFORMATION: The VA will not disclose information collected on this form to any source other than what has been authorized under the Privacy Act of 1974 or Title 38, Code of Federal Regulations 1.576 for routine uses (i.e., civil or criminal law enforcement, congressional communications, epidemiological or research studies, the collection of money owed to the United States, litigation in which the United States is a party or has an interest, the administration of VA Programs and delivery of VA benefits, verification of identity and status, and personnel administration) as identified in the VA system of records, 58VA21/22, Compensation, Pension, Education and Rehabilitation Records - VA, published in the Federal Register. Your obligation to respond is required to obtain or retain benefits. VA uses your SSN to identify your claim file. Providing your SSN will help ensure that your records are properly associated with your claim file. Giving us your SSN account information is voluntary. Refusal to provide your SSN by itself will not result in the denial of benefits. The VA will not deny an individual benefits for refusing to provide his or her SSN unless the disclosure of the SSN is required by Federal Statute of law in effect prior to January 1, 1975, and still in effect. The requested information is considered relevant and necessary to determine maximum benefits under the law. The responses you submit are considered confidential (38 U.S.C. 5701). Information submitted is subject to verification through computer matching programs with other agencies.

RESPONDENT BURDEN: We need this information to obtain evidence in support of your claim for benefits (38 U.S.C. 501(a) and (b)). Title 38, United States Code, allows us to ask for this information. We estimate that you will need an average of 15 minutes to review the instructions, find the information, and complete this form. VA cannot conduct or sponsor a collection of information unless a valid OMB control number is displayed. You are not required to respond to a collection of information if this number is not displayed. Valid OMB control numbers can be located on the OMB Internet Page at www.whitehouse.gov/omb/library/OMBINV.html#VA. If desired, you can call 1-800-827-1000 to get information on where to send comments or suggestions about this form.

FIRST NAME - MIDDLE NAME - LAST NAME OF VETERAN *(Type or print)* | SOCIAL SECURITY NO. | VA FILE NO.

David Scott Jones | 111-11-1111 | C/CSS -

The following statement is made in connection with a claim for benefits in the case of the above-named veteran:

This is an informal claim for a non-service-connected death pension. I am requesting Aid and Attendance pension benefits. I, Mary Jones, Social Security number 101-10-1010, was legally married to David Jones (deceased), a veteran of World War II. Attached is a photocopy of David Jones' discharge record. I will file a formal claim ASAP and will attach a copy of this informal claim to my formal claim.

I CERTIFY THAT the statements on this form are true and correct to the best of my knowledge and belief.

SIGNATURE | | DATE SIGNED
Mary L. Jones | surviving spouse of David Jones | 02-10-2009

ADDRESS | | TELEPHONE NUMBERS *(Include Area Code)*
| | DAYTIME | EVENING
100 Friendship Road Pleasantville, OH 10101 | | 814-555-1212 | ——

PENALTY: The law provides severe penalties which include fine or imprisonment, or both, for the willful submission of any statement or evidence of a material fact, knowing it to be false.

VA FORM AUG 2004 **21-4138** | EXISTING STOCKS OF VA FORM 21-4138, JUN 2000, WILL BE USED | CONTINUE ON REVERSE

(A blank copy of this form was obtained from the VA Web site, http://www.vba.va.gov/pubs/forms/VBA-21-4138-ARE.pdf.)

Figure 6.3 Sample completed Form 21-22: Appointment of Veterans Service Organization as Claimant's Representative is an authorization for a VSO to be your representative for your informal claim. This example provides information for a veteran claimant. For instructions on how to complete this form, see "Tips for Completing Form 21-22" in chapter 8.

OMB Control No. 2900-0321
Respondent Burden: 5 minutes

Department of Veterans Affairs — **APPOINTMENT OF VETERANS SERVICE ORGANIZATION AS CLAIMANT'S REPRESENTATIVE**

Note - If you would prefer to have an individual assist you with your claim, you may use VA Form 21-22a, " Appointment of Individual As Claimant's Representative."

IMPORTANT - PLEASE READ THE PRIVACY ACT AND RESPONDENT BURDEN ON REVERSE BEFORE COMPLETING THE FORM

1. LAST-FIRST-MIDDLE NAME OF VETERAN
Smith John Joseph

2. VA FILE NUMBER *(Include prefix)*

3A. NAME OF SERVICE ORGANIZATION RECOGNIZED BY THE DEPARTMENT OF VETERANS AFFAIRS *(See list on reverse side before selecting organization)*
American Legion

3B. JOB TITLE OF OFFICIAL REPRESENTATIVE AUTHORIZED TO ACT ON VETERAN'S BEHALF
Any service officer

INSTRUCTIONS - TYPE OR PRINT ALL ENTRIES

4. SOCIAL SECURITY NUMBER
000-00-0000

5. INSURANCE NUMBER(S) *(Include letter prefix)*

6A. SERVICE NUMBER(S)
35 000 000

6B. BRANCH OF SERVICE
Army

7. NAME OF CLAIMANT *(If other than veteran)*

8. RELATIONSHIP *(If other than veteran)*

9. ADDRESS OF CLAIMANT *(No. and street or rural route, city or P.O., State and ZIP Code)*
714 Happy Lane
Anytown PA 11111

10. CLAIMANT'S TELEPHONE NUMBER *(Include Area Code)*
A. DAYTIME
412-555-1212
B. EVENING

11. DATE OF THIS APPOINTMENT
01-05-2009

12. AUTHORIZATION FOR REPRESENTATIVE'S ACCESS TO RECORDS PROTECTED BY SECTION 7332, TITLE 38, U.S.C.
Unless I check the box below, I **do not authorize** VA to disclose to the service organization named on this appointment form any records that may be in my file relating to treatment for drug abuse, alcoholism or alcohol abuse, infection with the human immunodeficiency virus (HIV), or sickle cell anemia.

[X] I authorize the VA facility having custody of my VA claimant records to disclose to the service organization named in Item 3A all treatment records relating to drug abuse, alcoholism or alcohol abuse, infection with the human immunodeficiency virus (HIV), or sickle cell anemia. Redisclosure of these records by my service organization representative, other than to VA or the Court of Appeals for Veterans Claims, is not authorized without my further written consent. This authorization will remain in effect until the earlier of the following events: (1) I revoke this authorization by filing a written revocation with VA; or (2) I revoke the appointment of the service organization named above, either by explicit revocation or the appointment of another representative.

13. LIMITATION OF CONSENT - My consent in Item 12 for the disclosure of records relating to treatment for drug abuse, alcoholism or alcohol abuse, infection with the human immunodeficiency virus (HIV), or sickle cell anemia is limited as follows:

No limitations

I, the claimant named in Items 1 or 7, hereby appoint the service organization named in Item 3A as my representative to prepare, present and prosecute my claim for any and all benefits from the Department of Veterans Affairs based on the service of the veteran named in Item 1. I authorize the Department of Veterans Affairs to release any and all of my records, to include disclosure of my Federal tax information (other than as provided in Items 12 and 13), to that service organization appointed as my representative. It is understood that no fee or compensation of whatsoever nature will be charged me for service rendered pursuant to this power of attorney. I understand that the service organization I have appointed as my representative may revoke this power of attorney at any time, subject to 38 CFR 20.608. *Additionally, in those cases where a veteran's income is being developed because of an income verification necessitated by an Internal Revenue Service verification match, the assignment of the service organization as the veteran's representative is only valid for five years from the date this form is signed for purposes restricted to the verification match.* Signed and accepted subject to the foregoing conditions.

THIS POWER OF ATTORNEY DOES NOT REQUIRE EXECUTION BEFORE A NOTARY PUBLIC

14. SIGNATURE OF CLAIMANT *(Do Not Print)*
John Joseph Smith

15. DATE SIGNED
01-05-2009

VA USE ONLY	VA FORM 21-22-1 SENT TO: [ ] CER FILE [ ] EDU FILE [ ] INSURANCE FILE [ ] CH. 30 [ ] DEA FILE [ ] LG FILE	DATE SENT	ACKNOWLEDGED *(Date)*	REVOKED *(Reason and date)*

NOTE: As long as this appointment is in effect the organization named herein will be recognized as the sole agent for presentation of your claim before the Department of Veterans Affairs in connection with your claim or any portion thereof.

VA FORM NOV 2005 **21-22**   SUPERSEDES VA FORM 21-22, JUN 2003, WHICH WILL NOT BE USED.

(A blank copy of this form was obtained from the VA Web site, http://www.vba.va.gov/pubs/forms/VBA-21-22-ARE.pdf.)

DISCHARGE RECORD:
HOW TO IDENTIFY AND LOCATE
THIS DOCUMENT

Locating the veteran's discharge record is a vital step in the claim process as you need it to complete the application forms. While it is helpful (but not essential) to provide a copy of the discharge record if you file an informal claim, you *must* provide the discharge record when you file a formal claim. A discharge record is proof that a person is a veteran.

Discharge records, also known as separation documents, are commonly referred to as DD-214s. The form name varies depending on the service period. Form DD-214 applies from the Korean War to present, and WD AGO Form 53-55 (figure 7.1) applies to World War II.

Discharge record information is needed to complete appropriate sections of Forms 21-526 or 21-534 when applying for Aid and Attendance benefits or Housebound benefits. (See samples of completed Forms 21-526 and 21-534 in chapter 8.)

The veteran's discharge record will need to be attached to application Form 21-526 or 21-534. You should attach a *certified copy* (not the original discharge record). A photocopy of the discharge record is not the same as a certified copy. Personnel at the VA, a veterans service organization, or a county courthouse can make a certified copy of your original discharge record.

Figure 7.1 Sample discharge record. (This example was used to fill in sample Form 21-526.)

ENLISTED RECORD AND REPORT OF SEPARATION
HONORABLE DISCHARGE

1. LAST NAME - FIRST NAME - MIDDLE INITIAL	2. ARMY SERIAL NO.	3. GRADE	4. ARM OR SERVICE	5. COMPONENT
SMITH JOHN J	35 000 000	T/4	QMC	AUS

6. ORGANIZATION	7. DATE OF SEPARATION	8. PLACE OF SEPARATION
HQS 529TH QM GRP	11 APR 46	SEP CEN CAMP ATTERBURY IND

9. PERMANENT ADDRESS FOR MAILING PURPOSES	10. DATE OF BIRTH	11. PLACE OF BIRTH
130 SOUTH ST ALLEGHENY CO PITTSBURGH 3 PA	24 JAN 20	PITTSBURGH PA

12. ADDRESS FROM WHICH EMPLOYMENT WILL BE SOUGHT	13. COLOR EYES	14. COLOR HAIR	15. HEIGHT	16. WEIGHT	17. NO. DEPEND.
SEE 9	BLUE	BROWN	5-10	171 LBS.	0

18. RACE	19. MARITAL STATUS	20. U.S. CITIZEN	21. CIVILIAN OCCUPATION AND NO.
WHITE X NEGRO OTHER (specify)	SINGLE X MARRIED OTHER (specify)	YES X NO	NAUTICAL DESIGNER 0-00.03

MILITARY HISTORY

22. DATE OF INDUCTION	23. DATE OF ENLISTMENT	24. DATE OF ENTRY INTO ACTIVE SERVICE	25. PLACE OF ENTRY INTO SERVICE
17 JAN 44		7 FEB 44	CINCINNATI OHIO

SELECTIVE SERVICE DATA	26. REGISTERED	27. LOCAL S.S. BOARD NO.	28. COUNTY AND STATE	29. HOME ADDRESS AT TIME OF ENTRY INTO SERVICE
►	YES X NO	UNKNOWN	MIAMI OHIO	SEE 9

30. MILITARY OCCUPATIONAL SPECIALTY AND NO.	31. MILITARY QUALIFICATION AND DATE (i. e., infantry, aviation and marksmanship badges, etc.)
ADMINISTRATIVE NCO 502	NOT AVAIL

32. BATTLES AND CAMPAIGNS

RYUKYUS

33. DECORATIONS AND CITATIONS

ASIATIC-PACIFIC THEATER RIBBON W/1 BRONZE STAR;
GOOD CONDUCT MEDAL; VICTORY MEDAL WORLD WAR II;

34. WOUNDS RECEIVED IN ACTION

NONE

35. LATEST IMMUNIZATION DATES				36. SERVICE OUTSIDE CONTINENTAL U. S. AND RETURN		
SMALLPOX	TYPHOID	TETANUS	OTHER (specify)	DATE OF DEPARTURE	DESTINATION	DATE OF ARRIVAL
NOT AVAIL	NOT AVAIL	NOT AVAIL		26 DEC 44	AP	6 JAN 45

37. TOTAL LENGTH OF SERVICE				38. HIGHEST GRADE HELD			
CONTINENTAL SERVICE		FOREIGN SERVICE					
YEARS	MONTHS	DAYS	YEARS	MONTHS	DAYS		
0	10	26	1	3	8	T/4	24 MAR 46	US	3 APR 46

39. PRIOR SERVICE

NONE

40. REASON AND AUTHORITY FOR SEPARATION

AR 615-365 (CONVN OF GOVT) & LTR WD GAP 220.8

41. SERVICE SCHOOLS ATTENDED	42. EDUCATION (Years)		
NONE	GRAMMAR 8	HIGH SCHOOL 4	COLLEGE

33766

PAY DATA

43. LONGEVITY FOR PAY PURPOSES			44. MUSTERING OUT PAY		45. SOLDIER DEPOSITS	46. TRAVEL PAY	47. TOTAL AMOUNT, NAME OF DISBURSING OFFICER
YEARS	MONTHS	DAYS	TOTAL	THIS PAYMENT			FD
2	2	25	$200	$100	NONE	$7.85	205.71 A S BANDANAY LT COL

INSURANCE NOTICE

IMPORTANT IF PREMIUM IS NOT PAID WHEN DUE OR WITHIN THIRTY-ONE DAYS THEREAFTER, INSURANCE WILL LAPSE. MAKE CHECKS OR MONEY ORDERS PAYABLE TO THE TREASURER OF THE U. S. AND FORWARD TO COLLECTIONS SUBDIVISION, VETERANS ADMINISTRATION, WASHINGTON 25, D. C.

48. KIND OF INSURANCE	49. HOW PAID	50. Effective Date of Allotment Discontinuance	51. Date of Next Premium Due (One month after 50)	52. PREMIUM DUE EACH MONTH	53. INTENTION OF VETERAN TO
Nat. Serv. X U.S. Govt. None	Allotment X Direct to V.A.	30 APR 46	1 JUN 46	$6.50	Continue Continue Only Discontinue X

54.	55. REMARKS (This space for completion of above items or entry of other items specified in W. D. Directives)
RIGHT THUMB PRINT	ERC FROM 17 JAN 44 THRU 6 FEB 44 NO DAYS LOST UNDER AW 107 ASR-SCORE (2 SEP 45) 33 LAPEL BUTTON ISSUED SEPARATED ON PARTIAL SERVICE RECORD

56. SIGNATURE OF PERSON BEING SEPARATED	57. PERSONNEL OFFICER (Type name, grade and organization - signature)
John J Smith	T K SHUTON 1ST LT CAC

WD AGO FORM 53 - 55
1 November 1944

This form supersedes all previous editions of
WD AGO Forms 53 and 55 for enlisted persons
entitled to an Honorable Discharge, which
will not be used after receipt of this revision.

The following sections describe how to locate a discharge record.

HOME OR BANK

Look for the record at home or at a bank. Be sure to look where the veteran may have stored important papers or memorabilia. Check fireproof boxes and safe deposit boxes at the bank.

COUNTY COURTHOUSE

If the discharge record can't be found at home or at the bank, you should look for it at the county courthouse in the county where the veteran returned after the war. Many veterans were told by their commanding officers during the last days of service to file their discharge records at their county courthouses when they returned home. Many did just that, and in doing so, kept the records from being lost.

Contact a county VSO in the county where the veteran returned after the war; a county VSO can direct you to the appropriate person at the courthouse who can locate the discharge record if it was filed there. You may obtain the county VSO's contact information at the National Association of County Veteran Service Officers (NACVSO) Web site:

1. Go to http://www.nacvso.org.

2. On the home page, click on "Find a Service Officer."

3. To find a county VSO, select the appropriate state from the list that comes up. You will be redirected to the appropriate page if it is available. Note: Some states list their county VSOs when you click on the state link. For other states, you need to click on additional links to find a county VSO.

If a state does not list its county VSOs on the NACVSO Web site, call directory assistance to request the phone number of the appropriate county courthouse. Contact the courthouse to check if the veteran's discharge record is filed there.

Most states record or store discharge records, commonly referred to as DD-214s, at their county courthouses. To determine if a state does not record or store discharge records, you may search the NACVSO Web site:

1. Go to http://www.nacvso.org.

2. On the home page, click on "DD-214 Security."

3. Click on "State List."

4. If the state does not record or store discharge records, you will find it listed in the column under "States that Don't Record DD 214s at Counties." If you need to obtain your discharge record from one of these states, follow the procedure at the bottom of this page for requesting the record from the NPRC.

If the discharge record is located at a county courthouse, an employee at the courthouse can provide a certified copy of the record when requested by the appropriate person. Many county recorders and clerks require identification and may restrict access to the veteran's immediate family. Because of the rise in identity theft and fraudulent filing of pensions, the majority of states have rules requiring that you explain why you are requesting the veteran's discharge record. In most cases, the next of kin requests the record; be prepared to provide identification and proof that you are the next of kin. When inquiring about the record, use keywords such as: *military discharge record or DD-214*. Be prepared to give the veteran's full name, Social Security number, and date and place of birth.

NATIONAL PERSONNEL RECORDS CENTER

If the discharge record is not available at home, at the bank, or at the county courthouse, you must request a certified copy from the NPRC in one of the following four ways:

1. Use the eVetRecs system on the Internet.

2. Use Standard Form 180 (SF 180). Refer to the sample completed form in figure 7.2a.

3. Write a letter to the NPRC in St. Louis, Missouri.

4. Hire an independent researcher who will go to the NPRC.

Each of the above ways is discussed in further detail in this chapter.

Since 1956, official military personnel files have been stored at the NPRC in St. Louis. More than 34 million veterans' files are located there. The NPRC receives thousands of requests a day for discharge records, which are stored in 12-by-9½-inch paper folders in immense storage areas the size of football fields. The NPRC has no computerized recordkeeping system.[1]

A devastating fire on July 12, 1973, left the top floor of the NPRC in ruins. About 16 million to 18 million military personnel files were destroyed. Eighty percent of the records for Army personnel discharged between November 1, 1912, and January 1, 1960, were burned. About 75 percent of the records for Air Force personnel with surnames from Hubbard through Z discharged between September 25, 1947, and January 1, 1964, were also destroyed. The NPRC had no indices to the records, and no duplicate copies of the records destroyed in the fire were maintained. Incredibly, not even microfilm had been used. If a veteran has a photocopy of his or her discharge record, enclosing a copy with the request for the certified copy will help expedite the search if the record is charred.[2]

The NPRC reconstructs a veteran's discharge record even if it has been burned and issues a certification of military service. Alternative sources of records, such as payroll information, are often used to complete the request. Many state and federal agencies, particularly the VA, assist the NPRC with discharge record reconstruction.[3]

Note: The NPRC also handles requests for replacement service medals and decorations. See appendix 2 for the procedure to request these replacements.

When requesting a discharge record, you will need to provide the following information:

▶ Veteran's full name as used during military service

▶ Branch of service

▶ Approximate dates of services

▶ Service number or Social Security number

▶ Date and place of birth, especially if the service number is not known[4]

If you suspect the record may have been involved in the 1973 fire, also include the following information:

- ▶ Place of discharge

- ▶ Last unit of assignment

- ▶ Place of entry into service, if known[5]

You may wish to include the following optional information as well:

- ▶ The purpose or reason for your request, such as applying for veteran pension benefits

- ▶ Any emergency or deadline related to your request, such as the veteran or surviving spouse has a critical or terminal illness[6]

Using the eVetRecs System

An Internet request using eVetRecs is the quickest method for contacting the NPRC to request a discharge record. *Only veterans or the next of kin of deceased veterans may use eVetRecs.* Next of kin includes the father, mother, son, daughter, sister, brother, or unremarried surviving spouse of the deceased veteran.[7]

You may submit record inquiries at the eVetRecs Web site:

1. Go to http://www.archives.gov/veterans/evetrecs/.

2. Read the instructions on the Web page and then click on "Request Military Records" at the bottom of the page. This will launch a separate window.

3. Enter the required information in the system to create your customized request form.

4. Print, sign, and date the signature verification form. *Each request must be signed and dated by the veteran or the next of kin.*

5. Mail or fax your signature verification form to the NPRC, and it will process your request. *You must do this within the first twenty days of entering your online information,* or your request will be removed from the system.

If mailing the verification form, be sure to use the address specified by eVetRecs.

If faxing the verification form, use the NPRC fax number: 314-801-9195.

The online request can expedite the process of obtaining a discharge record. The NPRC will process the request only after it receives the signature verification form. The request has a barcode to minimize delays. The system, designed to provide better service on a request for a discharge record, eliminates the records center's mailroom processing time.

If the veteran or surviving spouse is critically ill or receiving hospice care for a terminal illness, be sure to state this fact in the "Comments" section of the eVetRecs form for priority service.[8]

Using Standard Form 180: Request Pertaining to Military Records

If you are not the veteran or the deceased veteran's next of kin, you may use SF 180 to request a discharge record. If you are a veteran or the next of kin of a deceased veteran and do not have access to the Internet, you may also use SF 180 to request a discharge record. (See the sample completed SF 180 in figure 7.2a.)

Mail your signed and dated form to the address specified on SF 180 (see figure 7.2b).

If the veteran or surviving spouse is critically ill or receiving hospice care for a terminal illness, state this in the "Purpose" section of the SF 180 for priority service.[9]

You can obtain Standard Form 180 in one of the following three ways:

1. Download a copy of SF 180 in PDF format from the National Archives and Records Administration (NARA) Web site:

   a. Go to http://www.archives.gov/forms/.

   b. Click on "Request Pertaining to Military Records" (which is the title of SF 180).

2. Request a copy from the National Personnel Records Center, 9700 Page Avenue, St. Louis, Missouri 63132-5100.

3. Contact a local veterans service organization and request that the form be mailed to you.

Figure 7.2a Sample completed Standard Form 180 (SF180): Request Pertaining to Military Records, page 1.

Standard Form 180 (Rev. 09/08) (Page 1)
Prescribed by NARA (36 CFR 1228.168(b))

Authorized for local reproduction
Previous edition unusable

OMB No. 3095-0029 Expires 10/31/2011

REQUEST PERTAINING TO MILITARY RECORDS

* Requests from veterans or deceased veteran's next-of-kin may be submitted online by using eVetRecs at http://www.archives.gov/veterans/evetrecs/ *

(To ensure the best possible service, please thoroughly review the accompanying instructions before filling out this form. Please print clearly or type.)

SECTION I - INFORMATION NEEDED TO LOCATE RECORDS (Furnish as much as possible.)

1. NAME USED DURING SERVICE (last, first, and middle)	2. SOCIAL SECURITY NO.	3. DATE OF BIRTH	4. PLACE OF BIRTH
Brown, James Larry	555-55-5555	06-16-1924	Swisstown, PA

5. SERVICE, PAST AND PRESENT (For an effective records search, it is important that all service be shown below.)

	BRANCH OF SERVICE	DATE ENTERED	DATE RELEASED	OFFICER	ENLISTED	SERVICE NUMBER (If unknown, write "unknown")
a. ACTIVE COMPONENT	Army Air Force	02-19-1943	10-29-1945		x	unknown
b. RESERVE COMPONENT						
c. NATIONAL GUARD						

6. IS THIS PERSON DECEASED? If "YES" enter the date of death.
[X] NO [ ] YES

7. IS (WAS) THIS PERSON RETIRED FROM MILITARY SERVICE?
[X] NO [ ] YES

SECTION II – INFORMATION AND/OR DOCUMENTS REQUESTED

1. CHECK THE ITEM(S) YOU WOULD LIKE TO REQUEST A COPY OF:

[X] **DD Form 214 or equivalent.** This form contains information normally needed to verify military service. A copy may be sent to the veteran, the deceased veteran's next of kin, or other persons or organizations if authorized in Section III, below. NOTE: If more than one period of service was performed, even in the same branch, there may be more than one DD214. **Check the appropriate box below to specify a deleted or undeleted copy.** When was the DD Form(s) 214 issued? YEAR(S): **1945**

    [X] **UNDELETED:** Ordinarily required to determine eligibility for benefits. Sensitive items, such as, the character of separation, authority for separation, reason for separation, reenlistment eligibility code, separation (SPD/SPN) code, and dates of time lost are usually shown.

    [ ] **DELETED:** The following items are deleted: authority for separation, reason for separation, reenlistment eligibility code, separation (SPD/SPN) code, and for separations after June 30, 1979, character of separation and dates of time lost.

[ ] **All Documents in Official Military Personnel File (OMPF)**

[ ] **Medical Records** (Includes Service Treatment Records (outpatient), inpatient and dental records.) If hospitalized, provide facility name and date for each admission:

[ ] **Other** (Specify):

2. **PURPOSE:** (An explanation of the purpose of the request is **strictly voluntary**; however, such information may help to provide the best possible response and may result in a faster reply. Information provided will in no way be used to make a decision to deny the request.) Check appropriate box:

[X] Benefits [ ] Employment [ ] VA Loan Programs [ ] Medical [ ] Medals/Awards [ ] Genealogy [ ] Correction [ ] Personal
[ ] Other, explain:

SECTION III - RETURN ADDRESS AND SIGNATURE

1. **REQUESTER IS:** (Signature Required in # 3 below of veteran, next of kin, legal guardian, authorized government agent or "other" authorized representative. If "other" authorized representative, provide copy of authorization letter.)

[X] Military service member or veteran identified in Section I, above

[ ] Next of kin of deceased veteran (Must provide proof of death).
    Show relationship:

    (See item 2a on accompanying instructions.)

[ ] Legal guardian (Must submit copy of court appointment.)

[ ] Other (specify)

2. **SEND INFORMATION/DOCUMENTS TO:**
(Please print or type. See item 4 on accompanying instructions.)

James Larry Brown
Name

125 Rose Place
Street   Apt.

Happytown   PA   22222
City   State   Zip Code

3. **AUTHORIZATION SIGNATURE REQUIRED** (See items 2a or 3a on accompanying instructions.) I declare (or certify, verify, or state) under penalty of perjury under the laws of the United States of America that the information in this Section III is true and correct.

James Larry Brown
Signature Required - Do not print

02-27-2009   412) 888-0909
Date of this request   Daytime phone

Email address

*This form is available at *http://www.archives.gov/research/order/standard-form-180.pdf* on the National Archives and Records Administration (NARA) web site.*

(A blank copy of this form was obtained from the NARA Web site, http://www.archives.gov/research/order/standard-form-180.pdf.)

Figure 7.2b Standard Form 180, page 2 (for locating the address to mail your form).

Standard Form 180 (Rev. 09/08) (Page 2)
Prescribed by NARA (36 CFR 1228.168(b))

Authorized for local reproduction
Previous edition unusable

OMB No. 3095-0029 Expires 10/31/2011

LOCATION OF MILITARY RECORDS

The various categories of military service records are described in the chart below. For each category there is a code number which indicates the address at the bottom of the page to which this request should be sent. Please refer to the Instruction and Information Sheet accompanying this form as needed.

BRANCH	CURRENT STATUS OF SERVICE MEMBER	Personnel Record	Service Treatment Record
AIR FORCE	Discharged, deceased, or retired before 5/1/1994	14	14
	Discharged, deceased, or retired 5/1/1994 – 9/30/2004	14	11
	Discharged, deceased, or retired on or after 10/1/2004	1	11
	Active (including National Guard on active duty in the Air Force), TDRL, or general officers retired with pay	1	
	Reserve, retired reserve in nonpay status, current National Guard officers not on active duty in the Air Force, or National Guard released from active duty in the Air Force	2	
	Current National Guard enlisted not on active duty in the Air Force	13	
COAST GUARD	Discharge, deceased, or retired before 1/1/1898	6	
	Discharged, deceased, or retired 1/1/1898 – 3/31/1998	14	14
	Discharged, deceased, or retired on or after 4/1/1998	14	11
	Active, reserve, or TDRL	3	
MARINE CORPS	Discharged, deceased, or retired before 1/1/1905	6	
	Discharged, deceased, or retired 1/1/1905 – 4/30/1994	14	14
	Discharged, deceased, or retired 5/1/1994 – 12/31/1998	14	11
	Discharged, deceased, or retired on or after 1/1/1999	4	11
	Individual Ready Reserve	5	
	Active, Selected Marine Corps Reserve, TDRL	4	
ARMY	Discharged, deceased, or retired before 11/1/1912 (enlisted) or before 7/1/1917 (officer)	6	
	Discharged, deceased, or retired 11/1/1912 – 10/15/1992 (enlisted) or 7/1/1917 – 10/15/1992 (officer)	14	14
	Discharged, deceased, or retired after 10/16/1992	14	11
	Reserve; or active duty records of current National Guard members who performed service in the U.S. Army before 7/1/1972	7	
	Active enlisted (including National Guard on active duty in the U.S. Army) or TDRL enlisted	9	
	Active officers (including National Guard on active duty in the U.S. Army) or TDRL officers	8	
	Current National Guard enlisted and officer not on active duty in Army (including records of Army active duty performed after 6/30/1972)	13	
NAVY	Discharged, deceased, or retired before 1/1/1886 (enlisted) or before 1/1/1903 (officer)	6	
	Discharged, deceased, or retired 1/1/1886 – 1/30/1994 (enlisted) or 1/1/1903 – 1/30/1994 (officer)	14	14
	Discharged, deceased, or retired 1/31/1994 – 12/31/1994	14	11
	Discharged, deceased, or retired on or after 1/1/1995	10	11
	Active, reserve, or TDRL	10	
PHS	Public Health Service - Commissioned Corps officers only	12	

ADDRESS LIST OF CUSTODIANS (BY CODE NUMBERS SHOWN ABOVE) – Where to write/send this form

1	Air Force Personnel Center HQ AFPC/DPSSRP 550 C Street West, Suite 19 Randolph AFB, TX 78150-4721	6	National Archives & Records Administration Old Military and Civil Records (NWCTB-Military) Textual Services Division 700 Pennsylvania Ave., N.W. Washington, DC 20408-0001	11	Department of Veterans Affairs Records Management Center P.O. Box 5020 St. Louis, MO 63115-5020
2	Air Reserve Personnel Center /DSMR HQ ARPC/DPSSA/B 6760 E. Irvington Place, Suite 4600 Denver, CO 80280-4600	7	U.S. Army Human Resources Command ATTN: AHRC-PAV-V 1 Reserve Way St. Louis, MO 63132-5200	12	Division of Commissioned Corps Officer Support ATTN: Records Officer 1101 Wooton Parkway, Plaza Level, Suite 100 Rockville, MD 20852
3	Commander, CGPC-adm-3 USCG Personnel Command 4200 Wilson Blvd., Suite 1100 Arlington, VA 22203-1804	8	U.S. Army Human Resources Command ATTN: AHRC-MSR 200 Stovall Street Alexandria, VA 22332-0444	13	The Adjutant General (of the appropriate state, DC, or Puerto Rico)
4	Headquarters U.S. Marine Corps Personnel Management Support Branch (MMSB-10) 2008 Elliot Road Quantico, VA 22134-5030	9	Commander USAEREC ATTN: PCRE-F 8899 E. 56th St. Indianapolis, IN 46249-5301	14	National Personnel Records Center (Military Personnel Records) 9700 Page Ave. St. Louis, MO 63132-5100 http://www.archives.gov/veterans/evetrecs/
5	Marine Corps Mobilization Command 15303 Andrews Road Kansas City, MO 64147-1207	10	Navy Personnel Command (PERS-312E) 5720 Integrity Drive Millington, TN 38055-3120		

Writing a Letter to the NPRC

If you are not able to obtain SF 180, you may request a discharge record by sending a letter to the NPRC containing the information listed on page 43. The letter must be signed and dated. If the requestor is not the veteran, the requestor should clarify the next-of-kin relationship after his or her signature—for example, "Daughter of (name of veteran)." Mail the letter to the National Personnel Records Center, Military Personnel Records, 9700 Page Avenue, St. Louis, MO 63132-5100.

Figure 7.3 Sample letter to the NPRC requesting a discharge record.

Roberta Smith
100 Happy Lane
Utopia, PA 15200

February 2, 2009

NPRC
Military Personnel Records
9700 Page Avenue
St. Louis, MO 63132-5100

Dear NPRC:

I am requesting the discharge record for my father, John Robert Smith. His Social Security number is 000-00-0000. He was born on March 1, 1923, in Utopia, Pennsylvania. He was in World War II and served in the Army. He enlisted on December 8, 1941, and was discharged sometime in 1945. I am not sure of the exact date of discharge. Thank you for your help.

Sincerely,

Roberta Smith

Roberta Smith
Daughter of John Robert Smith

Hiring an Independent Researcher

If you need extensive research assistance to locate a discharge record, you may want to hire an independent researcher. You can find a list of independent researches at the NARA Web site:

1. Go to http://www.archives.gov/veterans/evetrecs/.

2. Click on "Other Methods and Sources to Obtain Service Records."

3. Click on "Researchers specializing in Military Records."

Checking the Status of Your Request

Once you have allowed sufficient time for the NPRC to process your request (approximately ten business days for non-fire-related records), you may check the status of your request through the NPRC Customer Service Center by sending an e-mail to mpr.status@nara.gov. Provide the veteran's name, and service number or Social Security number to allow the NPRC to access your request, and if you made your request using eVetRecs, include the eleven-digit request number you were provided. You will receive a return e-mail with a projected completion date for your request.

You may also telephone the NPRC Customer Service Line at 314-801-0800 on Monday through Friday between the hours of 7:30 AM and 5:00 PM CST.[10]

8

AID AND ATTENDANCE AND HOUSEBOUND PENSIONS: SAMPLE APPLICATION FORMS AND TIPS ON COMPLETING THE FORMS

Since you have located your discharge record, it is time to complete the application forms. When a veteran or surviving spouse applies for an Aid and Attendance pension or a Housebound pension, the VA determines if the applicant is eligible to receive either of these benefits. The veteran or surviving spouse uses the same application forms with the following exception: Form 21-526 is used for a wartime service veteran, and Form 21-534 is used for a surviving spouse of a deceased wartime service veteran. You should not complete both Form 21-526 and Form 21-534. If you have questions while completing your forms, be sure to ask your VSO for help. Tips for completing forms and sample completed forms begin on page 53.

Forms are available from the following sources:

- ▶ Veterans service organizations: American Legion, National Association of County Veteran Service Officers (NACVSO), Disabled American Veterans (DAV), and Veterans of Foreign Wars of the United States (VFW) (see appendix 1)

- ▶ VA regional offices (see appendix 1)

▶ The VA Web site

The forms listed below are available from the VA Web site:

▶ Form 21-2680, Examination for Housebound Status or Permanent Need for Regular Aid and Attendance

▶ Form 21-4138, Statement in Support of Claim

▶ Form 21-526, Veteran's Application for Compensation and/or Pension

▶ Form 21-534, Application for Dependency and Indemnity Compensation, Death Pension and Accrued Benefits by a Surviving Spouse or Child (Do Not select Form 21-534a)

▶ Form 21-8416, Medical Expense Report (Check with a VSO if you feel Form 21-8416b, Report of Medical, Legal, and Other Expenses Incident to Recovery for Injury or Death may be applicable to you.)

▶ Form 21-22, Appointment of Veterans Service Organization as Claimant's Representative (If you choose to have an individual represent you rather than a VSO, then select Form 21-22a, Appointment of Individual as Claimant's Representative. This book does not address the topic of appointing an individual as a claimant's representative.)

Use the following steps to obtain the latest version of the form:

1. Go to http://www.va.gov/vaforms/.

2. In the search box, type in the form number and click on "Search." The title of the form you requested will appear near the top of the Web page.

3. Click on the link to the requested form. Note: Some of the forms have more than one version, as indicated above. Be sure to choose the correct form.

Complete the appropriate forms. Forms 21-526 and 21-534 come with a set of instructions. Take time to read through the instructions at least once before completing the applicable form. You must also attach appropriate documentation to your forms as supporting evidence.

FORM 21-2680: EXAMINATION FOR HOUSEBOUND STATUS OR PERMANENT NEED FOR REGULAR AID AND ATTENDANCE

You should ask your physician to complete Form 21-2680 at the beginning of your application process because your physician may be unable to complete the form immediately. If the veteran or surviving spouse is in an assisted living facility, the director of nursing can coordinate with the house physician (if available) in filling out the form. Note: If you are residing in a nursing home and are applying for pension benefits because neither Medicare or Medicaid is paying for your care (see "Special Circumstances" in chapter 3), you do not have to ask a physician to complete this form because your need for care has already been established.

If the physician documents a memory impairment diagnosis, such as Alzheimer's or dementia, the VA will require that a fiduciary (an individual who has power of attorney) be designated because the veteran or surviving spouse is deemed incompetent. Inform the VA if a power of attorney has already been executed by the veteran or surviving spouse and attach power of attorney documents. The VA will still need to investigate the individual who has power of attorney to rule out any exploitation concern before allowing the designee to be a fiduciary. The investigation of the fiduciary can take at least another month, so keep this schedule in mind.

The primary reason for applying for pension benefits is that you have a permanent disability and have care needs because of your disability. For an Aid and Attendance pension, list the medical conditions that require care and the type of ADL care that needs to be provided, such as bathing, dressing, supervised walking, and medication management. For a Housebound pension, state the medical conditions that confine you to the home or immediate premises and the care that needs to be provided, such as transportation services. *The form must reflect your disability or disabilities and your care needs or the claim will be denied.*

Tips for Completing Form 21-2680

A sample completed Form 21-2680 is presented in figure 8.1. You may want to provide your physician with the form tips and the example (figure 8.1) to use as a reference when completing Form 21-2680.

Box 1—Fill in the veteran's name. If the form is being completed for a surviving spouse, write the veteran's (not the surviving spouse's) name in box 1.

Box 2—If the form is being completed for a veteran, leave box 2 blank. If the form is being completed for a surviving spouse, write the surviving spouse's name in box 2.

Box 3—If the form is being completed for a veteran, write "N/A" in box 3. If the form is being completed for a surviving spouse, write "surviving spouse" in box 3.

Box 4A—Fill in the veteran's Social Security number. If the form is being completed for a surviving spouse, write the veteran's (not the surviving spouse's) Social Security number in box 4A.

Box 4B—If the form is being completed for a veteran, write "N/A" in box 4B. If the form is being completed for a surviving spouse, write the surviving spouse's Social Security number in box 4B.

Box 10—The physician states the claimant's diagnoses. Diagnoses substantiate the level of assistance documented in boxes 20 through 34.

Box 19—The physician states the claimant's disabilities. Permanent disabilities (not temporary disabilities, such as fractured arms or legs) substantiate the claimant's need for care. Note: The primary reason a claimant applies for an Aid and Attendance pension or a Housebound pension is because of a permanent disability and the care needs related to that disability.

Boxes 21–27—In addition to checking the appropriate "Yes" or "No" boxes, the physician needs to provide written explanations, as indicated on the form.

Box 24A—Blindness alone can justify granting of the pension if the blindness interferes with the claimant's ability to perform ADLs. Note: The VA considers a claimant blind if the corrected visual acuity is 5/200 or less in both eyes or the concentric contraction of the visual field is five degrees or less; it is not sufficient to simply document macular degeneration.[1]

Box 24B—If the "Yes" box is checked in 24A, then in box 24B, the physician must state the claimant's visual acuity, such as 5/200, in the sections labeled "Left eye" and "Right eye." If the "No" box is checked in

24A, the physician either states the visual acuity of a claimant who has vision impairment interfering with the ability to perform ADLs or writes "N/A" in the sections labeled "Left eye" and "Right eye."

Box 26—If the "Yes" box is checked, the physician must explain why the claimant needs medication management. Note: Memory impairment diagnoses, such as Alzheimer's disease and dementia, are examples of disabilities that substantiate the need for medication management.

Boxes 29–31—The physician states the restrictions of the claimant's hands, arms, legs, neck, or back and the type of care these restrictions require.

Box 32—The physician lists other conditions that limit the claimant's ability to walk, to take care of himself or herself, or to travel beyond the home or immediate premises, and describes what a claimant does during a typical day. Note: If the claimant is applying for an Aid and Attendance pension, the physician can state the claimant needs ADL care in an assisted living facility or needs caregivers to provide ADL care in the home. If the claimant is applying for a Housebound pension, the physician can state that transportation services are needed and the reason why, for example, claimant needs transportation services due to the loss of a driver's license because of (name of disability).

Box 33—The physician describes under what circumstances the claimant is able to leave the home and immediate premises. Note: For a claimant who is applying for an Aid and Attendance pension, the physician can state what transportation services are needed. For a claimant who is applying for a Housebound pension, the physician can state that the claimant is confined to the home and immediate premises and needs transportation services in order to go food shopping or to keep doctors' appointments, for example.

Box 34—If the physician checks the "Yes" box, the physician also needs to specify the distance the claimant is able to travel, by either placing a checkmark in the applicable box or by stating the travel distance in the item labeled "Other."

Boxes 35A–36B—The physician prints his or her name, provides his or her signature and title, dates the form, and provides the name, address, and telephone number of his or her office.

Figure 8.1a Sample completed Form 21-2680: Examination for Housebound Status or Permanent Need for Regular Aid and Attendance, page 1.

OMB Control No. 2900-0721
Respondent Burden: 30 minutes

VA Department of Veterans Affairs

EXAMINATION FOR HOUSEBOUND STATUS OR PERMANENT NEED FOR REGULAR AID AND ATTENDANCE

1. FIRST NAME - MIDDLE NAME - LAST NAME OF VETERAN	2. FIRST NAME - MIDDLE NAME - LAST NAME OF CLAIMANT (If other than veteran)	3. RELATIONSHIP OF CLAIMANT TO VETERAN
John Joseph Smith		N/A

4A. VETERAN'S SOCIAL SECURITY NUMBER	4B. CLAIMANT'S SOCIAL SECURITY NUMBER	5. CLAIM NUMBER
000-00-0000	N/A	N/A

6. DATE OF EXAMINATION	7. HOME ADDRESS
01-30-2009	714 Happy Lane, Anytown PA 11111

8A. IS CLAIMANT HOSPITALIZED?	8B. DATE ADMITTED	9. NAME AND ADDRESS OF HOSPITAL
☐ YES ☒ NO (If "Yes," complete Items 8B and 9)		

NOTE: EXAMINER PLEASE READ CAREFULLY

The purpose of this examination is to record manifestations and findings pertinent to the question of whether the claimant is housebound (confined to the home or immediate premises) or in need of the regular aid and attendance of another person.

The report should be in sufficient detail for the VA decision makers to determine the extent that disease or injury produces physical or mental impairment, that loss of coordination or enfeeblement affects the ability: to dress and undress; to feed him/herself; to attend to the wants of nature; or keep him/herself ordinarily clean and presentable.

Findings should be recorded to show whether the claimant is blind or bedridden.

Whether the claimant seeks housebound or aid and attendance benefits, the report should reflect how well he/she ambulates, where he/she goes, and what he/she is able to do during a typical day.

10. COMPLETE DIAGNOSIS (Diagnosis needs to equate to the level of assistance described in questions 20 through 34)
Severe COPD, kyphosis of thoracic spine, coronary artery disease, mild dementia, hypertension

11A. AGE	11B. SEX	12. WEIGHT		13. HEIGHT
89	M	ACTUAL: LBS.	ESTIMATED: LBS. 180	FEET: 5 INCHES: 8

14. NUTRITION	15. GAIT
Good	poor balance

16. BLOOD PRESSURE	17. PULSE RATE	18. RESPIRATORY RATE	19. WHAT DISABILITIES RESTRICT THE LISTED ACTIVITIES/FUNCTIONS?
148/90	90	18	COPD, CAD, mild dementia

20. IF THE CLAIMANT IS CONFINED TO BED, INDICATE THE NUMBER OF HOURS IN BED
From 9 PM To 9 AM: From 9 AM To 9 PM: Not confined to bed

21. IS THE CLAIMANT ABLE TO FEED HIM/HERSELF? (If "No," provide explanation)
☐ YES ☒ NO   Needs food cut up

22. IS CLAIMANT ABLE TO PREPARE OWN MEALS? (If "Yes," provide explanation)
☐ YES ☒ NO

23. DOES THE CLAIMANT NEED ASSISTANCE IN BATHING AND TENDING TO OTHER HYGIENE NEEDS? (If "Yes," provide explanation)
☒ YES ☐ NO   Needs bathing and shaving assistance, needs incontinence care

24A. IS THE CLAIMANT LEGALLY BLIND? (If "Yes," provide explanation)	24B. CORRECTED VISION	
☐ YES ☒ NO	LEFT EYE N/A	RIGHT EYE N/A

25. DOES THE CLAIMANT REQUIRE NURSING HOME CARE? (If "Yes," provide explanation)
☐ YES ☒ NO

26. DOES CLAIMANT REQUIRE MEDICATION MANAGEMENT? (If "Yes," provide explanation)
☒ YES ☐ NO   Needs medication management due to mild dementia

27. DOES THE CLAIMANT HAVE THE ABILITY TO MANAGE HIS/HER OWN FINANCIAL AFFAIRS? (If "No," provide explanation)
☐ YES ☒ NO   Needs assistance with financial affairs due to mild dementia

VA FORM JUN 2008 **21-2680**

SUPERSEDES VA FORM 21-2680, OCT 1992, WHICH WILL NOT BE USED.

(A blank copy of this form was obtained from the VA Web site, http://www.vba.va.gov/pubs/forms/VBA-21-2680-ARE.pdf.)

Figure 8.1b Sample completed Form 21-2680, page 2.

28. POSTURE AND GENERAL APPEARANCE *(Attach a separate sheet of paper if additional space is needed)*

Kyphosis of thoracic spine, well nourished, barrel chested

29. DESCRIBE RESTRICTIONS OF EACH UPPER EXTREMITY WITH PARTICULAR REFERENCE TO GRIP, FINE MOVEMENTS, AND ABILITY TO FEED HIM/HERSELF, TO BUTTON CLOTHING, SHAVE AND ATTEND TO THE NEEDS OF NATURE *(Attach a separate sheet of paper if additional space is needed)*

Requires assistance to button shirt, requires food to be cut up due to weak hand grip, needs assistance with personal hygiene including shaving, bathing and toileting

30. DESCRIBE RESTRICTIONS OF EACH LOWER EXTREMITY WITH PARTICULAR REFERENCE TO THE EXTENT OF LIMITATION OF MOTION, ATROPHY, AND CONTRACTURESOR OTHER INTERFERENCE. IF INDICATED, COMMENT SPECIFICALLY ON WEIGHT BEARING, BALANCE AND PROPULSION OF EACH LOWER EXTREMITY.

Poor balance, needs assistance with dressing of the lower extremities, requires supervision of ambulation with wheeled walker

31. DESCRIBE RESTRICTION OF THE SPINE, TRUNK AND NECK

Kyphosis of thoracic spine contributing to dyspnea on exertion

32. SET FORTH ALL OTHER PATHOLOGY INCLUDING THE LOSS OF BOWEL OR BLADDER CONTROL OR THE EFFECTS OF ADVANCING AGE, SUCH AS DIZZINESS, LOSS OF MEMORY OR POOR BALANCE ,THAT AFFECTS CLAIMANT'S ABILITY TO PERFORM SELF-CARE, AMBULATE OR TRAVEL BEYOND THE PREMISES OF THE HOME, OR, IF HOSPITALIZED, BEYOND THE WARD OR CLINICAL AREA. DESCRIBE WHERE THE CLAIMANT GOES AND WHAT HE OR SHE DOES DURING A TYPICAL DAY.

Incontinence of bowel and bladder requiring incontinence care, poor balance requiring wheeled walker for ambulation, needs 24 hour sypervision in an assisted living facility for ADL care

33. DESCRIBE HOW OFTEN PER DAY OR WEEK AND UNDER WHAT CIRCUMSTANCES THE CLAIMANT IS ABLE TO LEAVE THE HOME OR IMMEDIATE PREMISES

Mr. Smith is unable to drive and must be transported to doctor appointments

34. ARE AIDS SUCH AS CANES, BRACES, CRUTCHES, OR THE ASSISTANCE OF ANOTHER PERSON REQUIRED FOR LOCOMOTION? *(If so, specify and describe effectiveness in terms of distance that can be traveled, as in Item 32 above)*

[X] YES   *(If "YES," give distance)(Check applicable box or specify distance)*   [ ] 1 BLOCK   [ ] 5 or 6 BLOCKS   [ ] 1 MILE   OTHER *(Specify distance)* 50 feet
[ ] NO

35A. PRINTED NAME OF EXAMINING PHYSICIAN	35B. SIGNATURE AND TITLE OF EXAMINING PHYSICIAN	35C. DATE SIGNED
Markus Wellby	*Markus Wellby MD*	01-30-2009

36A. NAME AND ADDRESS OF MEDICAL FACILITY	36B. TELEPHONE NUMBER OF MEDICAL FACILITY *(Include Area Code)*
Professional Care Associates 250 Maple Street Anytown PA 11111	412-777-3000

PRIVACY ACT NOTICE: The VA will not disclose information collected on this form to any source other than what has been authorized under the Privacy Act of 1974 or Title 38, Code of Federal Regulations 1.576 for routine uses (i.e., civil or criminal law enforcement, congressional communications, epidemiological or research studies, the collection of money owed to the United States, litigation in which the United States is a party or has an interest, the administration of VA programs and delivery of VA benefits, verification of identity and status, and personnel administration) as identified in the VA system of records, 58VA21/22/28, Compensation, Pension, Education and Vocational Rehabilitation Records - VA, and published in the Federal Register. Your obligation to respond is required to obtain or retain benefits. Giving us your Social Security Number (SSN) account information is mandatory. Applicants are required to provide their SSN under Title 38, U.S.C. U.S.C. 5701(c) (1). The VA will not deny an individual benefits for refusing to provide his or her SSN unless the disclosure of the SSN is required by a Federal Statute of law in effect prior to January 1, 1975, and still in effect. The requested information is considered relevant and necessary to determine maximum benefits provided under the law. The responses you submit are considered confidential (38 U.S.C. 5701). Information that you furnish may be utilized in computer matching programs with other Federal or state agencies for the purpose of determining your eligibility to receive VA benefits, as well as to collect any amount owed to the United States by virtue of your participation in any benefit program administered by the Department of Veterans Affairs.

RESPONDENT BURDEN: We need this information to determine your eligibility for aid and attendance or housebound benefits. Title 38, United States Code 1521 (d) and (e), 1115 (1)(e), 1311(c) and (d), 1315 (h), 1122, 1541 (d) (e), and 1502(b) and (c) allows us to ask for this information. We estimate that you will need an average of 30 minutes to review the instructions, find the information, and complete this form. VA cannot conduct or sponsor a collection of information unless a valid OMB control number is displayed. You are not required to respond to a collection of information if this number is not displayed. Valid OMB control numbers can be located on the OMB Internet page at www.whitehouse.gov/omb/library/OMBINV.VA.EPA.html#VA. If desired, you can call 1-800-827-1000 to get information on where to send comments or suggestions about this form.

VA FORM 21-2680, JUN 2008

FORM 21-4138: STATEMENT IN SUPPORT OF CLAIM

To complete Form 21-4138, you will need to attach a letter from your care provider to support your claim. You should ask your care provider for the letter at the beginning of your application process because your care provider may be unable to write the letter immediately.

Tips for Completing Form 21-4138

A sample completed Form 21-4138 is presented in figure 8.2 and a sample provider letter is presented in figure 8.3. Be sure to refer to them to see how to complete the form and how the provider should write the letter.

In the boxes at the top of the form, fill in the veteran's name and Social Security number. If you are the surviving spouse, fill in the veteran's name and veteran's Social Security number, not yours, in these boxes.

In the section labeled "The following statement is made in connection with a claim for benefits in the case of the above-named veteran," write "See attached letter from provider."

In the signature box at the bottom of the page:

▶ If you are the veteran making the claim, sign your name.

▶ If you are the surviving spouse making the claim, provide your signature and write "surviving spouse of (name of veteran)."

Attach to this form a letter from the provider of care. Examples of a provider of care are an assisted living facility or nonmedical home-care service.

Figure 8.2 Sample completed Form 21-4138: Statement in Support of Claim.

OMB Approved No. 2900-0075
Respondent Burden: 15 minutes

Department of Veterans Affairs **STATEMENT IN SUPPORT OF CLAIM**

PRIVACY ACT INFORMATION: The VA will not disclose information collected on this form to any source other than what has been authorized under the Privacy Act of 1974 or Title 38, Code of Federal Regulations 1.576 for routine uses (i.e., civil or criminal law enforcement, congressional communications, epidemiological or research studies, the collection of money owed to the United States, litigation in which the United States is a party or has an interest, the administration of VA Programs and delivery of VA benefits, verification of identity and status, and personnel administration) as identified in the VA system of records, 58VA21/22, Compensation, Pension, Education and Rehabilitation Records - VA, published in the Federal Register. Your obligation to respond is required to obtain or retain benefits. VA uses your SSN to identify your claim file. Providing your SSN will help ensure that your records are properly associated with your claim file. Giving us your SSN account information is voluntary. Refusal to provide your SSN by itself will not result in the denial of benefits. The VA will not deny an individual benefits for refusing to provide his or her SSN unless the disclosure of the SSN is required by Federal Statute of law in effect prior to January 1, 1975, and still in effect. The requested information is considered relevant and necessary to determine maximum benefits under the law. The responses you submit are considered confidential (38 U.S.C. 5701). Information submitted is subject to verification through computer matching programs with other agencies.

RESPONDENT BURDEN: We need this information to obtain evidence in support of your claim for benefits (38 U.S.C. 501(a) and (b)). Title 38, United States Code, allows us to ask for this information. We estimate that you will need an average of 15 minutes to review the instructions, find the information, and complete this form. VA cannot conduct or sponsor a collection of information unless a valid OMB control number is displayed. You are not required to respond to a collection of information if this number is not displayed. Valid OMB control numbers can be located on the OMB Internet Page at www.whitehouse.gov/omb/library/OMBINV.html#VA. If desired, you can call 1-800-827-1000 to get information on where to send comments or suggestions about this form.

FIRST NAME - MIDDLE NAME - LAST NAME OF VETERAN *(Type or print)*	SOCIAL SECURITY NO.	VA FILE NO.
John Joseph Smith	000-00-0000	C/CSS -

The following statement is made in connection with a claim for benefits in the case of the above-named veteran:

See attached letter from provider

I CERTIFY THAT the statements on this form are true and correct to the best of my knowledge and belief.

SIGNATURE	DATE SIGNED
John Joseph Smith	02-15-2009

ADDRESS	TELEPHONE NUMBERS *(Include Area Code)*	
714 Happy Lane	DAYTIME	EVENING
Anytown PA 11111	412-555-1212	

VA FORM AUG 2004 **21-4138**	EXISTING STOCKS OF VA FORM 21-4138, JUN 2000, WILL BE USED	CONTINUE ON REVERSE

(A blank copy of this form was obtained from the Department of Veterans Affairs Web site, http://www.vba.va.gov/pubs/forms/VBA-21-4138-ARE.pdf.)

Figure 8.3 Sample Letter from Provider.

Meadowland Assisted Living
714 Happy Lane
Anytown, PA 11111

January 30, 2009

To Whom It May Concern:

John Smith is a resident who has been living permanently at Meadowland Assisted Living since December 15, 2008. He is paying $2,650/month for his care. Of that cost, John pays the full amount. He requires personal care, including bathing and medication management. If you have any questions regarding his care, call me at 412-555-1212.

Sincerely,

Jane Friendly

Jane Friendly
Administrator

FORM 21-526: VETERAN'S APPLICATION FOR COMPENSATION AND/OR PENSION

Form 21-526 can be used to apply for the following types of benefits: compensation, basic pension, and Aid and Attendance and Housebound pensions. The instructions below apply to living wartime service veterans who are applying for the Aid and Attendance pension or Housebound pension only, not for veterans interested in applying for a basic pension or compensation.

Tips for Completing Form 21-526

A sample completed Form 21-526 is presented in figure 8.4. Be sure to refer to it to see how to complete the form.

Note: If you leave a box blank or unchecked, your claim will be delayed and you will have wasted at least a month. Be thorough and review all your work. Read the instructions at least once before completing the form, and print legibly.

Part A: General Information

Section I: Tell us what you are applying for

Box 2a—You have no VA file number if you have never filed for benefits. If you have ever filed for any veteran benefit, a VA file number exists and should be written on the form. If you received pharmacy benefits, for example, a VA file number will be on record. The file number can be found on all VA correspondence. If in doubt, leave the box blank until you check with a VSO, who can look up the VA file number for you.

Section III: Tell us about your active duty

Boxes 14a–14g—Your discharge record will contain the information needed for these boxes, such as the date and place you entered and left active service, your service number, your grade or rank, and the branch of service.

You must attach your discharge record (also known as a separation document or DD-214) to this form. You should attach a *certified copy* of the discharge record, not the original. A photocopy or notarized copy will not substitute for a certified copy. As mentioned in chapter 7, personnel at the VA, an authorized veterans service organization, or the county courthouse can make a certified copy of your discharge record.

Section VIII: Give us direct deposit information

Boxes 22–24—Attach a voided blank check so that direct deposit payments may be made to your bank account. You should also fill in these boxes with your bank account information in case the voided blank check gets separated from the form. If you do not want direct deposit, write a letter to the VA as instructed on the form.

Section IX: Give us your signature

Boxes 25–26—You (the wartime service veteran) must provide a signature and date.

Boxes 27a–28b—If you sign by marking an X, then two witnesses must also complete these boxes.

Part B: Compensation

Part B does not pertain to wartime service veterans applying for Aid and Attendance pensions or Housebound pensions. Draw a line through both pages 1 and 2 and write "pension only" on each page. Be sure to provide your name and Social Security number at the bottom of page 2.

Part C: Dependency

Section I: Tell us about your marriage

Box 1—Note: This section has a check box labeled "Surviving Spouse," which in this instance applies to a veteran whose spouse has died. In the example (figure 8.4h), the wartime service veteran is widowed, so a check mark appears in the box for surviving spouse.

Boxes 2-21f —If you do not have any dependents, draw a line through all boxes in the remainder of part C. If you have any dependents, complete the remainder of part C, sections I–III. Attach copies of marriage certificates, divorce decrees, death certificates, birth records, and adoption records, as applicable. Dependents generally include spouses and unmarried biological children, adopted children, and stepchildren under the age of eighteen. If a child is older than eighteen, then to be considered a dependent, he or she must have become permanently incapable of self-support before turning eighteen years of age or must be in an approved school and under age twenty-three.[2]

Be sure to provide your name and Social Security number at the bottom of page 3.

Part D: Pension

Section I: Tell us about your disability and background

Box 1a—For disabilities that prevent you from working, list appropriate disabilities that have been documented by your physician. (Box 19 on Form 21-2680, the physician examination form, is a good source from which to obtain disabilities.) Note: A note in section I states that if you are a veteran who is age sixty-five or older or determined to be disabled by the Social Security Administration, you do not have to submit medical evidence with your application. This statement applies to veterans who are applying for basic pensions and not to those who are applying for Aid and Attendance pensions or Housebound pensions. If you are a resident in an assisted living facility or are receiving nonmedical home care or are confined to your home because of a permanent disability, attach Form 21-2680 (physician examination) as evidence of your disability.

Box 2—Check the "Yes" box because you are claiming a special monthly pension.

Section II: Tell us your work history

For many wartime service veterans, this section does not apply. In the example (figure 8.4l), this section does not apply, so a line is drawn through it. If you think that your work history is applicable, check with a VSO before completing this section.

Section III: Tell us if you are in a nursing home

Box 6a—Check the "No" box if you are a resident in an assisted living facility or are receiving nonmedical home care or are confined to your home because of a permanent disability. If you are in a nursing home, check with a VSO before answering boxes 6a–6d. You must meet certain requirements, as mentioned in "Special Circumstances" in chapter 3, in order to apply for benefits.

Section IV: Tell us the net worth of you and your dependents

Boxes 7a–7h—Fill in every box and write "None" or "0" where applicable. If the veteran does not have any dependents, then in the sections labeled "Spouse" and "Children," draw lines through boxes 7a–7h and write "N/A" in each section. Leaving a box blank can cause delays in processing your claim. Attach copies of your net worth documents, such as statements for

CDs, savings accounts, etc. (See "Examples of assets that contribute toward net worth" in chapter 3.)

Section V: Tell us about the income you have received and you expect to receive

Boxes 8–12f—Fill in every box and write "None" or "0" where applicable. If the veteran does not have any dependents, then in the sections labeled "Spouse" and "Children," draw lines through boxes 11a–12f and write "N/A" in each section. Leaving a box blank can cause delays in processing your claim. Attach proof of all income, such as a copy of your Social Security award letter, the pension letter from a previous employer, bank interest statements, etc. (See the "Income" section in chapter 3.)

Section VI: Tell us any information concerning Medical, Legal or Other Expenses

Most veterans have only medical expense deductions and not other types of expenses. In the example (figure 8.4n), the veteran has only deductible medical expenses.

Boxes 13a–13e—You have two options for this section as follows:

▶ Option 1: List all eligible out-of-pocket expenses on the form and attach proof of all listed expenses. If you are in an assisted living facility or receiving nonmedical home care, be sure to attach your monthly invoice as it is a medical expense.

▶ Option 2: If you need more space than provided in this section to list deductible medical expenses, list all of them on Form 21-8416. In boxes 13a–13e, write *"See enclosed medical expense report Form 21-8416."* (A sample Form 21-8416 is presented in figure 8.6.)

If you think you have legal or other expense deductions, check with a VSO as to their eligibility.

Be sure to provide your name and Social Security number at the bottom of page 4.

Note: Form 21-4142, Authorization and Consent to Release Information to the VA (which prints out when you print Form 21-526 online), is rarely used. It is used when a Form 21-2680 is unable to be completed. Check with a VSO if you feel this situation applies to you.

Figure 8.4a Sample completed Form 21-526: Veteran's Application for Compensation and/or Pension, part A, page 1(application form for wartime service veterans).

OMB Approved No. 2900-0001
Respondent Burden: 1 hour 30 minutes

Department of Veterans Affairs

(DO NOT WRITE IN THIS SPACE)

VETERAN'S APPLICATION FOR COMPENSATION AND/OR PENSION,
VA Form 21-526, Part A: General information

Please read the attached "General Instructions" before you fill out this form.

SECTION I **Tell us what you are applying for**	**1.** What are you applying for? If you are unsure please refer to the "General Instructions" page 2 Section 1: Preparing your application	
Check the box that says what you are applying for. Be sure to complete the other Parts you need.	☐ Compensation — Fill out Part A of VA Form 21-526 and Parts B and C	
	☒ Pension — Fill out Part A of VA Form 21-526 and Parts C and D	
	☐ Compensation and Pension — Fill out Part A of VA Form 21-526 and Parts B, C and D	

2a. Have you ever filed a claim with VA?
☒ No *(If "No," skip Item 2b and go to Item 3)*
(If "Yes," provide file number below)
☐ Yes *(Go to 2b)*

2b. I filed a claim for
☐ Compensation ☐ Pension
☐ Other

SECTION II **Tell us about you**

We need information about you to process your claim faster.

3. What is your name?
John   Joseph   Smith
First   Middle   Last   Suffix (If applicable)

4. What is your Social Security number?
000-00-0000

5. What is your sex?
☒ Male ☐ Female

6a. Did you serve under another name?
☐ Yes *(If "Yes," go to Item 6b)*
☒ No *(If "No," go to Item 7)*

6b. Please list the other name(s) you served under

Give us your current mailing address in the space provided. If it will change within the next three months, give us that new address in block 29 "Remarks." Also in block 29, give us the date you think you will be at the new address.

7. What is your address?
714 Happy Lane
Street address, Rural Route, or P.O. Box   Apt. number
Anytown   PA   11111   USA
City   State   ZIP Code   Country

8. What are your telephone numbers?
Daytime 412-555-1212
Evening

9. What is your e-mail address?

10. What is your date of birth?
01-24-1920

11. Where were you born? (City, State and Country)
Pittsburgh, PA, USA

OWCP used to be called the U.S. Bureau of Employees Compensation

12a. Are you receiving disability benefits from the Office of Workers' Compensation *(OWCP)*?
☐ Yes ☒ No
(If "Yes," answer 12b and 12c also)

12b. When was the claim filed?

12c. What disability are you receiving benefits for?

13a. What is the name of your nearest relative or other person we could contact if necessary?
Robert J. Smith

13b. What is his/her telephone number?
Daytime 724-333-1600
Evening

13c. What is this person's address?
501 Duck Lane
Anytown PA 1111

13d. How is this person related to you?
son

VA FORM
JAN 2004 **21-526**

SUPERSEDES STOCKS OF VA FORM 21-526, APR 2003
WHICH WILL NOT BE USED

21-526, Part A   *page 1*

(A blank copy of this form was obtained from the VA Web site, http://www.vba.va.gov/pubs/forms/VBA-21-526-ARE.pdf.)

Figure 8.4b Sample completed Form 21-526, part A, page 2.

SECTION III — Tell us about your active duty	

1. Enter complete information for all periods of service. If more space is needed use Item 29 "Remarks."

2. Attach your original DD214 or a certified copy to this form. (We will return original documents to you.)

14a. I entered active service the **first** time. . .	14b. Place:	14c. My service number was . . .	
02-07-1944 *mo day yr*	Cincinnati, Ohio	35 000 000	
14d. I left this active service. . . .	14e. Place:	14f. Branch of Service	14g. Grade, rank, or rating
04-11-1946 *mo day yr*	Sep Cen Camp Atterbury IN	Army	T/4
14h. I entered my **second** period of active service. . . . *mo day yr*	14i. Place:	14j. My service number was . . .	
14k. I left this active service. . . . *mo day yr*	14l. Place:	14m. Branch of Service	14n. Grade, rank, or rating

15a. Did you serve in Vietnam? ☐ Yes ☒ No *(If "Yes," answer Item 15b also)*	15b. When were you in Vietnam? *from* _____ *to* _____ *mo day yr* | *mo day yr*

The VA has a registry of veterans who served in the Gulf War. This area has also been called the "Persian Gulf." If you served there, we will include your name in the registry. If you want your medical information included, you must check "Yes" in Item 16b. For more information about the registry, see page 4 of the General Instructions for VA Form 21-526.

16a. Were you stationed in the Gulf after August 1, 1990? ☐ Yes ☒ No *(If "Yes," answer Item 16b also)*	16b. Do you want to have medical and other information about you included in the "Gulf War Veterans' Health Registry?" ☐ Yes ☐ No
17a. Have you ever been a prisoner of war? ☐ Yes ☒ No *(If "Yes," answer Items 17b, 17c, and 17d also)*	17b. What country or government imprisoned you?
17c. When were you confined? *from* _____ *to* _____ *mo day yr* | *mo day yr*	17d. What was the name of the camp or sector and what are the names of the city and country near its location?

SECTION IV — Tell us about your reserve duty	

18a. Are you currently assigned to an active reserve unit? ☐ Yes ☒ No *(If "Yes," answer Item 18b also)*	18b. What is the name, mailing address, and telephone number of your current unit?
18c. Were you previously assigned to an active reserve unit within the last 2 years? ☐ Yes ☒ No *(If "Yes," answer Item 18d also)*	18d. What is the name, mailing address, and telephone number of that unit?

21-526, Part A   *page 2*

Figure 8.4c Sample completed Form 21-526, part A, page 3.

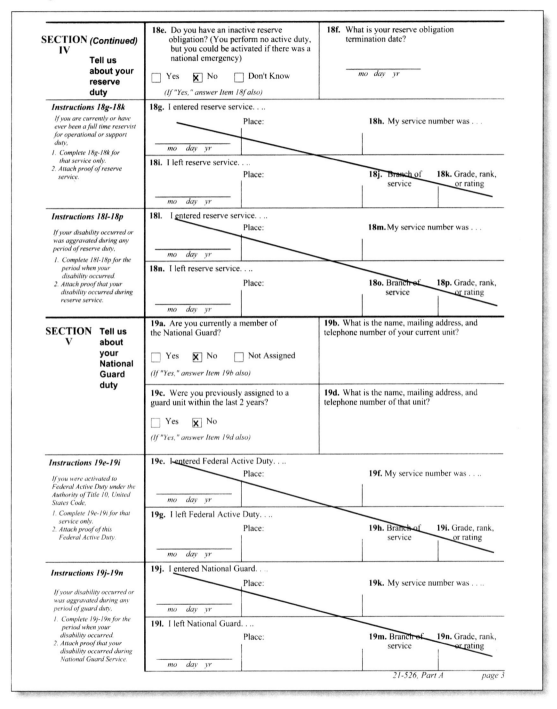

SECTION *(Continued)* IV **Tell us about your reserve duty**	**18e.** Do you have an inactive reserve obligation? (You perform no active duty, but you could be activated if there was a national emergency) ☐ Yes ☒ No ☐ Don't Know *(If "Yes," answer Item 18f also)*	**18f.** What is your reserve obligation termination date? _____ _____ _____ *mo day yr*
Instructions 18g-18k *If you are currently or have ever been a full time reservist for operational or support duty,* *1. Complete 18g-18k for that service only.* *2. Attach proof of reserve service.*	**18g.** I entered reserve service. . . . Place: _____ _____ _____ *mo day yr* **18i.** I left reserve service. . . . Place: _____ _____ _____ *mo day yr*	**18h.** My service number was . . . **18j.** Branch of service **18k.** Grade, rank, or rating
Instructions 18l-18p *If your disability occurred or was aggravated during any period of reserve duty,* *1. Complete 18l-18p for the period when your disability occurred.* *2. Attach proof that your disability occurred during reserve service.*	**18l.** I entered reserve service. . . . Place: _____ _____ _____ *mo day yr* **18n.** I left reserve service. . .. Place: _____ _____ _____ *mo day yr*	**18m.** My service number was . . . **18o.** Branch of service **18p.** Grade, rank, or rating
SECTION V **Tell us about your National Guard duty**	**19a.** Are you currently a member of the National Guard? ☐ Yes ☒ No ☐ Not Assigned *(If "Yes," answer Item 19b also)*	**19b.** What is the name, mailing address, and telephone number of your current unit?
	19c. Were you previously assigned to a guard unit within the last 2 years? ☐ Yes ☒ No *(If "Yes," answer Item 19d also)*	**19d.** What is the name, mailing address, and telephone number of that unit?
Instructions 19e-19i *If you were activated to Federal Active Duty under the Authority of Title 10, United States Code,* *1. Complete 19e-19i for that service only.* *2. Attach proof of this Federal Active Duty.*	**19e.** I entered Federal Active Duty. . . . Place: _____ _____ _____ *mo day yr* **19g.** I left Federal Active Duty. . . . Place: _____ _____ _____ *mo day yr*	**19f.** My service number was . . .. **19h.** Branch of service **19i.** Grade, rank, or rating
Instructions 19j-19n *If your disability occurred or was aggravated during any period of guard duty,* *1. Complete 19j-19n for the period when your disability occurred.* *2. Attach proof that your disability occurred during National Guard Service.*	**19j.** I entered National Guard. . . . Place: _____ _____ _____ *mo day yr* **19l.** I left National Guard. . . . Place: _____ _____ _____ *mo day yr*	**19k.** My service number was . . .. **19m.** Branch of service **19n.** Grade, rank, or rating

21-526, Part A *page 3*

Figure 8.4d Sample completed Form 21-526, part A, page 4.

SECTION VI	**Tell us about your travel status**	**20a.** Were you injured while traveling to or from your military assignment? *(If "Yes," answer Items 20b thru 20e and Section I of Part B: Compensation)* ☐ Yes ☒ No **20b.** When did your injury happen? *mo day yr* **20c.** Where did your injury happen? *(City,State,Country)* **20d.** Where were you treated? *(Provide name and address of doctor's office, hospital, etc.)* **20e.** What agency did you file an accident report with?

SECTION VII **Tell us about your military benefits**	**21a.** Are you receiving or will you receive retired or retainer pay that is based on your military service? ☐ Yes ☒ No *(If "Yes," answer Items 21b thru 21f. If "No," skip to Item 22)* **21b.** What branch of service is paying or will pay your retired or retainer pay? **21c.** What is the monthly amount? $ _____

When you file this application, you are telling us that you want to get VA compensation instead of military retired pay. If you currently receive military retired pay, you should be aware that we will reduce your retired pay by the amount of any compensation that you are awarded. VA will notify the Military Retired Pay Center of all benefit changes.

You must sign 21e if you want to keep getting military retired pay instead of VA compensation.

Please see page 4 of the General Instructions for VA Form 21-526.

If you have gotten both military retired pay and VA compensation, some of the amount you get may be recouped by VA, or in the case of VSI, by the Department of Defense.

21d. What is your retirement based on?
☐ Length of service ☐ Disability ☐ TDRL (Temporary Disability Retired List)

21e. Sign here if you want to receive military retired pay *instead of* VA compensation

_____

21f. Have you received or will you receive any of the following military benefits? **(Please check the appropriate boxes and tell us the amount)**

Benefit	*Amount*
(1) ☐ Lump Sum Readjustment Pay	$
(2) ☐ Separation pay under 10 USC 1174	$
(3) ☐ Special Separation Benefit (SSB)	$
(4) ☐ Voluntary Separation Incentive (VSI)	$
(5) ☐ Disability Severance Pay *(name of disability _____)*	$
(6) ☐ Other *(tell us the type of benefit _____)*	$

SECTION VIII **Give us direct deposit information**

If benefits are awarded we will need more information in order to process any payments to you. Please read the paragraph starting with, ***"All federal payments..."*** and then either:

1. Attach a voided check, or

2. Answer questions 22-24 to the right.

All federal payments beginning January 2, 1999, must be made by electronic funds transfer (EFT) also called Direct Deposit. Please attach a voided personal check or deposit slip or provide the information requested below in Items 22, 23 and 24 to enroll in Direct Deposit. If you do not have a bank account we will give you a waiver from Direct Deposit, just check the box below in Item 22. The Treasury Department is working on making bank accounts available to you. Once these accounts are available, you will be able to decide whether you wish to sign-up for one of the accounts or continue to receive a paper check. You can also request a waiver if you have other circumstances that you feel would cause you a hardship to be enrolled in Direct Deposit. You can write to: Department of Veterans Affairs, 125 S. Main Street Suite B, Muskogee OK 74401-7004, and give us a brief description of why you do not wish to participate in Direct Deposit.

22. Account number (Please check the appropriate box and provide that account number, if applicable)
☒ Checking ☐ I certify that I **do not** have an account with a financial institution or certified payment agent
☐ Savings
Account number   **10-2222-2222**

23. Name of financial institution
Thrifty Bank

24. Routing or transit number
0 11 0000 11

21-526, Part A   *page 4*

Figure 8.4e Sample completed Form 21-526, part A, page 5.

SECTION IX Give us your signature	I certify and authorize the release of information:
1. Read the box that starts, "I certify and authorize the release of information:"	I certify that the statements in this document are true and complete to the best of my knowledge. I authorize any person or entity, including but not limited to any organization, service provider, employer, or government agency, to give the Department of Veterans Affairs any information about me except protected health information, and I waive any privilege which makes the information confidential.

	25. Your signature *John Joseph Smith*	26. Today's date 02-15-2009
2. Sign the box that says, "Your signature."	27a. Signature of witness (If claimant signed above using an "X")	27b. Printed name and address of witness
3. If you sign with an "X", then you must have 2 people you know witness you as you sign. They must then sign the form and print their names and addresses also.	28a. Signature of witness (If claimant signed above using an "X")	28b. Printed name and address of witness

SECTION X	29. Remarks *(If you need more space to answer a question or have a comment about a specific item number on this form please identify your answer or statement by the part and item number). (See page 5 "Tips For Filling Out Your VA Form 21-526.")*
Remarks - Use this space for any additional statements that you would like to make concerning your application for Compensation and/or Pension *IMPORTANT* *Penalty: The law provides severe penalties which include fine or imprisonment, or both, for the willful submission of any statement or evidence of a material fact, knowing it to be false, or for the fraudulent acceptance of any payment which you are not entitled to.*	

21-526, Part A   *page 5*

Figure 8.4f Sample completed Form 21-526, part B, page 1.

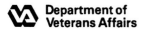

Department of Veterans Affairs

VA Form 21-526, Part B: Compensation

Use this form to apply for compensation. Remember that you must also fill out a VA Form 21-526, Part A: General Information, for your application to be processed. Be sure to write your name and Social Security number in the space provided on page 2.

SECTION I	Tell us about your disability	In the table below, tell us more about your disability or disabilities. Be sure to:
		 ● List all disabilities you believe are related to military service.
		 ● List all the treatments you received for your disabilities, including
		    ● treatments you received in a military facility before and after discharge.
		    ● treatments you received from civilian and VA sources before, during, and after your service.

1. What disability are you claiming?	2. When did your disability begin?	3. When were you treated?		4a. What medical facility or doctor treated you?	4b. What is the address of that medical facility or doctor?
		from	*to*		
	mo day yr	*mo day yr*	*mo day yr*		
		from	*to*		
	mo day yr	*mo day yr*	*mo day yr*		
		from	*to*		
	mo day yr	*mo day yr*	*mo day yr*		
		from	*to*		
	mo day yr	*mo day yr*	*mo day yr*		
		from	*to*		
	mo day yr	*mo day yr*	*mo day yr*		
		from	*to*		
	mo day yr	*mo day yr*	*mo day yr*		
		from	*to*		
	mo day yr	*mo day yr*	*mo day yr*		
		from	*to*		
	mo day yr	*mo day yr*	*mo day yr*		
		from	*to*		
	mo day yr	*mo day yr*	*mo day yr*		

pension only

VA FORM JAN 2004 **21-526**   *21-526, Part B*   *page 1*

Figure 8.4g Sample completed Form 21-526, part B, page 2.

SECTION II — Tell us if any of the disabilities you listed on Page 1 were because of exposures			
5a. Were you exposed to Agent Orange or other herbicides? ☐ Yes ☐ No	**5b.** What is your disability?	**5c.** In what country were you exposed?	
6a. Were you exposed to asbestos? ☐ Yes ☐ No *(If "Yes," answer Item 6b and 6c also)*	**6b.** What is your disability? **6c.** When and how were you exposed?		
7a. Were you exposed to mustard gas? ☐ Yes ☐ No *(If "Yes," answer Item 7b and 7c also)*	**7b.** What is your disability? **7c.** When and how were you exposed?		
8a. Were you exposed to ionizing radiation? ☐ Yes ☐ No *(If "Yes," answer Items 8b, 8c, and 8d also)*	**8b.** What is your disability?	**8c.** When was your last exposure? _mo day yr_	
8d. How were you exposed to radiation?	☐ Atmospheric testing ☐ Nagasaki/Hiroshima ☐ Other, describe		
9a. Were you exposed to an environmental hazard in the Gulf War? ☐ Yes ☐ No *(If "Yes," answer Items 9b and 9c also)*	**9b.** What is your disability?	**9c.** What was the hazard?	
10a. Did you have a separation or retirement physical examination? ☐ Yes ☐ No *(If "Yes," answer Items 10b and 10c also)*	**10b.** When was the exam? _mo day yr_	**10c.** Where did the exam occur?	

pension only

SECTION III — Tell us how your disabilities listed on Page 1 are related to your military service	**11. Explanation**

Your Name	Your Social Security Number
John Joseph Smith	000-00-0000

21-526 , Part B   page 2

Figure 8.4h Sample completed Form 21-526, part C, page 1.

VA **Department of Veterans Affairs**

VA Form 21-526, Part C: Dependency
Use this form to tell us more about your dependents. Remember that you must also fill out a VA Form 21-526, Part A: General Information, Part B and/or Part D, for your application to be processed. Be sure to write your name and Social Security number in the space provided on page 3.

SECTION I	Tell us about your marriage

NOTE: You should provide a copy of your marriage certificate

1. What is your marital status?

☐ Married ☒ Surviving Spouse ☐ Divorced ☐ Never Married

(If your spouse died, you are "divorced," or "never married" skip to Section III beginning on page 2)

2. When were you married?

_____
month   day   year

3. Where did you get married?

(city/state or country)

_____

4. What is your spouse's name?

First   Middle   Last

5. What is your spouse's birthday?

_____
month   day   year

6. What is your spouse's Social Security number?

_____

7a. Is your spouse also a veteran?

☐ Yes   ☐ No

(If "Yes," answer Item 7b also)

7b. What is your spouse's VA file number (If any)?

_____

8. Do you live with your spouse?

☐ Yes *(If "Yes," go to Item 12)*
☐ No   *(If "No," go to Item 9)*

9. What is your spouse's address?

_____
Street address, Rural Route, or P.O. Box   Apt. number

_____
City   State   Zip code   Country

10. Tell us why you are not living with your spouse

11. How much do you contribute monthly to your spouse's support?

$ _____

12. How were you married?

a. ☐ Ceremony by a clergyman or other authorized public official
b. ☐ Common-law

c. ☐ Tribal
d. ☐ Proxy
e. ☐ Other *(please describe in the space below)*

_____
_____
_____

VA Form
JAN 2004 **21-526**

21-526, Part C   *page 1*

Figure 8.4i Sample completed Form 21-526, part C, page 2.

SECTION II	Tell us about any previous marriages	In the table below, tell us about:
	NOTE: *You should provide copies of divorce decrees or death certificates.*	• Your previous marriages, and • Your spouse's previous marriages

Your previous marriages

13a. How many times have you been married before? _____

13b. When were you married?	13c. Where were you married? *(city/state or country)*	13d. Who were you married to? *(first, middle initial, last)*	13e. When did your marriage end?	13f. Why did your marriage end? *(death, divorce)*	13g. Where did your marriage end? *(city/state or country)*
mo day yr			*mo day yr*		
mo day yr			*mo day yr*		

Your spouse's previous marriages

14a. How many times has your current spouse been married before? _____

14b. When was your spouse married?	14c. Where was your spouse married? *(city/state or country)*	14d. Who was your spouse married to? *(first, middle initial, last)*	14e. When did your spouse's marriage end?	14f. Why did your spouse's marriage end? *(death, divorce)*	14g. Where did your spouse's marriage end? *(city/state or country)*
mo day yr			*mo day yr*		
mo day yr			*mo day yr*		

SECTION III	Tell us about your other dependents	In this section we want to know whether your parents are financially dependent on you (Question 15) and more about your **dependent children**. VA may recognize a veteran's biological children, adopted children, and stepchildren as dependent. These children must be unmarried and: • be under the age of 18, **or** • be at least 18 but under 23 and pursuing an approved course of education, **or** • have become permanently unable to support themselves before reaching the age of 18.

	15. Are your parents financially dependent on you? ☐ Yes ☐ No *(If "Yes," we will request additional information from you later)*

| *You should provide: a copy of the public record of birth for each child or a copy of the court record of adoption for each adopted child.* | 16. Do you have dependent children?

 ☐ Yes

 (If "No," Skip Items 17-21f). Go to the bottom of page 3 and write your name and Social Security number)

 ☐ No | 17. How many dependent children do you have?

 _____

 Give us more information about these children in the tables on the next page (Items 18 through 21f) |

21-526, Part C   *page 2*

Figure 8.4j Sample completed Form 21-526, part C, page 3.

SECTION III   **Tell us about your dependents (continued)**

18a. What is the name of your unmarried child(ren)? *(first, middle initial, last)*	18b. Date and place of birth *(city/state or country)*	18c. Social Security Number	19a. Biological	19b. Adopted	19c. Stepchild	20a. 18-23 yrs. old and in school	20b. Seriously disabled before age 18	20c. Child previously married
	mo day yr Place:		☐	☐	☐	☐	☐	☐
	mo day yr Place:		☐	☐	☐	☐	☐	☐
	mo day yr Place:		☐	☐	☐	☐	☐	☐
	mo day yr Place:		☐	☐	☐	☐	☐	☐

Tell us about your dependents listed above who *don't live with you*

21a. Do all the children listed above live with you?

☐ Yes   *(If "Yes," skip Items 21b thru 21f and write your name and Social Security number below)*

☐ No   *(If "No," complete Item 21b and the table below (Items 21c -21f) and write your name and Social Security number below)*

21b. How many of the children do not live with you?

_____

21c. What is the name of your child? *(first, middle initial, last)*	21d. What is your child's complete address?	21e. What is the name of the person your child lives with (If applicable)? *(first, middle initial, last)*	21f. How much do you contribute each month to the support of your child?
			$
			$
			$
			$

Your name	**Your Social Security Number**
John Joseph Smith	000-00-0000

Figure 8.4k Sample completed Form 21-526, part D, page 1.

Department of Veterans Affairs

VA Form 21-526, Part D: Pension

Use this form to apply for pension. Remember that you must also fill out a VA Form 21-526, Part A: General Information, for your application to be processed. Be sure to write your name and Social Security number in the space provided on page 4.

SECTION I Tell us about your disability and background	**1a.** What disability(ies) prevent you from working? COPD Mild dementia Coronary artery disease

1b. When did the disability(ies) begin?

01-01-2001
month day year

Complete this section if you are claiming pension because of permanent and total disability not caused by your military service.

2. Are you claiming a special monthly pension because you need the regular assistance of another person, are blind, nearly blind, or having severe visual problems, or are housebound?

[X] Yes   [ ] No

3a. Are you now, or have you recently been hospitalized or given outpatient or home-based care?

[X] Yes   [ ] No

(If "Yes," answer Items 3b and 3c also)

Attach current medical evidence showing that you are permanently and totally disabled.

3b. Tell us the dates of the recent hospitalization or care.

Began 06-01-2008
month day year

Ended 06-15-2008
month day year

3c. What is the name and complete mailing address of the facility or doctor?

Bently General Hospital
400 Dutch Avenue
Anytown PA 11111

Note: If you are a veteran who is age 65 or older, or determined to be disabled by the Social Security Administration, you DO NOT have to submit medical evidence with your application.

4a. Are you now employed?

[ ] Yes   [X] No

(If "No," answer Item 4b also)

4b. When did you last work?

01-31-1985
month day year

4c. Were you self-employed before becoming totally disabled?

[ ] Yes   [X] No

(If "Yes," answer Item 4d and 4e also)

4d. What kind of work did you do?

4e. Are you still self-employed?

[ ] Yes   [ ] No

(If "Yes," answer Item 4f also)

4f. What kind of work do you do now?

4g. Have you claimed or are you receiving disability benefits from the Social Security Administration (SSA)?

[ ] Yes   [X] No

4h. Circle the highest year of education you completed:

Grade school: [ ] 1 [ ] 2 [ ] 3 [ ] 4
[ ] 5 [ ] 6 [ ] 7 [ ] 8
[ ] 9 [ ] 10 [ ] 11 [ ](12)

College: [ ] 1 [ ] 2 [ ] 3 [ ] 4 [ ] over 4

4i. List the other training or experience you have and any certificates that you hold.

VA Form
JAN 2004 **21-526**

21-526, Part D   Page 1

Figure 8.4l Sample completed Form 21-526, part D, page 2.

SECTION II	Tell us your work history	In the table below, tell us about all of your employment, including self-employment, for one year before you became disabled to the present.					
5a. What was the name and address of your employer?		5b. What was your job title?	5c. When did your work begin?	5d. When did your work end?	5e. How many days were lost due to disability?	5f. What were your total annual earnings?	
			mo day yr	*mo day yr*		$	
			mo day yr	*mo day yr*		$	
			mo day yr	*mo day yr*		$	

SECTION III	Tell us if you are in a nursing home	In this section, tell us if you are in a nursing home. If you are in a nursing home, give us more information about the nursing home.

To get your claim processed faster, provide a statement by an official of the nursing home that tells us that you are a patient in the nursing home because of a physical or mental disability and tells us the daily charge for your care.	**6a.** Are you now in a nursing home? ☐ Yes ☒ No *(If "Yes," answer Item 6b also)*	**6b.** What is the name and complete mailing address of the facility or doctor?
	6c. Does Medicaid cover all or part of your nursing home costs? ☐ Yes ☐ No *(If "No," answer Item 6d also)*	**6d.** Have you applied for Medicaid? ☐ Yes ☐ No

SECTION IV	Tell us the net worth of you and your dependents	In this section, we ask you to give us specific information about your net worth and the net worth of your dependents. You will need to enter this information in the tables on page 3. You must include all assets in your net worth except those items you use everyday (See definition of net worth below.) You should subtract from the market value of your real estate any amounts that you owe on it (such as mortgages, liens, etc.) You can subtract mortgages on any property, and the value of the house or part of a building that you live in as your primary residence. You can report farms or buildings that you or a dependent own by reporting its value as "real property."
*VA cannot pay you pension if your **net worth** is sizeable.*		Definitions: Net worth is the market value of all interest and rights in any kind of property less any mortgages or other claims against the property. However, net worth does not include the house you live in or a reasonable area of land it sits on. Net worth also does not include the value of personal things you use everyday like your vehicle, clothing, and furniture. Go to Page 3 and fill out the table.

21-526, Part D Page 2

Figure 8.4m Sample completed Form 21-526, part D, page 3.

SECTION IV (Continued)	Tell us about your net worth and your dependents' net worth.				
	For items 7a-h: provide the amounts. If none, write "0" or "None"				
				Child(ren)	
Source	Veteran	Spouse	I. Name: *(first, middle initial, last)*	II. Name: *(first, middle initial, last)*	III. Name: *(first, middle initial, last)*
7a. Cash, non-interest bearing bank accounts	None	N/A			
7b. Interest bearing bank accounts, certificates of deposit (CDs)	20,000			N/A	
7c. IRAs, Keogh Plans, etc.	None				
7d. Stocks and bonds	None				
7e. Mutual funds	None				
7f. Value of business assets	None				
7g. Real property (not your home)	None				
7h. All other property	None				

SECTION V	Tell us about the income you have received and you expect to receive	In this section, we ask you to give us specific information about the income you have received and the income you expect to receive from all sources. You will need to enter this information in the tables on Page 4. In these tables, Report the total amounts before you take out deductions for taxes, insurance, etc. Do not report the same information in both tables. If you expect to receive a payment, but you don't know how much it will be, write "Unknown" in the space. If you do not receive any payments from one of the sources that we list, write "0" or "None" in the space. If you are receiving monthly benefits, give us a copy of your most recent award letter. This will help us determine the amount of benefits you should be paid.

Payments from any source will be counted, unless the law says that they don't need to be counted. VA will determine any amount that does not count.	**8.** Will you receive any income from rental property or from operation of a business within 12 months of the day you sign this form? ☐ Yes ☒ No	**9.** Will you receive any income from the operation of a farm within 12 months of the day you sign this form? ☐ Yes ☒ No	**10.** Do you expect to receive money from a civilian agency, corporation, or individual, because of personal injury or death within 12 months of the day you sign this form? ☐ Yes ☒ No

21-526, Part D   Page 3

Figure 8.4n Sample completed Form 21-526, part D, page 4.

SECTION V (Continued)   **Monthly Income - Tell us the income you and your dependents receive every month.**

For Items 11a-12f if none write "0" or "None"

Sources of recurring monthly income	Veteran	Spouse	Child(ren) I. Name: *(first, middle initial, last)*	II. Name: *(first, middle initial, last)*	III. Name: *(first, middle initial, last)*
11a. Social Security	1,000	N/A			
11b. U.S. Civil Service	None			N/A	
11c. U.S. Railroad Retirement	None				
11d. Military Retired Pay	None				
11e. Black Lung Benefits	None				
11f. Supplemental Security (SSI)/ Public Assistance	None				
11g. Other income received monthly *(Please write in the source below:)* work pension	800				

Next 12 months - Tell us about other income for you and your dependents

Sources of income for the next 12 months	Veteran	Spouse	Child(ren) I. Name: *(first, middle initial, last)*	II. Name: *(first, middle initial, last)*	III. Name: *(first, middle initial, last)*
12a. Gross wages and salary	None	N/A			
12b. Total interest and dividends	200			N/A	
12c. Worker's compensation for injury	None				
12d. Unemployment compensation	None				
12e. Other military benefit *(Please write in the source below:)*	None				
12f. Other one-time benefit *(Please write in the source below:)*	None				

SECTION VI

IMPORTANT - Items 13A through 13E should be completed only if you are applying for nonservice-connected pension.

Tell us any information concerning, Medical, Legal or Other Expenses - Family medical expenses actually paid by you may be deductible from your income. Show the amount of unreimbursed medical expenses you paid for yourself or relatives you are under an obligation to support. Also, show medical, legal or other expenses you paid because of a disability for which civilian disability benefits have been awarded. When determining your income, we may be able to deduct them from the disability benefits for the year in which the expenses are paid. **Do not** include any expenses for which you were reimbursed. Show the Medicare deduction in line 1. If more space is needed attach a separate sheet.

13A. AMOUNT PAID BY YOU	13B. DATE PAID	13C. PURPOSE *(Doctor's fees, hospital charges, Attorney fees, etc.)*	13D. PAID TO *(Name of doctor, hospital, pharmacy, Attorney, etc.)*	13E. DISABILITY OR RELATIONSHIP OF PERSON FOR WHOM EXPENSES PAID
		See enclosed medical expense report Form 21-8416		

Your Name John Joseph Smith	Your Social Security Number 000-00-0000

21-526, Part D   *Page 4*

FORM 21-534: APPLICATION FOR DEPENDENCY AND INDEMNITY COMPENSATION, DEATH PENSION AND ACCRUED BENEFITS BY A SURVIVING SPOUSE OR CHILD

Form 21-534 can be used to apply for dependency and indemnity compensation (DIC), death pension, and accrued benefits. The instructions below apply to surviving spouses of deceased wartime service veterans who are applying for Aid and Attendance pensions or Housebound pensions; the VA categorizes Aid and Attendance and Housebound pensions for surviving spouses as death pensions. The instructions below do not address death pensions for surviving dependent children of wartime service veterans. The instructions below do not address DIC situations, where a veteran died in service or died as the result of a service-connected disability or where a veteran rated totally disabled from a service-connected disability died from a non-service-connected condition. The instructions below also do not address applying for accrued benefits.

Tips for Completing Form 21-534

A sample completed Form 21-534 is presented in figure 8.5. Be sure to refer to it to see how to complete the form.

Note: If you leave a box blank or unchecked, your claim will be delayed and you will have wasted at least a month. Be thorough and review all your work. Read the instructions at least once before completing the form, and print legibly.

Section I: Tell us what you are applying for and what you and the deceased veteran have applied for

Box 2 or 4—There is no VA file number if the deceased veteran or the surviving spouse has never filed for benefits. If the deceased veteran or surviving spouse has ever filed for any veteran benefit, a VA file number exists and should be written on the form. The file number can be found on all VA correspondence. If in doubt, leave the box blank until you check with a VSO, who can look up the VA file number for you.

Box 7—Check the "No" box because you are filing for a death pension.

Section II: Tell us about you and the deceased veteran

Attach a copy of the veteran's death certificate.

Section III: Tell us about the veteran's active duty service

Boxes 21a–21g—The veteran's discharge record will contain the information needed for these boxes, such as the date and place the veteran entered and left active service, his or her service number, his or her grade or rank, and the branch of service.

You must attach the veteran's discharge record (also known as a separation document or DD-214) to this form. Attach a *certified copy* of the discharge record, not the original. A photocopy or notarized copy will not substitute for a certified copy. As mentioned in chapter 7, personnel at the VA, an authorized veterans service organization, or the county courthouse can make a certified copy of the discharge record.

Section IV: Tell us about your and the veteran's marital history

Attach a copy of your marriage certificate showing your marriage to the deceased wartime service veteran.

Boxes 26–27—If there was any period of marriage separation before the veteran died and the separation was by court order, attach a copy of the court order of the separation.

Section V: Tell us about the unmarried children of the veteran

This section does not apply to surviving spouses of deceased wartime service veterans applying for Aid and Attendance pensions or Housebound pensions. Draw a line through boxes 28a–30d.

Section VI: Tell us if you are housebound, in a nursing home or require aid and attendance

Box 31—Check the "Yes" box. Note: If you are a resident in an assisted living facility or are receiving nonmedical home care or are confined to your home because of a permanent disability, attach Form 21-2680 (physician examination) as evidence of your disability.

Boxes 32a–32d—If you are in a nursing home, check with a VSO before answering boxes 32a–32d. You must meet certain requirements, as mentioned in "Special Circumstances" in chapter 3, in order to apply for benefits.

Section VII: Tell us the net worth of you and your dependents

Boxes 33a–33f—Fill in every box and write "None" or "0" where applicable. If the surviving spouse does not have any dependents, then in the section labeled "Children," draw a line through boxes 33a–33f and write "N/A" in this section. (See definition of dependents in the "Pension Rates" section of chapter 4.) Leaving a box blank can cause delays in processing your claim. Attach copies of your net worth documents, such as statements for CDs, savings accounts, etc. (See "Examples of assets that contribute toward net worth" in chapter 3.)

Section VIII: Tell us about the income of you and your dependents

Boxes 34a–39d—Fill in every box and write "None" or "0" where applicable. If the surviving spouse does not have any dependents, then in the sections labeled "Children," draw lines through boxes 38a–39d and write "N/A" in each section. Leaving a box blank can cause delays in processing your claim. Attach proof of all income, such as a copy of your Social Security award letter, the pension letter from a previous employer, bank interest statements, etc. (See the "Income" section in chapter 3.)

Section IX: Tell us about medical, last illness, burial or other unreimbursed expenses

Most surviving spouses have only medical expense deductions and not other types of expenses. In the example (figure 8.5g), the surviving spouse has only deductible medical expenses.

Boxes 40a–40e—You have two options for this section as follows:

▶ Option 1: List all eligible out-of-pocket expenses on the form and attach proof of all listed expenses. Since the surviving spouse in the example has only unreimbursed medical expenses and there is enough room on the form, all the expenses are listed there (figure 8.5g). If you are in an assisted living facility or receiving nonmedical home care, be sure to attach your monthly invoice as it is a medical expense.

▶ Option 2: If you need more space than provided in this section to list deductible medical expenses, list all of them on Form 21-8416. In boxes 40a–40e, write "See enclosed medical expense report Form 21-8416." (A sample Form 21-8416 is presented in figure 8.6.)

If you think you have legal or other expense deductions, check with a VSO as to their eligibility.

Section X: Give us direct deposit information

Boxes 41–43—Attach a voided blank check so that direct deposit payments may be made to your bank account. You should also fill in these boxes with your bank account information in case the voided blank check gets separated from the form. If you do not want direct deposit, write a letter to the VA as instructed on the form.

Section XI: Give us your signature

Boxes 44–45—You (the surviving spouse) must provide a signature and date.

Boxes 46a–47b—If you sign by marking an X, then two witnesses must also complete these boxes.

Note: Form SSA-24, Application for Survivors Benefits which prints out when you print Form 21-534 online is rarely used. In my experience, surviving spouses of wartime service veterans already receive Social Security benefits; if you are not receiving Social Security benefits and decide to apply for them by completing this form, contact a VSO if you have any questions.

Figure 8.5a Sample completed Form 21-534: Application for Dependency and Indemnity Compensation, Death Pension and Accrued Benefits by a Surviving Spouse or Child, page 1 (application form for surviving spouses of deceased wartime service veterans).

OMB Approved No. 2900-0004
Respondent Burden: 1 hour 15 minutes

Department of Veterans Affairs

Application for Dependency and Indemnity Compensation, Death Pension and Accrued Benefits by a Surviving Spouse or Child (Including Death Compensation if Applicable)
VA Form 21-534

Please read the attached "General Instructions" before you fill out this form.

VA DATE STAMP
(DO NOT WRITE IN THIS SPACE)

SECTION I — Tell us what you are applying for and what you and the deceased veteran have applied for	
1. Did the veteran ever file a claim with VA? ☐ YES ☒ NO *(If "Yes," answer Item 2)*	2. What is the VA file number?
3. Has the surviving spouse or child ever filed a claim with VA? ☐ YES ☒ NO *(If "Yes," answer Items 4 through 6)*	4. What is the VA file number?
5. What is the name of the person on whose service the claim was filed? First Middle Last	
6. What is your relationship to that person?	
7. Are you claiming service connection for cause of death? ☐ YES ☒ NO	

SECTION II — Tell us about you and the deceased veteran	
8. What is the veteran's name? **David** **Scott** **Jones** First Middle Last Suffix *(If applicable)*	
9. What is the veteran's Social Security number? **111-11-1111**	10a. Did the veteran serve under another name? ☐ YES ☒ NO *(If "Yes," answer Items 10b)*
10b. Please list the other name(s) the veteran served under:	11. What is the veteran's date of birth? **01-24-1923** mo day yr
12. What is the veteran's date of death? **02-11-2000** mo day yr	13. Was the veteran a former prisoner of war? ☐ YES ☒ NO
14. What is your name? *(First, Middle, Last Name)* **Mary Louise Jones**	15. What is your relationship to the veteran? *(check one)* ☒ Surviving Spouse ☐ Child

Attach a copy of the death certificate unless the veteran died in active service of the Army, Navy, Air Force, Marine Corps, or Coast Guard, or in a U.S. government institution.

16. What is your address?
100 Friendship Road
Street address, Rural Route, or P.O. Box   Apt. number
Pleasantville   **OH**   **10101**   **USA**
City   State   ZIP Code   Country

17. What are your telephone numbers? *(Include Area Code)* **814-555-1212**	18. What is your e-mail address?
19. What is your Social Security number? **101-10-1010**	20. What is your date of birth? **10-05-1924** mo day yr

VA FORM JUN 2005 **21-534**   SUPERSEDES VA FORM 21-534, JUN 1998, WHICH WILL NOT BE USED.   *PAGE 1*

(A blank copy of this form was obtained from the VA Web site, http://www.vba.va.gov/pubs/forms/VBA-21-534-ARE.pdf.)

Figure 8.5b Sample completed Form 21-534, page 2.

SECTION III	Tell us about the veteran's active duty service	Note: Skip to Section IV if the veteran was receiving VA compensation or pension at the time of his/her death.			
		21a. Entered Active Service *(first period)* **03-01-1944** mo day yr	21b. Place **Pleasantville Ohio**	21c. Service Number **34 000 111**	
1. Enter complete information for all periods of service. If more space is needed use Item 48 "Remarks."		21d. Left This Active Service **05-11-1946** mo day yr	21e. Place **Sep Gen Camp Blooming IN**	21f. Branch of Service **Army**	21g. Grade, Rank, or Rating **Corporal**
2. If the veteran never filed a claim with VA, attach the original DD214 or a certified copy for each period of service listed. We will return original documents to you.		21h. Entered Active Service *(second period)* ——— mo day yr	21i. Place	21j. Service Number	
		21k. Left This Active Service ——— mo day yr	21l. Place	21m. Branch of Service	21n. Grade, Rank, or Rating

SECTION IV	Tell us about your and the veteran's marital history	Note: Skip to Section V if the veteran was receiving additional VA benefits for you as his/her spouse at the time of his/her death *unless* you remarried after the veteran's death.
Attach a copy of your marriage certificate showing your marriage to the veteran.		You must furnish complete information about **all** marriages of the surviving spouse and the veteran. If you need additional space, please attach a separate sheet of paper providing the requested information about the marriages.

The veteran's marriages

22a. How many times was the veteran married? **1**

22b. Date of Marriage	22c. Place *(city/state or country)*	22d. To whom married *(first, middle initial, last name)*	22e. Date marriage ended	22f. Place *(city/state or country)*	22g. How marriage ended *(death, divorce)*
11-02-1950 mo day yr	**Pleasantville OH**	**Mary L Jones**	**02-11-2000** mo day yr	**Pleasantville OH**	**death**
mo day yr			mo day yr		

The surviving spouse's marriages. Note: Items 23a through 27 should be completed by the veteran's surviving spouse. If the claimant is not the surviving spouse, skip to Section V.

23a. How many times were you married? **1**   23b. Have you remarried since the death of the veteran? ☐ YES ☒ NO

23c. Date of Marriage	23d. Place *(city/state or country)*	23e. To whom married *(first, middle initial, last name)*	23f. Date marriage ended	23g. Place *(city/state or country)*	23h. How marriage ended *(death, divorce)*
11-02-1950 mo day yr	**Pleasantville OH**	**David S Jones**	**02-11-2000** mo day yr	**Pleasantville OH**	**death**
mo day yr			mo day yr		

VA FORM 21-534, JUN 2005   *PAGE 2*

Figure 8.5c Sample completed Form 21-534, page 3.

SECTION IV Tell us about your and the veteran's marital history (continued)

Answer Item 24 only if you were married to the veteran for less than one year. ▶	24. Was a child born to you and the veteran during your marriage or prior to your marriage? ☐ YES ☐ NO	25. Are you expecting the birth of a child of the veteran? ☐ YES ☒ NO
	26. Did you live continuously with the veteran from the date of marriage to the date of his/her death? ☒ YES ☐ NO *(If "No", answer Item 27)*	27. What was the cause of the separation? Give the reason, date(s), and duration of the separation. If the separation was by court order, attach a copy of the order.

SECTION V Tell us about the unmarried children of the veteran

Note: You should provide a copy of the public record of birth or a copy of the court record of adoption for each child listed in Item 28a *unless* the veteran was receiving additional VA benefits for the child.

If you need additional space, please attach a separate sheet of paper providing the requested information about each child.

Note: Skip to Section VI if you are not claiming benefits for any children that meet the following criteria.

VA recognizes the veteran's biological children, adopted children, and stepchildren as dependents. These children must be unmarried and:

- under age 18, or
- between 18 and 23 and pursuing an approved course of education, or
- of any age if they became permanently unable to support themselves before reaching age 18.

"Seriously disabled" (Item 29e) means that the child became permanently unable to support himself/herself before reaching age 18. Furnish a statement from an attending physician or other medical evidence which shows the nature and extent of the physical or mental impairment.

Note to surviving spouse: If entitlement to DIC is established, a "seriously disabled" child over age 18 is entitled to receive DIC benefits in his or her own right. A veteran's child who is seriously disabled and over age 18 must submit a separate VA Form 21-534 to apply for benefits.

28a. Name of child *(First, middle initial, Last)*	28b. Date and place of birth *(City/State or Country)*	28c. Social Security Number	29a. Biological	29b. Adopted	29c. Stepchild	29d. 18 - 23 yrs old and in school	29e. Seriously disabled	29f. Child previously married
	mo day yr		☐	☐	☐	☐	☐	☐
	mo day yr		☐	☐	☐	☐	☐	☐
	mo day yr		☐	☐	☐	☐	☐	☐

VA FORM 21-534, JUN 2005

PAGE 3

Figure 8.5d Sample completed Form 21-534, page 4.

SECTION V Tell us about the unmarried children of the veteran (continued)

Tell us about the children listed above that don't live with you.

30a. Name of child *(first, middle initial, last)*	30b. Child's Complete Address	30c. Name of person the child lives with *(if applicable)*	30d. Monthly amount you contribute to child's support
			$
			$
			$
			$

SECTION VI Tell us if you are housebound, in a nursing home or require aid and attendance	31. Are you claiming aid and attendance allowance and/or housebound benefits because you need the regular assistance of another person, are having severe visual problems, or are housebound?	32a. Are you now in a nursing home?
If you answered "yes" to Item 31 and are not in a nursing home, submit a statement from your doctor showing the extent of your disabilities. If you are in a nursing home, attach a statement signed by an official of the nursing home showing the date you were admitted to the nursing home, the level of care you receive, the amount you pay out-of-pocket for your care, and whether Medicaid covers all or part of your nursing home costs.	[X] YES [ ] NO *(If "No," skip to section VII)*	[ ] YES [X] NO *(If "Yes," answer Items 32b and 32c also)*
	32b. What is the name and complete mailing address of the facility?	32c. Does Medicaid cover all or part of your nursing home costs? [ ] YES [ ] NO *(If "No," answer Item 32d also)*
	32d. Have you applied for Medicaid? [ ] YES [ ] NO	

VA FORM 21-534, JUN 2005

PAGE 4

86

Figure 8.5e Sample completed Form 21-534, page 5.

SECTION VII — Tell us the net worth of you and your dependents	VA cannot pay you pension if your net worth is sizeable. Net worth is the market value of all interest and rights you have in any kind of property less any mortgages or other claims against the property. However, net worth does not include the house you live in or a reasonable area of land it sits on. Net worth also does not include the value of personal things you use everyday like your vehicle, clothing, and furniture. You must report net worth for yourself and all persons for whom you are claiming benefits.

Note: If you are filing this application on behalf of a minor or incompetent child of the veteran and you are the child's custodian, you must report your net worth as well as the net worth of the child for whom benefits are claimed.

For Items 33a through 33f, provide the amounts. If none, write "0" or "None."

Source	Surviving spouse or Custodian of children	Child(ren) Name: *(first, middle initial, last)*	Name: *(first, middle initial, last)*	Name: *(first, middle initial, last)*
33a. Cash, bank accounts, certificates of deposit (CDs)	10,000		N/A	
33b. IRAs, Keogh Plans, etc.	None			
33c. Stocks, bonds, mutual funds	10,000			
33d. Value of business assets	None			
33e. Real property *(not your home)*	None			
33f. All other property	None			

SECTION VIII — Tell us about the income of you and your dependents	Report the total amounts before you take out deductions for taxes, insurance, etc. Do not report the same information in both tables. If you expect to receive a payment, but you don't know how much it will be, write "Unknown" in the space. If you do not receive any payments from one of the sources that we list, write "0" or "None" in the space. If you are receiving monthly benefits, give us a copy of your most recent award letter. This will help us determine the amount of benefits you should be paid.

Payments from any source will be counted, unless the law says that they don't need to be counted. Report **all** income, and VA will determine any amount that does not count.

Note: If you are filing this application on behalf of a minor of whom you are the custodian, you must report your income as well as the income of each child for whom benefits are claimed.

34a. Have you claimed or are you receiving benefits from the Social Security Administration on your own behalf or on behalf of child(ren) in your custody? [X] YES [ ] NO *(If "Yes," answer item 34b)*	34b. Is Social Security based on your own employment? [X] YES [ ] NO
35. Has a surviving spouse or child filed a claim for compensation from the Office of Worker's Compensation Programs based on the death of the veteran? [ ] YES [X] NO	36. Has a court awarded damages based on the death of the veteran or is a claim or legal action for damages pending? [ ] YES [X] NO

37. Have you claimed or are you receiving Survivor Benefit Plan (SBP) annuity from a service department based on the death of the veteran?   [ ] YES [X] NO

VA FORM 21-534, JUN 2005

PAGE 5

Figure 8.5f Sample completed Form 21-534, page 6.

SECTION VIII Tell us about the income of you and your dependents (continued)

Monthly Income - Tell us the income you and your dependents receive every month

Source	Surviving spouse or Custodian of children	Child(ren)		
		Name: *(first, middle initial, last)*	Name: *(first, middle initial, last)*	Name: *(first, middle initial, last)*
38a. Social Security	1,000			
38b. U.S. Civil Service	None		N/A	
38c. U.S. Railroad Retirement	None			
38d. Military Retirement	None			
38e. Black Lung Benefits	None			
38f. Supplemental Security Income (SSI)/ Public Assistance	None			
38g. Other income received monthly *(Please write source below:)*	None			

Expected income next 12 months - Tell us about other income for you and your dependents

Report expected income for the 12 month period following the veteran's death. If the claim is filed more than one year after the veteran died, report the expected income for the 12 month period from the date you sign this application.

Sources of income for the next 12 months	Surviving spouse or Custodian of children	Child(ren)		
		Name: *(first, middle initial, last)*	Name: *(first, middle initial, last)*	Name: *(first, middle initial, last)*
39a. Gross wages and salary	None		N/A	
39b. Total dividends and interest	200			
39c. Other income expected *(Please write source below:)*	None			
39d. Other income expected *(Please write source below:)*	None			

VA FORM 21-534, JUN 2005

PAGE 6

Figure 8.5g Sample completed Form 21-534, page 7.

SECTION IX	Family medical expenses and certain other expenses actually paid by you may be deductible from your income. Show the amount of any continuing family medical expenses such as the monthly Medicare deduction or nursing home costs you pay. Also, show unreimbursed last illness and burial expenses and educational or vocational rehabilitation expenses you paid. Last illness and burial expenses are unreimbursed amounts paid by you for the veteran's or his/her child's last illness and burial and the veteran's just debts. Educational or vocational rehabilitation expenses are amounts paid for courses of education, including tuition, fees, and materials. **Do not** include any expenses for which you were reimbursed. If you receive reimbursement after you have filed this claim, promptly advise the VA office handling your claim. If more space is needed attach a separate sheet.
Tell us about medical, last illness, burial or other unreimbursed expenses	

40a. Amount paid by you	40b. Date Paid	40c. Purpose (Medicare deduction, nursing home costs, burial expenses, etc.)	40d. Paid to (Name of nursing home, hospital, funeral home, etc.)	40e. Relationship of person for whom expenses paid
$ 96.40/mo	04-01-08 mo day yr to 03-01-09	Medicare Part B	Social Security	self
$ 135/mo	04-01-08 mo day yr to 03-01-09	Medicare HMO	High Med Security Blue	self
$ 1,080/mo	01-15-09 mo day yr to 03-15-09	nonmedical home care	Visiting Care Inc.	self
$ 60/mo	04-01-08 mo day yr to 03-01-09	medications	Thrifty Pharmacy	self

SECTION X	All Federal payments beginning January 2, 1999, must be made by electronic funds transfer (EFT) also called Direct Deposit. Please attach a voided personal check or deposit slip or provide the information requested below in Items 41, 42, and 43 to enroll in Direct Deposit. If you do not have a bank account we will give you a waiver from Direct Deposit, just check the box below in Item 41. The Treasury Department is working on making bank accounts available to you. Once these accounts are available, you will be able to decide whether you wish to sign-up for one of the accounts or continue to receive a paper check. You can also request a waiver if you have other circumstances that you feel would cause you a hardship to be enrolled in Direct Deposit. You can write to: Department of Veterans Affairs, 125 S. Main Street Suite B, Muskogee OK 74401-7004, and give us a brief description of why you do not wish to participate in Direct Deposit.
Give us direct deposit information	
If benefits are awarded we will need more information in order to process any payments to you. Please read the paragraph starting with, **"All Federal payments..."** and then either:	

If benefits are awarded we will need more information in order to process any payments to you. Please read the paragraph starting with, **"All Federal payments..."** and then either:

1. Attach a voided check, or

2. Answer questions 41-43 to the right.

41. Account number *(Please check the appropriate box and provide that account number, if applicable)*

[X] Checking   [ ] I certify that I **do not** have an account with a financial institution or certified payment agent

[ ] Savings

Account number   0015556666

42. Name of financial institution

Big Star Bank

43. Routing or transit number

021000088

Figure 8.5h Sample completed Form 21-534, page 8.

| SECTION XI — Give us your signature | I certify and authorize the release of information: I certify that the statements in this document are true and complete to the best of my knowledge. I authorize any person or entity, including but not limited to any organization, service provider, employer, or government agency, to give the Department of Veterans Affairs any information about me except protected health information, and I waive any privilege which makes the information confidential. |

SECTION XI Give us your signature

1. Read the box that starts, "I certify and authorize the release of information:"

2. Sign the box that says, "Your signature."

3. If you sign with an "X," then you must have 2 people you know witness you as you sign. They must then sign the form and print their names and addresses also.

44. Your signature	45. Today's date
Mary Louise Jones	03-28-2009

46a. Signature of witness *(If claimant signed above using an "X")*	46b. Printed name and address of witness
47a. Signature of witness *(If claimant signed above using an "X")*	47b. Printed name and address of witness

SECTION XII

Remarks - Use this space for any additional statements that you would like to make concerning your application.

IMPORTANT

Penalty: The law provides severe penalties which include fine or imprisonment, or both, for the willful submission of any statement or evidence of a material fact, knowing it to be false, or for the fraudulent acceptance of any payment which you are not entitled to.

48. Remarks *(If you need more space to answer a question or have a comment about a specific item number on this form please identify your answer or statement by the part and item number)*

VA FORM 21-534, JUN 2005

PAGE 8

FORM 21-8416: MEDICAL EXPENSE REPORT

Form 21-8416 may be used to document all unreimbursed medical expenses of the wartime service veteran or surviving spouse. This form gets attached to Form 21-526 or Form 21-534 (as applicable). Generally, unreimbursed expenses are recurring expenses, such as costs of medications, medical insurance (Medicare deduction, Security Blue, etc.), assisted living, and nonmedical home care. If you are confined to your home because of a permanent disability, the costs of transportation services count as medical expenses. Noteworthy nonrecurring expenses such as hospitalizations may also be listed; the VA will annualize these expenses. You must attach proof of all out-of-pocket medical expenses to this form. If you live in an assisted living facility or receive nonmedical home care, be sure to attach your monthly invoice as this is a medical expense.

Remember, unreimbursed medical expenses reduce countable income. *If unreimbursed medical expenses exceed income (and when you are in assisted living or receive nonmedical home care, this is often the case), you will receive the maximum pension.* If you fail to list all unreimbursed medical expenses, you may not receive the appropriate pension amount you are entitled to. Check with a VSO if you are not sure if a particular expense is an allowable medical expense.

Tips for Completing Form 21-8416

A sample completed Form 21-8416 is presented in figure 8.6. Be sure to refer to it to see how to complete the form.

Box 1—Fill in the name of the veteran. If you are the surviving spouse, fill in the veteran's name, not yours, in box 1.

Box 3A—If you are the veteran claimant, fill in your name and address. If you are the surviving spouse claimant, fill in your name and address.

Box 4—Fill in the veteran's Social Security number. If you are the surviving spouse, fill in the veteran's Social Security number, not yours, in box 4.

Boxes 7A–7B—Be sure you sign and date the form.

Figure 8.6a Sample completed Form 21-8416: Medical Expense Report, page 1.

OMB Control No. 2900-0161
Respondent Burden: 30 minutes

VA Department of Veterans Affairs

MEDICAL EXPENSE REPORT

1. NAME OF VETERAN (First, middle, last) John Joseph Smith		2. VA FILE NUMBER ____
3A. NAME AND ADDRESS OF CLAIMANT John Joseph Smith 714 Happy Lane Anytown PA 11111	3B. CHANGE OF ADDRESS (Check box if address in Item 3A is different from last address furnished to VA) ☐	3C. E-MAIL ADDRESS (If applicable) N/A
4. VETERAN'S SOCIAL SECURITY NO. 000-00-0000		

NOTE: Family medical expenses actually paid by you may be deductible from your income. Report the actual amount of unreimbursed medical expenses you paid for yourself or relatives who are members of your household. Do not report any expenses you did not pay or expenses for which you were or will be reimbursed. Any expenses reasonably related to medical or dental care may be allowed as medical expenses. Examples of allowable medical expenses include the following: hospital expenses, office visits, drugs and medicines, eyeglasses, dental fees, medical insurance premiums (including the Medicare deduction), hearing aids, nursing home fees, home health services, and transportation for medical purposes (28.5 cents per mile, plus parking and tolls or fares for taxis, buses, etc.). If you are not sure whether a particular expense can be allowed, furnish a complete description of the purpose of the payment. We will let you know if an expense cannot be allowed. If more space is needed, attach a separate sheet of paper with columns corresponding to those on this form. Be sure to write your VA file number on any attachments.

You may be asked to verify the amounts you actually paid, so keep all receipts or other documentation of payments for at least 3 years after we make a decision on your medical expense claim. If you are unable to provide documentation of payments for at least 3 years after we make a decision of your medical expense claim. If you are unable to provide documentation of the claimed medical expenses when asked to do so by VA, your benefits will be retroactively reduced or terminated.

Report medical expenses for the period _____ thru _____ . If no dates appear on this line, refer to the accompanying letter or Eligibility Verification Report for the dates your medical expense report should cover.

5. ITEMIZATION OF MEDICAL EXPENSES

A. PURPOSE (Physician or Hospital Charges Eyeglasses, Oxygen Rental, Medical Insurance, etc.)	B. AMOUNT PAID BY YOU	C. DATE PAID (Mo/Day/Yr)	D. NAME OF PROVIDER (Name of doctor, dentist, hospital, lab, etc.)	E. FOR WHOM PAID (Self, spouse, child)
MEDICARE (PART B)	96.40	Mar 1, 2008 –Feb 1, 2009	Social Security	self
PRIVATE MEDICAL INSURANCE	135/mo	Mar 1, 2008 –Feb 1, 2009	High Med Security Blue	self
Assisted Living Facility	2,650/mo	Dec 1, 2008 –Feb 1, 2009	Meadowland Assisted Living	self
Medications	119/mo	Mar 1, 2008 –Feb 1, 2009	Giant Red Pharmacy	self

IMPORTANT: Be sure to sign this form in Item 7A on the reverse side. Unsigned reports will be returned.

VA FORM SEP 2008 **21-8416** SUPERSEDES VA FORM 21-8416, NOV 2004, WHICH WILL NOT BE USED.

(A blank copy of this form was obtained from the VA Web site, http://www.vba.va.gov/pubs/forms/VBA-21-8416-ARE.pdf.)

Figure 8.6b Sample completed Form 21-8416, page 2.

5. ITEMIZATION OF MEDICAL EXPENSES *(Continued)*				
A. PURPOSE *(Physician or Hospital Charges Eyeglasses, Oxygen Rental, Medical Insurance, etc.)*	B. AMOUNT PAID BY YOU	C. DATE PAID *(Mo/Day/Yr)*	D. NAME OF PROVIDER *(Name of doctor, dentist, hospital, lab, etc.)*	E. FOR WHOM PAID *(Self, spouse, child)*

I have not and will not receive reimbursement for these expenses. I certify that the above information is true.

6A. DAYTIME TELEPHONE NO. *(Include Area Code)*	6B. EVENING TELEPHONE NO. *(Include Area Code)*
412-555-1212	

7A. SIGNATURE OF CLAIMANT *(Do NOT print)*	7B. DATE
John Joseph Smith	02-15-2009

PENALTY: The law provides severe penalties which include fine or imprisonment, or both, for the willful submission of any statement or evidence of a material fact, knowing it is false, or fraudulent acceptance of any payment to which you are not entitled.

PRIVACY ACT NOTICE: VA will not disclose information collected on this form to any source other than what has been authorized under the Privacy Act of 1974 or Title 38, code of Federal Regulations 1.576 for routine uses (i.e., civil or criminal law enforcement, congressional communications, epidemiological or research studies, the collection of money owed to the United States, litigation in which the United States is a party or has an interest, the administration of VA programs and delivery of VA benefits, verification of identity and status, and personnel administration) as identified in the VA system of records, 58VA21/22/28 Compensation, Pension, Education, and Vocational Rehabilitation Records - VA, and published in the Federal Register. Your obligation to respond is required to obtain or retain benefits. The requested information is considered relevant and necessary to determine maximum benefits provided under law. VA uses your SSN to identify your claim file. Providing your SSN will help ensure that your records are properly associated with your claim file. Giving us your SSN account information is voluntary. Refusal to provide your SSN by itself will not result in the denial of benefits. VA will not deny an individual benefits for refusing to provide his or her SSN unless the disclosure of the SSN is required by a Federal Statute of law in effect prior to January 1, 1975, and still in effect. The responses you submit are considered confidential (38 U.S.C. 5701). Information submitted is subject to verification through computer matching programs with other agencies.

RESPONDENT BURDEN: We need this information to determine whether medical expenses you paid may be used to reduce the amount of income we count in determining eligibility to benefits (38 U.S.C. 1503). Title 38, United States Code, allows us to ask for this information. We estimate that you will need an average of 30 minutes to review the instructions, find the information, and complete this form. VA cannot conduct or sponsor a collection of information unless a valid OMB control number is displayed. You are not required to respond to a collection of information if this number is not displayed. Valid OMB control numbers can be located on the OMB Internet Page at www.whitehouse.gov/omb/library/OMBINV.VA.EPA.html#VA. If desired, you can call 1-800-827-1000 to get information on where to send comments or suggestions about this form.

VA FORM 21-8416, SEP 2008

FORM 21-22: APPOINTMENT OF VETERANS SERVICE ORGANIZATION AS CLAIMANT'S REPRESENTATIVE

Note: If you filed an informal claim and have already completed Form 21-22, you do not need to complete the form again for the formal claim.

Use Form 21-22 only if you are using county or regional veterans service organization personnel—such as a county VSO, or a regional VSO of the American Legion, DAV, or VFW— to represent you. You do not need to be a member of a veterans service organization for the organization to represent you. Wartime service veterans and surviving spouses who applied for the Aid and Attendance and Housebound pensions often found it very helpful to have the regional or county VSOs represent them. (See the list of veterans service organizations in appendix 1.)

How to Choose a Veteran Service Officer

VSOs are invaluable in answering questions, looking up previous communications the veteran may have made with the VA, and checking application forms for errors. VSOs can also check on the status of claims after filing. You should be confident in the ability of the VSO. You may interview several before choosing your VSO. If the VSO does not seem capable of helping you, get a second opinion from another VSO, just as you would do if you were getting medical or legal advice. Some VSOs are less experienced and may not be informed about all the details of the VA pension program. Ask how many years of experience the VSO has in filing Aid and Attendance and Housebound pension claims and ask for a business card and e-mail address so you can contact the VSO to check on your claim. When scheduling a meeting with a VSO, be sure to bring all supporting documents. (See "Supporting Documents" at the end of this chapter for a list of documents.) The county VSOs and the regional VSOs located at organizations such as the American Legion, DAV, and VFW, are often very helpful and knowledgeable in filing claims. (See the lists of veterans service organizations in appendix 1.)

Tips for Completing Form 21-22

A sample completed Form 21-22 is presented in figure 8.7. Be sure to refer to it to see how to complete the form.

Box 1—Fill in the veteran's name. If you are the surviving spouse, fill in the veteran's name, not yours, in box 1.

Box 2—There is no VA file number if the veteran has never filed for benefits. If the wartime service veteran has ever filed for any veteran benefit, a VA file number exists and should be written on the form. If the veteran received pharmacy benefits, for example, a VA file number will be on record. The file number can be found on all VA correspondence. If in doubt, leave the box blank until you check with the VSO, who can look up the VA file number for you.

Box 4—Fill in the veteran's Social Security number. If you are the surviving spouse, fill in the veteran's Social Security number, not yours, in box 4.

Box 5—This box applies to VA life insurance; if in doubt, leave the box blank until you check with the VSO to see if this question is applicable to you.

Box 7—If the veteran is the claimant, draw a line in the box. If the surviving spouse is the claimant, fill in the surviving spouse's name.

Box 8—If the veteran is the claimant, draw a line in the box. If the surviving spouse is the claimant, then fill in "surviving spouse" as the relationship to the deceased veteran.

Box 12—Check the box authorizing the veterans service organization's representative to have access to your records.

Box 13—Write "No Limitations" in this box.

Box 14—If you are the veteran making the claim, sign your name. If you are the surviving spouse, provide your signature and write "surviving spouse of (name of veteran)."

Figure 8.7 Sample completed Form 21-22: Appointment of Veterans Service Organization as Claimant's Representative.

OMB Control No. 2900-0321
Respondent Burden: 5 minutes

VA Department of Veterans Affairs

APPOINTMENT OF VETERANS SERVICE ORGANIZATION AS CLAIMANT'S REPRESENTATIVE

Note - If you would prefer to have an individual assist you with your claim, you may use VA Form 21-22a, " Appointment of Individual As Claimant's Representative."

IMPORTANT - PLEASE READ THE PRIVACY ACT AND RESPONDENT BURDEN ON REVERSE BEFORE COMPLETING THE FORM

1. LAST-FIRST-MIDDLE NAME OF VETERAN	2. VA FILE NUMBER *(Include prefix)*
Smith John Joseph	

3A. NAME OF SERVICE ORGANIZATION RECOGNIZED BY THE DEPARTMENT OF VETERANS AFFAIRS *(See list on reverse side before selecting organization)*
American Legion

3B. JOB TITLE OF OFFICIAL REPRESENTATIVE AUTHORIZED TO ACT ON VETERAN'S BEHALF
Any service officer

INSTRUCTIONS - TYPE OR PRINT ALL ENTRIES

4. SOCIAL SECURITY NUMBER	5. INSURANCE NUMBER(S) *(Include letter prefix)*
000-00-0000	

6A. SERVICE NUMBER(S)	6B. BRANCH OF SERVICE
35 000 000	Army

7. NAME OF CLAIMANT *(If other than veteran)*	8. RELATIONSHIP *(If other than veteran)*

9. ADDRESS OF CLAIMANT *(No. and street or rural route, city or P.O., State and ZIP Code)*	10. CLAIMANT'S TELEPHONE NUMBER *(Include Area Code)*	
714 Happy Lane	A. DAYTIME 412-555-1212	B. EVENING
Anytown PA 11111	11. DATE OF THIS APPOINTMENT 02-15-2009	

12. AUTHORIZATION FOR REPRESENTATIVE'S ACCESS TO RECORDS PROTECTED BY SECTION 7332, TITLE 38, U.S.C.
Unless I check the box below, I **do not authorize** VA to disclose to the service organization named on this appointment form any records that may be in my file relating to treatment for drug abuse, alcoholism or alcohol abuse, infection with the human immunodeficiency virus (HIV), or sickle cell anemia.

[X] I authorize the VA facility having custody of my VA claimant records to disclose to the service organization named in Item 3A all treatment records relating to drug abuse, alcoholism or alcohol abuse, infection with the human immunodeficiency virus (HIV), or sickle cell anemia. Redisclosure of these records by my service organization representative, other than to VA or the Court of Appeals for Veterans Claims, is not authorized without my further written consent. This authorization will remain in effect until the earlier of the following events: (1) I revoke this authorization by filing a written revocation with VA; or (2) I revoke the appointment of the service organization named above, either by explicit revocation or the appointment of another representative.

13. LIMITATION OF CONSENT - My consent in Item 12 for the disclosure of records relating to treatment for drug abuse, alcoholism or alcohol abuse, infection with the human immunodeficiency virus (HIV), or sickle cell anemia is limited as follows:

No limitations

I, the claimant named in Items 1 or 7, hereby appoint the service organization named in Item 3A as my representative to prepare, present and prosecute my claim for any and all benefits from the Department of Veterans Affairs based on the service of the veteran named in Item 1. I authorize the Department of Veterans Affairs to release any and all of my records, to include disclosure of my Federal tax information (other than as provided in Items 12 and 13), to that service organization appointed as my representative. It is understood that no fee or compensation of whatsoever nature will be charged me for service rendered pursuant to this power of attorney. I understand that the service organization I have appointed as my representative may revoke this power of attorney at any time, subject to 38 CFR 20.608. *Additionally, in those cases where a veteran's income is being developed because of an income verification necessitated by an Internal Revenue Service verification match, the assignment of the service organization as the veteran's representative is only valid for five years from the date this form is signed for purposes restricted to the verification match.* Signed and accepted subject to the foregoing conditions.

THIS POWER OF ATTORNEY DOES NOT REQUIRE EXECUTION BEFORE A NOTARY PUBLIC

14. SIGNATURE OF CLAIMANT *(Do Not Print)*	15. DATE SIGNED
John Joseph Smith	02-15-2009

VA USE ONLY	VA FORM 21-22-1 SENT TO: [ ] CER FILE [ ] EDU FILE [ ] INSURANCE FILE [ ] CH. 30 [ ] DEA FILE [ ] LG FILE	DATE SENT	ACKNOWLEDGED *(Date)*	REVOKED *(Reason and date)*

NOTE: As long as this appointment is in effect the organization named herein will be recognized as the sole agent for presentation of your claim before the Department of Veterans Affairs in connection with your claim or any portion thereof.

VA FORM NOV 2005 **21-22**   SUPERSEDES VA FORM 21-22, JUN 2003, WHICH WILL NOT BE USED.

(A blank copy of this form was obtained from the VA Web site, http://www.vba.va.gov/pubs/forms/VBA-21-22-ARE.pdf.)

SUPPORTING DOCUMENTS

The following is a summary of supporting documents to be attached to the application (as applicable):

- ▶ *Certified copy* of the veteran's discharge record
- ▶ Voided blank check from the account where pension payments will be deposited
- ▶ Marriage certificate copy—can be obtained from the county of marriage
- ▶ For a court-ordered marriage separation, a copy of the court order of the separation
- ▶ Divorce decree copy
- ▶ Death certificate copy—can be obtained from the funeral home or county courthouse
- ▶ For dependent children, copies of birth records; for adopted children, copies of adoption records
- ▶ Net worth documents—copies of statements for CDs, stocks, savings accounts, and so on
- ▶ Proof of all income, such as a copy of the Social Security award letter stating the monthly amount received, a work pension letter, and interest statements
- ▶ Proof of out-of-pocket medical expenses, such as medical insurance premiums, cost of assisted living, nonmedical home care, transportation services, and medication costs
- ▶ For court-appointed guardians, a certified copy of the court order of the appointment
- ▶ Power of attorney documents
- ▶ Proof of reserve service, if the veteran has ever been a full-time reservist

9

PHARMACY AND OTHER HEALTH BENEFITS: FREE HEALTHCARE FOR AID AND ATTENDANCE AND HOUSEBOUND PENSION RECIPIENTS

Veterans receiving either an Aid and Attendance pension or Housebound pension are eligible to receive free prescription medications and other health benefits such as incontinence supplies, eyeglasses, and hearing aids.[1] Paying for prescription medications is often as much of a concern as paying for caregivers. This chapter explains the application procedure for receiving pharmacy and other health benefits.

Note: Surviving spouses of veterans are not eligible for these benefits unless they are veterans themselves.

To obtain free pharmacy and other health benefits, you must be enrolled in the VA healthcare system. You can enroll by completing Form 10-10EZ, Application for Health Benefits, which is available from a VSO or from the VA Web site. Use the following steps to obtain the latest version of the form:

1. Go to the https://www.1010ez.med.va.gov/sec/vha/1010ez/.

2. Click on "viewing or printing the 10-10EZ," near the top of the page.

Tips for Completing Form 10-10EZ

A sample completed Form 10-10EZ is presented in figure 9.1. Be sure to refer to it to see how to complete the form.

Section I: General Information

Box 13—Write in the name of the VA healthcare facility where you prefer to receive care. (See the list of VA facilities in appendix 1.) Note: To receive a hearing aid, you must schedule an audiology test with a VA medical center because VA clinics do not offer this service.

Box 14—Check the "Yes" box if you want the VA to schedule a doctor's appointment for you when your application is processed. Note: Pharmacy benefits do not begin automatically; you must first have a physical with a VA physician. At your doctor's appointment, the VA physician will write your prescriptions for the VA mail-order pharmacy.

Section II: Insurance Information

Attach copies of *all health insurance cards (both sides)* to the form. If you are covered under a spouse's health insurance, be sure to include a copy of both sides of that insurance card also.

Section IV: Military Service Information

Attach a copy of your discharge record.

Be sure you sign and date the form at the bottom of page 3.

Forms should be faxed or mailed to the *eligibility department* at the VA medical center or clinic where you prefer to receive care. (See the list of VA facilities in appendix 1.) After your application has been processed, the VA will send you a letter notifying you of your eligibility, and if you checked "Yes" in Box 14 in section I, you will also be informed of your doctor's appointment.

Contact a VSO for questions related to VA health benefits.

Note: Veterans who are not eligible to receive Aid and Attendance and Housebound pensions and therefore cannot receive free pharmacy benefits may be eligible to receive discounted pharmacy benefits. (See appendix 2 for eligibility requirements for discounted prescription medications.)

Figure 9.1a Sample completed Form 10-10EZ: Application for Health Benefits, page 1.

OMB Approved No. 2900-0091
Estimated Burden Avg. 45 min.

Department of Veterans Affairs

APPLICATION FOR HEALTH BENEFITS

SECTION I - GENERAL INFORMATION

Federal law provides criminal penalties, including a fine and/or imprisonment for up to 5 years, for concealing a material fact or making a materially false statement. (See 18 U.S.C. 1001)

1. VETERAN'S NAME *(Last, First, Middle Name)*
Smith, John Joseph

2. OTHER NAMES USED
——

3. MOTHER'S MAIDEN NAME
Baker

4. GENDER
[X] MALE [ ] FEMALE

5. ARE YOU SPANISH, HISPANIC, OR LATINO?
[ ] YES [X] NO

6. WHAT IS YOUR RACE? *(You may check more than one.) (Information is required for statistical purposes only.)*
[ ] AMERICAN INDIAN OR ALASKA NATIVE [ ] BLACK OR AFRICAN AMERICAN
[ ] ASIAN [X] WHITE [ ] NATIVE HAWAIIAN OR OTHER PACIFIC ISLANDER

7. SOCIAL SECURITY NUMBER
000-00-0000

9. DATE OF BIRTH *(mm/dd/yyyy)*
01-24-1920

10. RELIGION
Catholic

8. CLAIM NUMBER
——

9A. PLACE OF BIRTH *(City and State)*
Pittsburgh, PA

11. PERMANENT ADDRESS *(Street)*
714 Happy Lane

11A. CITY
Anytown

11B. STATE
PA

11C. ZIP CODE *(9 digits)*
11111-2010

11D. COUNTY
Allegheny

11E. HOME TELEPHONE NUMBER *(Include area code)*
412-555-1212

11F. E-MAIL ADDRESS
——

11G. CELLULAR TELEPHONE NUMBER *(Include area code)*

11H. PAGER NUMBER *(Include area code)*

12. TYPE OF BENEFIT(S) APPLIED FOR *(You may check more than one)*
[X] HEALTH SERVICES [ ] NURSING HOME [ ] DOMICILIARY [ ] DENTAL

13. IF APPLYING FOR HEALTH SERVICES OR ENROLLMENT, WHICH VA MEDICAL CENTER OR OUTPATIENT CLINIC DO YOU PREFER?
Dept. of Veterans Affairs Medical Center, University Drive, Pittsburgh, PA

14. DO YOU WANT AN APPOINTMENT WITH A VA DOCTOR OR PROVIDER AS SOON AS ONE BECOMES AVAILABLE?
[X] YES [ ] NO I am only enrolling in case I need care in the future.

15. HAVE YOU BEEN SEEN AT A VA HEALTH CARE FACILITY?
[ ] YES, **LOCATION:** [X] NO

16. CURRENT MARITAL STATUS *(Check one)*
[ ] MARRIED [ ] NEVER MARRIED [ ] SEPARATED [X] WIDOWED [ ] DIVORCED [ ] UNKNOWN

17. NAME, ADDRESS AND RELATIONSHIP OF NEXT OF KIN
Robert J. Smith (son)
501 Duck Lane
Anytown PA 11111

17A. NEXT OF KIN'S HOME TELEPHONE NUMBER *(Include area code)*
724-333-1600

17B. NEXT OF KIN'S WORK TELEPHONE NUMBER *(Include area code)*
412-123-4567

18. NAME, ADDRESS AND RELATIONSHIP OF EMERGENCY CONTACT
same as above

18A. EMERGENCY CONTACT'S HOME TELEPHONE NUMBER *(Include area code)*
same as above

18B. EMERGENCY CONTACT'S WORK TELEPHONE NUMBER *(Include area code)*
same as above

19. INDIVIDUAL TO RECEIVE POSSESSION OF YOUR PERSONAL PROPERTY LEFT ON PREMISES UNDER VA CONTROL AFTER YOUR DEPARTURE OR AT THE TIME OF DEATH. NOTE: THIS DOES NOT CONSTITUTE A WILL OR TRANSFER OF TITLE *(Check one)*
[ ] EMERGENCY CONTACT [X] NEXT OF KIN

VA FORM JUL 2008 **10-10EZ**
PREVIOUS EDITIONS OF THIS FORM ARE NOT TO BE USED
PAGE 1

(A blank form was obtained from the VA Web site, https://www.1010ez.med.va.gov/sec/vha/1010ez/Form/vha-10-10ez.pdf.)

Figure 9.1b Sample completed Form 10-10EZ, page 2.

APPLICATION FOR HEALTH BENEFITS, Continued	VETERAN'S NAME (Last, First, Middle) Smith, John Joseph	SOCIAL SECURITY NUMBER 000-00-0000

SECTION II - INSURANCE INFORMATION (Use a separate sheet for additional information)

1. ARE YOU COVERED BY HEALTH INSURANCE? (Including coverage through a spouse or another person) ☒ YES ☐ NO

2. HEALTH INSURANCE COMPANY NAME, ADDRESS AND TELEPHONE NUMBER
High Med Security Blue
500 Insurance Road
Pittsburgh PA 15222
800-222-1010

3. NAME OF POLICY HOLDER
John Joseph Smith

4. POLICY NUMBER
XYZ 987654321

5. GROUP CODE
1111 1111

	YES	NO	
6. ARE YOU ELIGIBLE FOR MEDICAID?	☐	☒	
7. ARE YOU ENROLLED IN MEDICARE HOSPITAL INSURANCE PART A?	☒	☐	7A. EFFECTIVE DATE (mm/dd/yyyy) 02-01-1985
8. ARE YOU ENROLLED IN MEDICARE HOSPITAL INSURANCE PART B?	☒	☐	8A. EFFECTIVE DATE (mm/dd/yyyy) 02-01-1985

9. NAME EXACTLY AS IT APPEARS ON YOUR MEDICARE CARD
John Joseph Smith

10. MEDICARE CLAIM NUMBER

11. IS NEED FOR CARE DUE TO ON THE JOB INJURY? (Check one) ☐ YES ☒ NO

12. IS NEED FOR CARE DUE TO ACCIDENT? (Check One) ☐ YES ☒ NO

SECTION III - EMPLOYMENT INFORMATION

1. VETERAN'S EMPLOYMENT STATUS (Check one) ☐ FULL TIME ☐ NOT EMPLOYED
If employed or retired, complete item 1A ☐ PART TIME ☒ RETIRED
01-31-1985 Date of retirement (mm/dd/yyyy)

1A. COMPANY NAME, ADDRESS AND TELEPHONE NUMBER
ABC Company   412-222-7777
100 Work Blvd
Anytown PA 11111

2. SPOUSE'S EMPLOYMENT STATUS (Check one)   N/A   ☐ FULL TIME ☐ NOT EMPLOYED
If employed or retired, complete item 2A ☐ PART TIME ☐ RETIRED
Date of retirement (mm/dd/yyyy)

2A. COMPANY NAME, ADDRESS AND TELEPHONE NUMBER

SECTION IV - MILITARY SERVICE INFORMATION

1. LAST BRANCH OF SERVICE	1A. LAST ENTRY DATE	1B. LAST DISCHARGE DATE	1C. DISCHARGE TYPE	1D. MILITARY SERVICE NUMBER
Army	02-07-1944	04-11-1946	Honorable	35 000 000

2. CHECK YES OR NO	YES	NO		YES	NO
A. ARE YOU A PURPLE HEART AWARD RECIPIENT?	☐	☒	E1. ARE YOU RECEIVING DISABILITY RETIREMENT PAY INSTEAD OF VA COMPENSATION?	☐	☒
B. ARE YOU A FORMER PRISONER OF WAR?	☐	☒	F. DO YOU NEED CARE OF CONDITIONS POTENTIALLY RELATED TO SERVICE IN SW ASIA DURING THE GULF WAR?	☐	☒
C. DO YOU HAVE A VA SERVICE-CONNECTED RATING?	☐	☒	G. WERE YOU EXPOSED TO AGENT ORANGE WHILE SERVING IN VIETNAM?	☐	☒
C1. IF YES, WHAT IS YOUR RATED PERCENTAGE? %			H. WERE YOU EXPOSED TO RADIATION WHILE IN THE MILITARY?	☐	☒
D. DID YOU SERVE IN COMBAT AFTER 11/11/1998?	☐	☒	I. DID YOU RECEIVE NOSE AND THROAT RADIUM TREATMENTS WHILE IN THE MILITARY?	☐	☒
E. WAS YOUR DISCHARGE FROM MILITARY FOR A DISABILITY INCURRED OR AGGRAVATED IN THE LINE OF DUTY?	☐	☒	J. DO YOU HAVE A SPINAL CORD INJURY?	☐	☒

SECTION V - PAPERWORK REDUCTION ACT AND PRIVACY ACT INFORMATION

The Paperwork Reduction Act of 1995 requires us to notify you that this information collection is in accordance with the clearance requirements of Section 3507 of the Paperwork Reduction Act of 1995. We may not conduct or sponsor, and you are not required to respond to, a collection of information unless it displays a valid OMB number. We anticipate that the time expended by all individuals who must complete this form will average 45 minutes. This includes the time it will take to read instructions, gather the necessary facts and fill out the form.

Privacy Act Information: VA is asking you to provide the information on this form under 38 U.S.C. Sections 1705, 1710, 1712, and 1722 in order for VA to determine your eligibility for medical benefits. Information you supply may be verified through a computer-matching program. VA may disclose the information that you put on the form as permitted by law. VA may make a "routine use" disclosure of the information as outlined in the Privacy Act systems of records notices and in accordance with the VHA Notice of Privacy Practices. Providing the requested information is voluntary, but if any or all of the requested information is not provided, it may delay or result in denial of your request for health care benefits. Failure to furnish the information will not have any effect on any other benefits to which you may be entitled. If you provide VA your Social Security Number, VA will use it to administer your VA benefits. VA may also use this information to identify veterans and persons claiming or receiving VA benefits and their records, and for other purposes authorized or required by law.

VA FORM JUL 2008 **10-10EZ**   PAGE 2

Figure 9.1c Sample completed Form 10-10EZ, page 3.

APPLICATION FOR HEALTH BENEFITS, Continued	VETERAN'S NAME *(Last, First, Middle)* Smith, John Joseph	SOCIAL SECURITY NUMBER 000-00-0000

SECTION VI - FINANCIAL DISCLOSURE

Disclosure allows VA to accurately determine whether certain veterans will be charged copayments for care and medications, their eligibility for other services and enrollment priority. Veterans are not required to disclose their financial information; however, VA is not currently enrolling new applicants who decline to provide their financial information unless they have a special eligibility factor. **Recent combat veterans (e.g., OEF/OIF) who were discharged within the past 5 years or were discharged more than 5 years ago and applying for enrollment by Jan. 27, 2011 are eligible for enrollment without disclosing their financial information** but like other veterans may provide it to establish their eligibility for travel reimbursement, cost-free medication and/or medical care for services unrelated to military experience.

☐ **No, I do not wish to provide financial information in Sections VII through X.** I understand that VA is not enrolling new applicants who do not provide this information and who do not have a special eligibility factor (e.g., recently discharged combat veteran, compensable service connection, receipt of VA pension or Medicaid benefits.) If I am enrolled, I agree to pay applicable VA copayments. *Sign and date the form in Section XII.*

☒ **Yes, I will provide my household financial information for last calendar year.** Complete applicable sections VII through X. *Sign and date the form in Section XII.*

SECTION VII - DEPENDENT INFORMATION *(Use a separate sheet for additional dependents)*

1. SPOUSE'S NAME *(Last, First, Middle Name)* deceased	2. CHILD'S NAME *(Last, First, Middle Name)*
1A. SPOUSE'S MAIDEN NAME	2A. CHILD'S RELATIONSHIP TO YOU *(Check one)* ☐ Son ☐ Daughter ☐ Stepson ☐ Stepdaughter
1B. SPOUSE'S SOCIAL SECURITY NUMBER	2B. CHILD'S SOCIAL SECURITY NUMBER / 2C. DATE CHILD BECAME YOUR DEPENDENT *(mm/dd/yyyy)*
1C. SPOUSE'S DATE OF BIRTH *(mm/dd/yyyy)* / 1D. DATE OF MARRIAGE *(mm/dd/yyyy)*	2D. CHILD'S DATE OF BIRTH *(mm/dd/yyyy)*
1E. SPOUSE'S ADDRESS AND TELEPHONE NUMBER *(Street, City, State, ZIP)*	2E. WAS CHILD PERMANENTLY AND TOTALLY DISABLED BEFORE THE AGE OF 18? ☐ YES ☐ NO
	2F. IF CHILD IS BETWEEN 18 AND 23 YEARS OF AGE, DID CHILD ATTEND SCHOOL LAST CALENDAR YEAR? ☐ YES ☐ NO
3. IF YOUR SPOUSE OR DEPENDENT CHILD DID NOT LIVE WITH YOU LAST YEAR ENTER THE AMOUNT YOU CONTRIBUTED TO THEIR SUPPORT. SPOUSE $ CHILD $	2G. EXPENSES PAID BY YOUR DEPENDENT CHILD FOR COLLEGE, VOCATIONAL REHABILITATION OR TRAINING *(e.g., tuition, books, materials)* $

SECTION VIII - PREVIOUS CALENDAR YEAR GROSS ANNUAL INCOME OF VETERAN, SPOUSE AND DEPENDENT CHILDREN
(Use a separate sheet for additional dependents)

	VETERAN	SPOUSE	CHILD 1
1. GROSS ANNUAL INCOME FROM EMPLOYMENT *(wages, bonuses, tips, etc.)* EXCLUDING INCOME FROM YOUR FARM, RANCH, PROPERTY OR BUSINESS	$ —	$ —	$ —
2. NET INCOME FROM YOUR FARM, RANCH, PROPERTY OR BUSINESS	$ —	$ —	$ —
3. LIST OTHER INCOME AMOUNTS *(eg., Social Security, compensation, pension interest, dividends).* EXCLUDING WELFARE.	$ 24,000	$ —	$ —

SECTION IX - PREVIOUS CALENDAR YEAR DEDUCTIBLE EXPENSES

1. TOTAL NON-REIMBURSED MEDICAL EXPENSES PAID BY YOU OR YOUR SPOUSE *(e.g., payments for doctors, dentists, medications, Medicare, health insurance, hospital and nursing home)* VA will calculate a deductible and the net medical expenses you may claim.	$ 6,850
2. AMOUNT YOU PAID LAST CALENDAR YEAR FOR FUNERAL AND BURIAL EXPENSES FOR YOUR DECEASED SPOUSE OR DEPENDENT CHILD *(Also enter spouse or child's information in Section VII.)*	$ —
3. AMOUNT YOU PAID LAST CALENDAR YEAR FOR YOUR COLLEGE OR VOCATIONAL EDUCATIONAL EXPENSES *(e.g., tuition, books, fees, materials)* DO NOT LIST YOUR DEPENDENTS' EDUCATIONAL EXPENSES.	$ —

SECTION X - PREVIOUS CALENDAR YEAR NET WORTH *(Use a separate sheet for additional dependents)*

	VETERAN	SPOUSE	CHILD 1
1. CASH, AMOUNT IN BANK ACCOUNTS *(e.g., checking and savings accounts, certificates of deposit, individual retirement accounts, stocks and bonds)*	$ 20,000	$ —	$ —
2. MARKET VALUE OF LAND AND BUILDINGS MINUS MORTGAGES AND LIENS. *(e.g., second homes and non-income producing property. Do not count your primary home.)*	$ —	$ —	$ —
3. VALUE OF OTHER PROPERTY OR ASSETS *(e.g., art, rare coins, collectables)* MINUS THE AMOUNT YOU OWE ON THESE ITEMS. INCLUDE VALUE OF FARM, RANCH OR BUSINESS ASSETS. *Exclude household effects and family vehicles.*	$ —	$ —	$ —

SECTION XI - CONSENT TO COPAYMENTS

If you are a 0% SC veteran and do not receive VA monetary benefits or a NSC veteran (and you are not a Former POW, Purple Heart Recipient or VA pensioner) and your household income (or combined income and net worth) exceeds the established threshold, this application will be considered for enrollment, but only if you agree to pay VA copayments for treatment of your NSC conditions. **If you are such a veteran by signing this application you are agreeing to pay the applicable VA copayments as required by law.**

SECTION XII - ASSIGNMENT OF BENEFITS

I understand that pursuant to 38 U.S.C. Section 1729, VA is authorized to recover or collect from my health plan (HP) for the reasonable charges of nonservice-connected VA medical care or services furnished or provided to me. I hereby authorize payment directly to VA from any HP under which I am covered (including coverage provided under my spouse's HP) that is responsible for payment of the charges for my medical care, including benefits otherwise payable to me or my spouse.

ALL APPLICANTS MUST SIGN AND DATE THIS FORM. REFER TO INSTRUCTIONS WHICH DEFINE WHO CAN SIGN ON BEHALF OF THE VETERAN.

SIGNATURE OF APPLICANT *John Joseph Smith*	DATE 06-15-2009

VA FORM JUL 2008 **10-10EZ**	PAGE 3

EPILOGUE

Even if you are not eligible for an Aid and Attendance pension or a Housebound pension now, obtain an original or certified copy of the veteran's discharge record and keep it in a safe place, such as a fireproof box, so that it is available if you need to file at a future time. In addition, knowing the location of supporting documents, such as marriage and death certificates, is helpful to avoid delays if the time comes to file for Aid and Attendance benefits or Housebound benefits.

Pay it forward! Tell others about the Aid and Attendance and Housebound benefits. There is no greater satisfaction than helping veterans and their surviving spouses afford to live dignified lives in their retirement years.

Finally, a message to all veterans: Many thanks for your heroic service to our country. You not only protected the American Way, but you also made it possible. We can never repay the debt we owe you or those veterans who gave their lives for this country. Financial assistance in your remaining years is a fitting remembrance.

APPENDIX I

VETERANS SERVICE ORGANIZATIONS AND VA FACILITIES

V A facilities and veterans service organizations across the country (and even in other countries) can help you with your claims for Aid and Attendance and Housebound pensions. Veterans service organizations include the American Legion, National Association of County Veteran Service Officers (NACVSO), Disabled American Veterans (DAV), and Veterans of Foreign Wars of the United States (VFW).

AMERICAN LEGION

Service officers at American Legion offices are available for answering questions, checking forms, and filing pension claims with the VA.

ALABAMA

Dept of Veterans Affairs
PO Box 1391
Montgomery, AL 36102
Phone: 334-213-3321
Fax: 334-279-8086

ALASKA

American Legion Dept Svc Ofcr
2925 Debarr Rd, Ste 3103
Anchorage, AK 99508
Phone: 907-276-8211
Fax: 907-258-0756

ARIZONA

American Legion Dept Svc Ofcr
3333 N Central Ave, Ste 1048
Phoenix, AZ 85012
Phone: 602-627-3281
Fax: 602-627-3285

ARKANSAS

PO Box 3280
Little Rock, AR 72203
Phone: 501-221-3192
Fax: Not available

CALIFORNIA

The American Legion
1301 Clay St, Rm 1135N
Oakland, CA 94612
Phone: 510-834-0310
Fax: 510-834-0507

The American Legion
Federal Bldg
11000 Wilshire Blvd, Rm 5201
Los Angeles, CA 90024
Phone: 310-473-6534
Fax: 310-479-4641

The American Legion
8810 Rio San Diego Dr, Rm 1173
San Diego, CA 92108
Phone: 619-400-5301
Fax: 619-688-0874

COLORADO

The American Legion
155 Van Gordon St
Denver, CO 80225
Phone: 303-914-5585
Fax: 303-914-5588

CONNECTICUT

American Legion Service Office
PO Box 310909
Newington, CT 06131
Phone: 860-594-6600
Fax: 860-667-3257

DELAWARE

American Legion Dept Svc Ofcr
1601 Kirkwood Hwy Elsmere
Wilmington, DE 19805
Phone: 302-998-9448
Fax: 302-633-5388

DISTRICT OF COLUMBIA

American Legion Dept Svc Ofcr of
DC
1722 I St NW, Rm 230
Washington, DC 20421
Phone: 202-530-9140
Fax: 202-530-0126

FLORIDA

Dept of Veterans Affairs
PO Box 31003
St. Petersburg, FL 33731
Phone: 727-319-7427
Fax: 727-319-7780

FRANCE

American Legion Dept Svc Ofcr
1000 Liberty Ave, Ste 432D
Pittsburgh, PA 15222
Phone: 412-395-6230
Fax: 412-395-6234

Note: The America Legion in France is managed by PA Dept Service Officer

GEORGIA

State Dept of Veterans Services
1700 Clairmont Rd
Decatur, GA 30033
Phone: 404-929-5345
Fax: 404-929-5502

HAWAII

American Legion Svc Ofcr
Spark Matsunaga Med Ctr
459 Patterson Rd
Honolulu, HI 96819
Phone: 808-946-6383
Fax: Not available

IDAHO

Idaho Division of Veterans Services
805 W Franklin St, Rm 201
Boise, ID 83702
Phone: 208-334-1245
Fax: 208-334-3549

ILLINOIS

American Legion Svc Ofcr
2122 W Taylor St, Ste 106
Chicago, IL 60612
Phone: 312-980-4266
Fax: 312-706-6675

INDIANA

American Legion Service Dept
575 N Pennsylvania St, Rm 325
Indianapolis, IN 46204
Phone: 317-916-3605
Fax: 317-226-6645

IOWA

American Legion Svc Ofcr
210 Walnut St, Rm 1033A
Des Moines, IA 50309
Phone: 515-323-7532
Phone: 1-800-944-2039
Fax: 515-323-7401

KANSAS

Colmery-O'Neil VA Med Ctr
2200 SW Gage Blvd
Topeka, KS 66622
Phone: 785-350-4489
Fax: 785-350-4417

KENTUCKY

American Legion Svc Ofcr
PO Box 3661
Louisville, KY 40201
Phone: 502-566-4478
Fax: 502-566-4371

LOUISIANA

Dept of Veterans Affairs
6640 Riverside Dr, Ste 210
Metairie, LA 70003
Phone: 504-833-8775
Fax: 504-838-8333

MAINE

The American Legion
PO Box 3411
Augusta, ME 04330
Phone: 207-623-5726
Fax: 207-621-4821

MARYLAND

American Legion Svc Ofcr
31 Hopkins Plaza
Baltimore, MD 21201
Phone: 410-230-4420
Fax: 410-230-4421

MASSACHUSETTS

American Legion Svc Ofcr
JFK Federal Bldg, Rm 1500D
Boston, MA 02202
Phone: 617-303-5693
Fax: 617-973-9560

MEXICO

The American Legion
6900 Almeda Rd, Rm 1019
Houston, TX 77030
Phone: 713-383-2702
Fax: 713-383-2759
Note: The American Legion in Mexico is managed by Texas Dept Service Office

MICHIGAN

The American Legion
477 Michigan Ave, Rm 1210
Detroit, MI 48226
Phone: 313-964-6640
Fax: 313-964-5697

MINNESOTA

American Legion Svc Ofcr
1 Veterans Dr 4H, Rm 104
Minneapolis, MN 55417
Phone: 612-467-3849
Fax: 612-727-5643

MISSISSIPPI

The American Legion
PO Box 534
Calhoun City, MS 38916
Phone: 662-628-1933
Fax: Not available

MISSOURI

The American Legion
400 S 18th St, Rm 106
St Louis, MO 63103
Phone: 314-552-9884
Fax: 314-231-7463

MONTANA

The American Legion Dept Svc
Ofcr
PO Box 1007
Ft Harrison, MT 59636
Phone: 406-495-2080
Fax: 406-495-2003

NEBRASKA

VA Regional Office
5631 S 48th St
Lincoln, NE 68516
Phone: 402-420-4021
Fax: 402-471-7070

NEVADA

For Northern Half of the State:
Nevada Office of Veterans Services
5460 Reno Corporate Dr # 131
Reno, NV 89521
Phone: 775-688-1653, Ext 31003
Fax: 775-688-1656

For Southern Half of the State:
Office of Veterans Services
950 W Owens, Rm 111
Las Vegas, NV 89106
Phone: 702-636-3070
Fax: 702-636-3079

NEW HAMPSHIRE

Norris Cotton Federal Bldg
275 Chestnut St, Rm 519
Manchester, NH 03101
Phone: 603-222-5784
Fax: 603-222-5787

NEW JERSEY

The American Legion
20 Washington Pl, Rm 436
Newark, NJ 07102
Phone: 973-623-6298
Fax: 973-504-8709

NEW MEXICO

American Legion Service Office
500 Gold St SW, Rm 3017
Albuquerque, NM 87102
Phone: 505-346-4878
Fax: 505-346-487

NEW YORK

American Legion Dept Svc Ofcr
245 W Houston St, Rm 315A
New York, NY 10014
Phone: 212-807-3066
Fax: 212-807-4029

American Legion Dept Svc Ofcr
130 S Elmwood Ave, Ste 614
Buffalo, NY 14202
Phone: 716-857-3361
Fax: 716-857-3488

NORTH CAROLINA

American Legion Dept Svc Ofcr
251 Main St, Rm 103B
Winston Salem, NC 27155
Phone: 336-631-5471
Fax: 336-714-0902

NORTH DAKOTA

American Legion
2101 N Elm St
Fargo, ND 58108
Phone: 701-451-4646
Fax: 701-293-9951

OHIO

American Legion Svc Ofcr
4100 W 3rd St
PO Box 335
Dayton, OH 45428
Phone: 937-268-6511, Ext 2967
Fax: 937-267-7605

American Legion Svc Ofcr
1240 E 9th St, Rm 923
Cleveland, OH 44199
Phone: 216-522-3504
Fax: 216-522-3233

VA Med Ctr
American Legion Dept Svc Ofcr
10701 East Blvd, 1B115
Cleveland, OH 44106
Phone: 216-791-3800, Ext 4155
Fax: 216-707-5948

VA Med Ctr
American Legion Dept Svc Ofcr
3200 Vine St, Rm B162G
Cincinnati, OH 45220
Phone: 513-475-6440
Fax: 513-475-6444

OKLAHOMA

American Legion Dept Svc Ofcr
125 S Main St
Muskogee, OK 74401
Phone: 918-781-7760
Fax: 918-781-7761

OREGON

American Legion
1220 SW 3rd Ave, Ste 1684
Portland, OR 97204
Phone: 503-412-4771
Fax: 503-412-4772

PENNSYLVANIA

The American Legion
135 E 38th St
Erie, PA 16504
Phone: 814-864-4240
Fax: 814-864-3405

American Legion Dept Svc Ofcr
1000 Liberty Ave, Ste 432D
Pittsburgh, PA 15222
Phone: 412-395-6230
Fax: 412-395-6234

VA Regional Office
American Legion Svc Ofcr
PO Box 42938
Philadelphia, PA 19144
Phone: 215-381-3032
Fax: 215-381-3500

The American Legion
1123 E End Blvd, Ste 5
Wilkes Barre, PA 18702
Phone: 570-821-2525
Fax: 570-821-2529

The American Legion
PO Box 2324
Harrisburg, PA 17105
Phone: 717-730-9100
Fax: 717-975-2836

PHILIPPINES

PSC 517 Box R C
FPO, AP 96517-1000
Phone: 63-45-322-6061
Fax: 63-45-322-1950

PUERTO RICO

The American Legion
PO Box 447
Saint Just, PR 00978
Phone: 787-772-7455
Fax: 787-792-5947

RHODE ISLAND

The American Legion
1005 Charles St
North Providence, RI 02904
Phone: 401-726-2126
Fax: 401-726-2464

SOUTH CAROLINA

American Legion Dept Svc Ofcr
1205 Pendleton St, Ste 369
Columbia, SC 29201
Phone: 803-734-0200
Fax: 803-734-0200

SOUTH DAKOTA

The American Legion
PO Box 67
Watertown, SD 57201
Phone: 605-886-3604
Fax: 605-886-2870

TENNESSEE

American Legion Svc Ofcr
2414 Harris Rd
Woodlawn, TN 37191
Phone: 931-553-5173
Fax: 931-553-5176

TEXAS

The American Legion
6900 Almeda Rd, Rm 1019
Houston, TX 77030
Phone: 713-383-2702
Fax: 713-383-2759

The American Legion
701 Clay Ave
Waco, TX 76799
Phone: 254-299-9960
Fax: 254-299-9965

UTAH

The American Legion
550 Foothill Dr, Ste 203
Salt Lake City, UT 84158
Phone: 801-326-2380
Fax: 801-326-2383

VERMONT

The American Legion
VAM & ROC
215 N Main St
White River Junction, VT 05009
Phone: 802-296-5166
Fax: 802-291-6266

VIRGINIA

The American Legion
270 Franklin Rd, SW, Rm 503
Roanoke, VA 24011
Phone: 540-857-7101
Fax: 540-857-6437

WASHINGTON

The American Legion
915 2nd Ave, Ste 1042
Seattle, WA 98174
Phone: 206-220-6223
Fax: 206-220-6104

WEST VIRGINIA

Huntington VA Regional Office
640 4th Ave, Rm 108
Huntington, WV 25701
Phone: 304-399-9395
Fax: 304-528-5738

WISCONSIN

VA Regional Office
5400 W National Ave # 164
Milwaukee, WI 53214
Phone: 414-902-5722
Fax: 414-902-9401

WYOMING

VA Hospital
2360 E Pershing Blvd
Cheyenne, WY 82001
Phone: 307-433-2750
Fax: 307-433-2788

NATIONAL ASSOCIATION OF COUNTY VETERAN SERVICE OFFICERS

Most counties have a veteran service officer who is available for answering questions, checking forms, and filing pension claims with the VA. NACVSO maintains a Web site that can help you locate the appropriate county VSO for your area. Not all counties provide a list of their service officers; some just refer you to a veterans' affairs office.

To find your county VSO on the NACVSO Web site,

1. Go to http://www.nacvso.org.

2. On the home page, click on "Find a Service Officer."

3. To find your local service officer, select your state from the list that comes up. You will be redirected to the appropriate page if it is available. Note: Some states list their county VSOs when you click on the state link. For other states, you need to click on additional links to find your county VSO.

If you do not have access to the Internet or your state does not list its county VSOs on the NACVSO Web site, consult your phone book. Go to the section titled, "County Government." Locate the veterans services information under the county courthouse listing. Call the number listed and ask for the county veteran service officer.

DISABLED AMERICAN VETERANS

Service officers at DAV offices are available for answering questions, checking forms, and filing pension claims with the VA.

ALABAMA

Disabled American Veterans
VA Regional Office
345 Perry Hill Rd, Rm 1-116
Montgomery, AL 36109
Phone: 334-213-3365
Fax: 334-213-5661

ALASKA

Disabled American Veterans
VA Regional Office
2925 DeBarr Road, Rm 3101
Anchorage, AK 99508
Phone: 907-257-4803
Fax: 907-257-7427

ARIZONA

Disabled American Veterans
VA Regional Office
3333 N Central Ave, Ste 1053
Phoenix, AZ 85012
Phone: 602-627-3286
Fax: 602-627-3295

ARKANSAS

Disabled American Veterans
VA Regional Office, Bldg 65, Rm 121
2200 Fort Roots Drive, (VA Med Ctr)
N Little Rock, AR 72114
Phone: 501-370-3838
Fax: 501-370-3729

CALIFORNIA

Disabled American Veterans
VA Regional Office Federal
    Building
11000 Wilshire Blvd, Rm 5227
W Los Angeles, CA 90024
Phone: 310-477-2539
Fax: 310-479-0100

Disabled American Veterans
VA Regional Office
10365 Old Placerville Rd
Ste 100
Sacramento, CA 95827
Phone: 916-364-6796
Fax: 916-364-1530

Disabled American Veterans
VA Regional Office Oakland
    Federal Bldg
1301 Clay St, Rm 1110, N
Oakland, CA 94612
Phone: 510-834-2921
Fax: 510-834-1331

Disabled American Veterans
VA Regional Office
8810 Rio San Diego Dr
Ste 1160
San Diego, CA 92108
Phone: 619-299-6916
Fax: 619-299-7092

COLORADO

Disabled American Veterans
VA Regional Office
155 Van Gordon St
PO Box 25126
Denver, CO 80225
Phone: 303-914-5570
Fax: 303-914-5584

CONNECTICUT

Disabled American Veterans
VA Med Ctr
555 Willard Ave
Newington, CT 06111
Mailing Address:
Disabled American Veterans
PO Box 310909
Newington, CT 06131
Phone: 860-594-6612
Fax: 860-667-1238

DELAWARE

Disabled American Veterans
VA Medical & Regional Office Ctr
1601 Kirkwood Hwy
Wilmington, DE 19805
Phone: 302-633-5324
Fax: 302-994-8424

DISTRICT OF COLUMBIA

Disabled American Veterans
VA Regional Office
1722 I St NW, Rm 210
Washington, DC 20421
Phone: 202-530-9260
Fax: 202-293-2120

Disabled American Veterans
Walter Reed Army Med Ctr
6900 Georgia Ave, NW
Bldg #11, Rm G-14
Washington, DC 20307
Phone: 202-356-1012, Ext 40572
Fax: Not available

FLORIDA

Disabled American Veterans
VA Regional Office
9500 Bay Pines Blvd, Rm 232
Bay Pines, FL 33744
Mailing Address:
Disabled American Veterans
PO Box 1437
St Petersburg, FL 33731
Phone: 727-319-7444
Fax: 727-319-7775

Disabled American Veterans
VA Med Ctr
1201 NW 16th St, Rm 2A146
Miami, FL 33125
Phone: 305-575-3130
Fax: 305-326-7510

Disabled American Veterans
1000 Legion Pl
Ste 1550
Orlando, FL 32801
Phone: 407-648-6130
Fax: 407-648-6199

Disabled American Veterans
West Palm Beach VA Med Ctr
Bldg 10, Rm 110-112
7305 N Military Trail
West Palm Beach, FL 33410
Phone: 561-422-8203
Fax: 561-422-8497

GEORGIA

Disabled American Veterans
VA Regional Office
1700 Clairmont Rd
Decatur, GA 30033
Phone: 404-929-5956
Fax: 404-929-5332

HAWAII

Disabled American Veterans
VAM&ROC, E-Wing
459 Patterson Rd, Rm 1-C103
Honolulu, HI 96819
Phone: 808-433-0490
Fax: 808-433-0493

IDAHO

Disabled American Veterans
VA Regional Office
805 W Franklin St, Rm 205
Boise, ID 83702
Phone: 208-334-1956
Fax: 208-342-2036

ILLINOIS

Disabled American Veterans
VA Regional Office
2122 W Taylor St, Ste 104
Chicago, IL 60612
Phone: 312-980-4242
Fax: 312-706-6673

INDIANA

Disabled American Veterans
VA Regional Office Federal Bldg
575 N Pennsylvania St, Rm 320
Indianapolis, IN 46204
Phone: 317-916-3615
Fax: 317-636-5567

IOWA

Disabled American Veterans
VA Regional Office,
1033 B Federal Bldg
2nd & Walnut Sts
Des Moines, IA 50309
Phone: 515-323-7539
Fax: 515-323-7403

KANSAS

Disabled American Veterans
VAM & ROC
5500 E Kellogg, Rm 112
Wichita, KS 67218
Phone: 316-688-6722
Fax: 316-688-6864

Disabled American Veterans
VA Med Ctr
4201 S Fourth St
Traffic Way
Leavenworth, KS 66048
Phone: 913-651-2402
Fax: 913-651-0366

KENTUCKY

Disabled American Veterans
VA Regional Office, Ste 390
321 W Main St, Rm 322
Louisville, KY 40202
Phone: 502-566-4482
Fax: 502-566-4487

LOUISIANA

Disabled American Veterans
VA Regional Office
701 Loyola Ave, Rm 1021
New Orleans, LA 70113
Mailing Address:
Disabled American Veterans
PO Box 1278
Gretna, LA 70054
Phone: 504-589-3868
Fax: 504-525-0220

MAINE

Disabled American Veterans
VA Regional Office - Med Ctr
Bldg 248, Rm 113, Route 17 E
Togus, ME 04330-3151
Mailing Address:
Disabled American Veterans
PO Box 3151
Augusta, ME 04330
Phone: 207-623-5725
Fax: 207-623-1528

MARYLAND

Disabled American Veterans
VA Regional Office Federal Bldg
Rm 1229, 31 Hopkins Plaza
Baltimore, MD 21201
Phone: 410-230-4440
Fax: 410-230-4441

MASSACHUSETTS

Disabled American Veterans
VA Regional Office
JFK Federal Bldg, Government Ctr
Rm 1575B
Boston, MA 02203
Phone: 617-303-5675
Fax: 617-227-4283

MICHIGAN

Disabled American Veterans
VA Regional Office McNamara
    Federal Bldg
477 Michigan Ave, Rm 1200
Detroit, MI 48226
Phone: 313-964-6595
Fax: 313-964-6576

MINNESOTA

Disabled American Veterans
VA Regional Office &
    Insurance Center
1 Federal Dr, Rm 192, Federal Bldg
Fort Snelling, MN 55111
Phone: 612-970-5665
Fax: 612-970-5671

MISSISSIPPI

Disabled American Veterans
VA Regional Office
1600 E Woodrow Wilson Ave
Rm 113
Jackson, MS 39216
Phone: 601-364-7178
Fax: 601-364-7209

MISSOURI

Disabled American Veterans
VA Regional Office
400 S 18th St, Rm 119
St Louis, MO 63103
Phone: 314-552-9883
Fax: 314-241-0338

MONTANA

Disabled American Veterans
VA Regional Office
3633 Veterans Dr, Ste 110B
PO Box 189
Fort Harrison, MT 59636
Phone: 406-495-2089
Fax: 406-495-2008

NEBRASKA

Disabled American Veterans
VA Regional Office
5631 S 48th St
Lincoln, NE 68516
Phone: 402-420-4025
Fax: 402-423-0728

NEVADA

Disabled American Veterans
National Service Office
5460 Reno Corporate Dr, Rm 102
Reno, NV 89511
Phone: 775-321-4895
Fax: 775-348-9519

Disabled American Veterans
Veterans Assistance Office
4800 Alpine Pl, Ste #7
Las Vegas, NV 89107
Phone: 702-878-7918
Fax: 702-878-7919

NEW HAMPSHIRE

Disabled American Veterans
VA Regional Office Norris Cotton
    Federal Bldg
275 Chestnut St, Rm 515
Manchester, NH 03101
Phone: 603-222-5788
Fax: 603-222-5798

NEW JERSEY

Disabled American Veterans
VA Regional Office
20 Washington Pl
Newark, NJ 07102
Phone: 973-297-3378
Fax: 973-297-3367

NEW MEXICO

Disabled American Veterans
VA Regional Office
500 Gold Ave, SW, Rm 3508
Albuquerque, NM 87102
Phone: 505-346-4864
Fax: 505-843-7282

NEW YORK

Disabled American Veterans
VA Regional Office
245 West Houston St, Rm 204
New York, NY 10014
Phone: 212-807-3157
Fax: 212-807-4016

Disabled American Veterans
Stratton VA Med Ctr
113 Holland Ave, Rm C308-5
Albany, NY 12208
Phone: 518-626-5690
Fax: 518-626-5696

Disabled American Veterans
VA Regional Office
130 S Elmwood Ave, Ste 620
Buffalo, NY 14202
Phone: 716-857-3354
Fax: 716-857-3487

Disabled American Veterans
VA Contact Office
344 W Genesee St, 2nd Fl
Syracuse, NY 13202
Phone: 315-423-5541
Fax: 315-422-3000

NORTH CAROLINA

Disabled American Veterans
VA Regional Office Federal Bldg
251 N Main St, Rm 115
Winston-Salem, NC 27102
Phone: 336-631-5481
Fax: 336-724-2101

NORTH DAKOTA

Disabled American Veterans
VA Regional Office
2101 N Elm, Rm 206
Fargo, ND 58102
Phone: 701-451-4636
Fax: 701-451-4672

OHIO

Disabled American Veterans
VA Regional Office
1240 E 9th St, Rm 1015
Cleveland, OH 44199
Phone: 216-522-3507
Fax: 216-621-6571

Disabled American Veterans
VA Contact Office
URS Tower, Ste 220
36 E 7th St
Cincinnati, OH 45202
Phone: 513-684-2676
Fax: 513-651-4280

OKLAHOMA

Disabled American Veterans
VA Regional Office
125 S Main St, Rm 1B30
Muskogee, OK 74401
Phone: 918-781-7764
Fax: 918-687-0606

OREGON

Disabled American Veterans
VA Regional Office Federal Bldg
1220 SW Third Ave, Rm #1692
Portland, OR 97204
Phone: 503-412-4750
Fax: 503-412-4751

PENNSYLVANIA

Disabled American Veterans
VA Regional Office &
    Insurance Center
PO Box 42938
Wissahickon & Manheim Sts
Philadelphia, PA 19101
Phone: 215-381-3065
Fax: 215-381-3498

Disabled American Veterans
VA Contact Office
1123 East End Blvd
Wilkes-Barre, PA 18702
Phone: 570-821-2520
Fax: 570-821-2524

Disabled American Veterans
VA Regional Office
1000 Liberty Ave, Rm 1606
Pittsburgh, PA 15222
Phone: 412-395-6241
Fax: 412-391-3085

PUERTO RICO

Disabled American Veterans
VA Ctr
150 Ave Carlos Chardon #232-2
San Juan, PR 00918
Phone: 787-772-7388
Fax: 787-772-7464

RHODE ISLAND

Disabled American Veterans
VA Regional Office
380 Westminster Mall
Providence, RI 02903
Phone: 401-223-3695
Fax: 401-274-1460

SOUTH CAROLINA

Disabled American Veterans
VA Regional Office, Ste 129
1801 Assembly St
Columbia, SC 29201
Phone: 803-255-4238
Fax: 803-255-4237

SOUTH DAKOTA

Disabled American Veterans
VA Regional Office
PO Box 5046, 2501 W 22nd St
Sioux Falls, SD 57117
Phone: 605-333-6896
Fax: 605-336-8158

TENNESSEE

Disabled American Veterans
VA Regional Office
US Court House, 110 9th Ave S
Nashville, TN 37203
Phone: 615-695-6384
Fax: 615-242-7494

TEXAS

Disabled American Veterans
VA Regional Office
One Veterans Plaza, 701 Clay St
Waco, TX 76799
Phone: 254-299-9932
Fax: 254-299-9925

Disabled American Veterans
VA Regional Office
6900 Almeda Rd, Rm 1033
Houston, TX 77030
Phone: 713-383-2715
Fax: 713-383-2719

Disabled American Veterans
VA Contact Office
5788 Eckhert Rd, Rm 2A112
San Antonio, TX 78240
Phone: 210-699-5064
Fax: 210-699-5082

Disabled American Veterans
Brooke Army Med Ctr
3851 Roger Brooke Dr, Ste 313-7
Fort Sam Houston, TX 78234
Phone: 210-916-5012
Fax: 210-916-4083

UTAH

Location (FedEx, UPS, etc.):
Disabled American Veterans
VA Regional Office
550 Foothill Dr, Rm G-3
Salt Lake City, UT 84113
Mailing (USPS Mail Only):
Disabled American Veterans
550 Foothill Dr
PO Box 581900
Salt Lake City, UT 84158
Phone: 801-326-2375
Fax: 801-326-2378

VERMONT

Disabled American Veterans
VA Med Ctr
215 N Main St
White River Junction, VT 05009
Phone: 802-296-5167
Fax: 802-295-9545

VIRGINIA

Disabled American Veterans
VA Regional Office Federal Bldg
210 Franklin Rd SW, Rm 505
Roanoke, VA 24011
Phone: 540-857-2373
Fax: 540-344-8205

WASHINGTON

Disabled American Veterans
VA Regional Office Federal Bldg
915 2nd Ave, Rm 1040
Seattle, WA 98174
Phone: 206-220-6225
Fax: 206-220-4171

WEST VIRGINIA

Disabled American Veterans
VA Regional Office
640 4th Ave, Rm 138
Huntington, WV 25701
Phone: 304-399-9350
Fax: 304-529-0389

WISCONSIN

Disabled American Veterans
VA Regional Office, Rm 162
5400 W National Ave
Milwaukee, WI 53214
Phone: 414-902-5736
Fax: 414-902-9440

WYOMING

(Itinerant Coverage by Denver, CO NSO office)

Disabled American Veterans
VAM & ROC
2360 E Pershing Blvd
Cheyenne, WY 82001
Phone: 307-433-2752
Fax: 307-433-2791

VETERANS OF FOREIGN WARS OF THE UNITED STATES

Service officers at VFW offices are available for answering questions, checking forms, and filing pension claims with the VA.

ALABAMA

VFW Dept Svc Ofcr
VA Regional Office
345 Perry Hill Rd, Rm 1-124
Montgomery, AL 36109
Phone: 334-213-3439
Fax: 334-213-3689

ALASKA

VFW Dept Svc Ofcr
VA Regional Office
2925 DeBarr Rd, Ste 3106
Anchorage, AK 99508
Phone: 907-276-8213
Fax: 907-278-6780

ARIZONA

VFW Dept Svc Ofcr
3333 N Central Ave, Rm 1049
Phoenix, AZ 85304
Phone: 602-627-3316
Fax: 602-627-3320

VFW Service and Liaison Ofcr
VA Med Ctr
Prescott, AZ 86313
Phone: 928-445-4860, Ext 6066
Fax: Not available

VFW Service and Liaison Ofcr
Sierra Vista VA Clinic
RWBA Community Health Clinic,
Bldg 45006
Fort Huachuca, AZ 85613
Phone: 520-458-2803
Fax: Not available

ARKANSAS

VFW Dept Svc Ofcr
VA Regional Office
2200 Fort Roots Dr
Bldg 65, Rm 119
North Little Rock, AR 72114
Phone: 501-370-3820
Fax: 501-370-3829

CALIFORNIA

Supervisor, VFW Service Office
Oakland Federal Bldg
1301 Clay St, Rm 1140N
Oakland, CA 94612
Phone: 510-835-1246
Fax: 510-835-8029

VFW Dept Svc Ofcr
Federal Bldg, Rm 5202
11000 Wilshire Blvd
Los Angeles, CA 90024
Phone: 310-235-7129
Fax: 310-575-9722

VFW Dept Svc Ofcr
VA Regional Office
8810 Rio San Diego Dr, Rm 1161
San Diego, CA 92108
Phone: 619-400-5322
Fax: 619-291-8516

COLORADO

VFW Dept Svc Ofcr
VA Regional Office
155 Van Gordon St, Rm #360
Box 25126
Denver, CO 80225
Phone: 303-914-5595/96/97
Fax: 303-914-5598

CONNECTICUT

VFW Dept Svc Ofcr
PO Box 310909
Rm 3133
555 Willard Ave
Newington, CT 06131
Phone: 860-594-6610
Fax: 860-667-1214

DELAWARE

VFW Dept Svc Ofcr
VAM & ROC
1601 Kirkwood Hwy, Rm 21
Wilmington, DE 19805
Phone: 302-633-5326
Fax: 302-633-5507

DISTRICT OF COLUMBIA

VFW National Service Office
    Supervisor
1722 Eye Street, NW
Ste 207
Washington, DC 20421
Phone: 202-530-9385
Fax: 202-775-9475

EUROPE

Veterans of Foreign Wars
Attn: Dept of Europe Svc Ofcr
CMR 454 Box F
APO AE 09250
Phone: 49-911-9602633
Fax: 49-911-60046025

FLORIDA

Director, Veterans Service Office
VFW Dept of Florida
VA Regional Office, Rm 217
(Mail: PO Box 1437)
St Petersburg, FL 33731
Phone: 727-319-7483
Fax: 727-319-7776

GEORGIA

VFW Dept Svc Ofcr
1700 Clairmont Rd, Room 1.318
Decatur, GA 30033
Phone: 404-929-5345
Fax: 404-929-5347

HAWAII

VFW Dept Svc Ofcr
Tripler Army Med Ctr
459 Patterson Rd, E-Wing,
    Rm 1-C104
Honolulu, HI 96819-1522
Phone: 808-433-0494/0495
Fax: 808-433-0388

IDAHO

VFW Dept Svc Ofcr
805 W Franklin St
Boise, ID 83702
Phone: 208-334-1245
Fax: 208-334-3549

ILLINOIS

VFW Dept Svc Ofcr
2122 W Taylor St, Rm 127
Chicago, IL 60612
Phone: 312-980-4284
Fax: 312-706-6680

INDIANA

VFW Dept Svc Ofcr
575 N Pennsylvania St, Rm 374
Indianapolis, IN 46204
Phone: 317-916-3629
Fax: 317- 226-5412

IOWA

VFW Dept Svc Ofcr
Federal Bldg, Rm 1033-C
Des Moines, IA 50309
Phone: 515-323-7546
Fax: 515-323-7405

KANSAS

VFW Dept Svc Ofcr
VAM & ROC
5500 E Kellogg
Wichita, KS 67218
Phone: 316-688-6801/6802
Fax: 316-688-6777

KENTUCKY

VFW Dept Svc Ofcr
PO Box 2105
Louisville, KY 40201
Phone: 502-566-4422
Fax: 502-566-4425

LATIN AMERICA/CARIBBEAN

Aparto 0843-02775
Panama, Republic of Panama
Phone: 011-507-227-5444, Ext 110
Fax: Not available

LOUISIANA

VFW Dept Svc Ofcr
PO Box 94095, CAP STA
Baton Rouge, LA 70804
Phone: 225-922-0500, Ext 201
Fax: 225-922-0511

MAINE

VFW Dept Svc Ofcr
Dept of VA Togus
PO Box 3311
Augusta, ME 04330
Phone: 207-623-5723
Fax: 207-626-4732

MARYLAND

VFW Dept Svc Ofcr
Fallon Federal Bldg
31 Hopkins Plaza, Rm 114E
Baltimore, MD 21201
Phone: 410-230-4480
Fax: 410-230-4481

MASSACHUSETTS

VFW Dept Svc Ofcr
John F Kennedy Federal Bldg
Government Ctr, Rm 1500-C
Boston, MA 02203
Phone: 617-303-5688
Fax: 617-227-2024

MICHIGAN

State Service Director
VFW Dept of Michigan
Patrick V McNamara Federal Bldg
477 Michigan Ave, Rm 1215
Detroit, MI 48226
Phone: 313-964-6510
Fax: 313-964-6545

MINNESOTA

Director, VFW Claims Division
Veterans of Foreign Wars of the US
Bishop Henry Whipple
    Federal Bldg
1 Federal Dr, Room 184
Fort Snelling, MN 55111
Phone: 612-970-5669
Fax: 612-970-5404

MISSISSIPPI

VFW Dept Svc Ofcr
1600 E Woodrow Wilson Blvd
Jackson, MS 39216
Phone: 601-364-7180
Fax: 601-364-7226

MISSOURI

VFW Dept Svc Ofcr
400 S 18th St, Rm 105
St Louis, MO 63103
Phone: 314-552-9886
Fax: 314-231-2957

MONTANA

VFW Dept Svc Ofcr
3633 Veterans Dr
Ste 110C
PO Box 52
Fort Harrison, MT 59636
Phone: 406-495-2086/2087
Fax: 406-495-2007

NEBRASKA

VFW Dept Svc Ofcr
5631 S 48th St
Lincoln, NE 68516
Phone: 402-420-4021/4023
Fax: 402-471-7070

NEVADA

VFW Dept Svc Ofcr
5460 Reno Corporate Dr, Rm 106
Reno, NV 89511
Phone: 775-321-4885
Fax: 775-321-4889

NEW HAMPSHIRE

VFW Dept Svc Ofcr
Norris Cotton Federal Bldg
275 Chestnut St
Manchester, NH 03101
Phone: 603-222-5780
Fax: 603-222-5783

NEW JERSEY

VFW Dept Svc Ofcr
20 Washington Pl
Newark, NJ 07102
Phone: 973-297-3226
Fax: 973-623-1244

NEW MEXICO

VFW Dept Svc Ofcr
500 Gold Ave, SW, Ste 3009
Albuquerque, NM 87102
Phone: 505-346-4881
Fax: 505-346-4880

NEW YORK

VFW Dept Svc Ofcr
245 W Houston St, Rm 207
New York, NY 10014
Phone: 212-807-3024/3164
Fax: 212-807-4023

VFW Dept Svc Ofcr
130 S Elmwood Ave, Ste 626
Buffalo, NY 14202
Phone: 716-857-3348/3349
Fax: 716-857-3484

VFW Dept Svc Ofcr
344 W Genesee St, Ste 205
Syracuse, NY 13202
Phone: 315-423-5539
Fax: 315-479-8993

NORTH CAROLINA

VFW Dept Svc Ofcr
VA Regional Office
251 N Main St
Winston-Salem, NC 27155
*(DO NOT OPEN IN VA MAIL
ROOM)*
Phone: 336-631-5457
Fax: 336-714-0901

NORTH DAKOTA

VFW Department Service Officer
VAM & ROC
2101 N Elm St, Ste 205
Fargo, ND 58102
Phone: 701-451-4635
Fax: 701-451-4670

OHIO

VFW State Service Ofcr
Federal Bldg
1240 E 9th St, Rm 1043
Cleveland, OH 44199
Phone: 216-522-3510/3511
Fax: 216-522-7335

OKLAHOMA

VFW Dept Svc Ofcr
VA Regional Office
125 S Main St
Muskogee, OK 74401
Phone: 918-781-7769
Fax: 918-686-6604

OREGON

VFW Dept Svc Ofcr
VA Regional Office
1220 SW 3rd Ave, Rm 1690
Portland, OR 97204
Phone: 503-412-4757
Fax: 503-412-4758

PACIFIC AREAS

Box R-CV
FPO, AP 96517
Phone: 63-45-892-2407
Fax: 63-45-892-2406

PENNSYLVANIA

VFW Dept Svc Ofcr
5000 Wissahickon Ave
(MAIL: VA Regional Office &
Insurance Center)
ATTN: VFW, PO Box 42938
Philadelphia, PA 19101
Phone: 215-842-2000, Ext 4213
          215-381-3123
Fax: 215-381-3491

VFW Dept Svc Ofcr
1000 Liberty Ave, Rm 1601
Pittsburgh, PA 15222
Phone: 412-395-6259/6260
Fax: 412-395-6261

VFW Dept Svc Ofcr
1123 E End Blvd, Bldg. 35, Ste 1
Wilkes-Barre, PA 18702
Phone: 570-821-2535/2536
Fax: 570-821-2539

PUERTO RICO

VFW Svc Ofcr
PO Box 33131
Veterans Plaza Station
San Juan, PR 00933
Phone: 787-772-7456
Fax: 787-772-7474

RHODE ISLAND

VFW Dept Svc Ofcr
VA Regional Office
380 Westminster St
Providence, RI 02903
Phone: 401-223-3689/3690
Fax: 401-272-2580

SOUTH CAROLINA

VFW Dept Svc Ofcr
1801 Assembly St, Rm 119
Columbia, SC 29201
Phone: 803-255-4304
Fax: 803-255-4303

SOUTH DAKOTA

VFW State Service Ofcr
VA Regional Office
2501 W 22nd St
PO Box 5046
Sioux Falls, SD 57117
Phone: 605-333-6869
Fax: 605-333-5386

TENNESSEE

Director of Claims
VFW Dept Svc Ofcr
VA Regional Office
110 9th Ave S, Rm 310-A
Nashville, TN 37203
Phone: 615-741-1863
Fax: 615-741-6231

VFW State Service Ofcr
90 E Spring St
Veterans Memorial Bldg
Cookeville, TN 38501
Phone: 931-526-6929
Fax: 931-372-2546

TEXAS

VFW Dept Svc Ofcr
One Veterans Plaza
701 Clay St
Waco, TX 76799
Phone: 254-299-9959
Fax: 254-299-9970

VFW Dept Svc Ofcr
6900 Almeda Rd
Houston, Texas 77030
Phone: 713-383-2750
Fax: 713-383-2760

UTAH

VFW Dept Svc Ofcr
550 Foothill Dr, Ste 203
PO Box 581900
Salt Lake City, UT 84158
Phone: 801-326-2385
Fax: 801-326-2388

VERMONT

VFW Dept Svc Ofcr
VAM & ROC
215 N Main St
White River Junction, VT 05009
Phone: 802-296-5168
Fax: 802-296-5198

VIRGINIA

VFW Dept Svc Ofcr
Poff Federal Bldg
270 Franklin Rd, SW, Rm 503
Roanoke, VA 24011
Phone: 540-857-7101
Fax: 540-857-6437 or 540-857-7573

WASHINGTON

VFW Dept Svc Ofcr
915 Second Ave, Rm 1044
Seattle, WA 98174
(DO NOT OPEN IN VA MAIL ROOM)
Phone: 206-220-6191
Fax: 206-220-6241

VFW Dept Svc Ofcr
2711 Oakes Ave
Everett, WA 98201
Phone: 425-304-1223
Fax: 425-339-5550

WEST VIRGINIA

VFW Dept Svc Ofcr
1321 Plaza E, Ste 109
Charleston, WV 25301
Phone: 304-558-3661
Fax: 304-558-3662

WISCONSIN

VFW Dept Svc Ofcr
VA Regional Office
5400 W National Ave, Rm 166
Milwaukee, WI 53214
Phone: 414-902-5748
Fax: 414-902-9412

WYOMING

VFW Dept Svc Ofcr
VAM & ROC
2360 E Pershing Blvd
Cheyenne, WY 82001
Phone: 307-778-7340
Fax: 307-778-7549

VA FACILITIES

Service representatives at VA regional offices are available for answering questions, checking forms, and filing pension claims with the VA. Healthcare services are available at VA medical centers and clinics.

Patients should call the telephone numbers listed to ask about clinic hours and services.

For more information or to search for a facility near you by zip code, visit http://www1.va.gov/directory/guide/home.asp?isFlash=1.

ALABAMA

VA Medical Centers:

700 S 19th St
Birmingham, AL 35233
Phone: 205-933-8101
    or toll free: 1-800-872-0328

215 Perry Hill Rd
Montgomery, AL 36109
Phone: 334-272-4670
    or toll free: 1-800-214-8387

3701 Loop Rd, East
Tuscaloosa, AL 35404
Phone: 205-554-2000
    or toll free: 1-888-269-3045

2400 Hospital Rd
Tuskegee, AL 36083
Phone: 334-727-0550
    or toll free: 1-800-214-8387

VA Clinics:

975 9th Ave
SW-Ste 400 at UAB West Medical
    Ctr West
Bessemer, AL 32055
Phone: 205-428-3495

2020 Alexander Dr
Dothan, AL 36301
Phone: 334-673-4166

Dothan Mental Health Ctr
3753 Ross Clark Cir, Ste 4
Dothan, AL 36301
Phone: 334-678-1903

206 Rescia Ave
Gadsden, AL 35906
Phone: 256-413-7154

301 Governor's Dr
Huntsville, AL 35801
Phone: 256-535-3100

3400 Hwy 78 East, Ste 215
Jasper, AL 35501
Phone: 205-221-7384

8075 Madison Blvd, Ste 101
Madison, AL 35758
Phone: 256-772-6220

1504 Springhill Ave
Mobile, AL 36604
Phone: 251-219-3900

96 Ali Way Creekside South
Oxford, AL 36203
Phone: 256-832-414

Florence Shoals Area Clinic
422 DD Cox Blvd
Sheffield, AL 35660
Phone: 256-381-9055

VA Regional Offices:

345 Perry Hill Rd
Montgomery, AL 36109
Phone statewide toll free:
    1-800-827-1000

2577 Government Blvd
Mobile, AL 36606
Phone: 251-478-5906

ALASKA

VA Medical Center:

2925 DeBarr Rd
Anchorage, AK 99508
Phone: 907-257-4700
    or toll free: 1-888-353-7574

VA Clinics:

Bldg 4076, Neeley Rd, Rm 1J-101
Fort Wainwright, AK 99703
Mailing address:
PO Box 74570
Fairbanks, AK 99707
Phone: 907-361-6370

11312 Kenai Spur Hwy, #39
Kenai, AK 99669
Phone: 907-283-2231

VA Regional Office:

2925 De Barr Rd
Anchorage, AK 99508
Phone statewide toll free:
    1-800-827-1000

VA Benefits Office:

PO Box 20069
Juneau, AK 99802
Phone: 907-586-7472

AMERICAN SAMOA

VA Clinic:

Fiatele Teo Army Reserve Bldg
Pago Pago, AS 96799
Mailing address:
PO Box 1005
Pago Pago, AS 96799
Phone: 684-699-3730

VA Benefits Office:

PO Box 1005
Pago Pago, AS 96799
Phone: 684-633-5073

ARIZONA

VA Medical Centers:

500 N Hwy 89
Prescott, AZ 86313
Phone: 928-445-4860
    or toll free: 1-800-949-1005

3601 S 6th Ave
Tucson, AZ 85723
Phone: 520-792-1450
    or toll free: 1-800-470-8262

650 E Indian School Rd
Phoenix, AZ 85012
Phone: 602-277-5551
or toll free: 1-800-554-7174

VA Clinics:

Anthem Medical Plaza
3618 W Anthem Way
Bldg D, #120
Anthem, AZ 85086
Phone: 623-551-6092

PO Box 16196
Camp Navajo Army Depot
Bellemont, AZ 86015
Phone: 928-226-1056

306 E Monroe Ave
Buckeye, AZ 85326
Phone: 623-386-4814

900 E Florence Blvd
Suites H & I
Casa Grande, AZ 85222
Phone: 520-629-4900

203 Candy Lane
Bldg 5B
Cottonwood, AZ 86326
Phone: 928-649-1523
or 928-649-1532

5860 S Hospital Dr
Ste 11
Globe, AZ 85501
Phone: 928-425-0027

380 W Hermosa Dr #140
Green Valley, AZ 85614
Phone: 520-629-4900
or toll free: 1-800-470-8262

1726 Beverly Ave
Kingman, AZ 86401
Phone: 928-692-0080
or 928-445-4860, Ext 6830

2035 Mesquite
Ste E
Lake Havasu City, AZ 86403
Phone: 928-680-0090

6950 E Williams Field Rd
Bldg 23
Mesa, AZ 85212
Phone: 602-222-6568/3315

1106 N Beeline Hwy
Payson, AZ 85541
Phone: 928-472-3148

1106 N Beeline Hwy
Safford, AZ 85546
Phone: 520-629-4900

2450 Show Low Lake Rd
Ste 1
Show Low, AZ 85901
Phone: 928-532-1069

101 Coronado Dr, Ste A
Sierra Vista, AZ 85635
Phone: 520-792-1450

10147 Grand Ave
Ste C1
Sun City, AZ 85351
Phone: 602-222-2630

2945 W Ina Rd
Tucson, AZ 85741
Phone: 520-629-4900

2555 E Gila Ridge Rd
Yuma, AZ 85365
Phone: 520-629-4900

VA Regional Office:

3333 N Central Ave
Phoenix, AZ 85012
Phone statewide toll free:
    1-800-827-1000

ARKANSAS

VA Medical Centers:

1100 N College Ave
Fayetteville, AR 72703
Phone: 479-443-4301
    or toll free: 1-800-691-8387

4300 W 7th St
Little Rock, AR 72205
Phone: 501-257-1000

2200 Fort Roots Dr
North Little Rock, AR 72114
Phone: 501-257-1000

VA Clinics:

460 W Oak St
El Dorado, AR 71730
Phone: 870-862-2489

1500 Dodson Ave
Sparks Medical Plaza
Fort Smith, AR 72917
Phone: 479-709-6850
    or toll free: 1-877-604-0798

707 N Main St
Harrison, AR 72601
Phone: 870-741-3592

1661 Airport Rd
Ste E
Hot Springs, AR 71913
Phone: 501-881-4112

223 E Jackson Ave
Jonesboro, AR 72401
Phone: 870-972-0063

1706 Hwy 71 N
Mena, AR 71953
Phone: 479-394-4800

10 Medical Plaza
Mountain Home, AR 72653
Phone: 870-424-4109

1101 Morgan St
Paragould, AR 72450
Phone: 870-236-9756

4010 Old Warren Rd
Pine Bluff, AR 71603
Phone: 870-541-9300

910 Realtor Ave
Texarkana, AR 71854
Phone: 870-216-2242

VA Regional Office:

2200 Fort Roots Dr, Bldg 65
North Little Rock, AR 72114
Phone statewide toll free:
    1-800-827-1000

CALIFORNIA

VA Medical Centers:

2615 E Clinton Ave
Fresno, CA 93703
Phone: 559-225-6100
    or toll free: 1-888-826-2838

4951 Arroyo Rd
Livermore, CA 94550
Phone: 925-373-4700

11201 Benton St
Loma Linda, CA 92357
Phone: 909-825-7084
    or toll free: 1-800-741-8387

5901 E 7th St
Long Beach, CA 90822
Phone: 562-826-8000
    or toll free: 1-888-769-8387

11301 Wilshire Blvd
Los Angeles, CA 90073
Phone: 310-478-3711
    or toll free: 1-800-952-4852

10535 Hospital Way
Mather, CA 95655
Phone: 916-366-5366
    or toll free: 1-800-382-8387

795 Willow Rd
Menlo Park, CA 94025
Phone: 650-416-9997

3801 Miranda Ave
Palo Alto, CA 94304
Phone: 650-493-5000
    or toll free: 1-800-455-0057

3350 La Jolla Village Dr
San Diego, CA 92161
Phone: 858-552-8585
    or toll free: 1-800-331-8387

4150 Clement St
San Francisco, CA 94121
Phone: 415-221-4810
    or toll free: 1-800-733-0502

VA Clinics:

Professional Ctr, 3rd Fl, #303
1801 W Romneya Dr
Anaheim, CA 92801
Phone: 714-780-5400

3605 Hospital Rd, Ste D
Atwater, CA 95301
Phone: 209-381-0105

11985 Heritage Oaks Pl
Auburn, CA 95603
Phone: 530-889-0872
    or toll free: 1-888-227-5404

1801 Westwind Dr
Bakersfield, CA 93301
Phone: 661-632-1800

Imperial Valley Clinic
528 G St
Brawley, CA 92227
Phone: 760-344-9085

1350 N 41st St, Ste 102
Capitola, CA 95010
Phone: 831-464-5519

280 Cohasset Rd
Chico, CA 95926
Phone: 530-879-5000
    or toll free: 1-800-382-8387

South Bay
835 Third Ave
Chula Vista, CA 91910
619-409-1600

East Los Angeles
5426 E Olympic Blvd
City of Commerce, CA 90040
Phone: 323-725-7557

800 Magnolia Ave, #101
Corona, CA 92879
Phone: 951-817-8820

815 E Pennsylvania Ave
Escondido, CA 92025
Phone: 760-466-7020

714 F St
Eureka, CA 95501
Phone: 707-442-5335

103 Bodin Cir
Travis Air Force Base
Fairfield, CA 94535
Phone: 707-437-1800
    or toll free: 1-800-382-8387

Stockton Clinic
7777 S Freedom Dr
French Camp, CA 95231
Phone: 209-946-3400

1251 Redondo Beach Blvd, 3rd Fl
Gardena, CA 90247
Phone: 310-851-4705

Antelope Valley
547 W Lancaster Blvd
Lancaster, CA 93536
Phone: 661-729-8655
    or toll free: 1-800-515-0031

Villages at Cabrillo
2001 River Ave, Bldg 28
Long Beach, CA 90806
Phone: 562-388-8000

351 E Temple St
Los Angeles, CA 90012
213-253-2677

West LA Ambulatory Care
11301 Wilshire Blvd
Los Angeles, CA 90073
Phone: 310-268-3526

3737 Martin Luther King Blvd,
    Ste 515
Lynwood, CA 90262
Phone: 310-537-6825

Clinic and Ctr for Rehabilitation
    & Extended Care
150 Muir Rd
Martinez, CA 94553
Phone: 925-372-2000
    or toll free: 1-800-382-8387

1524 McHenry Ave
Modesto, CA 95350
Phone: 209-557-6200

Sepulveda Clinic and
    Nursing Home
16111 Plummer St
North Hills, CA 91343
Phone: 818-891-7711
    or toll free: 1-800-516-4567

Mental Health Clinic
2505 W 14th St
Oakland Army Base
Oakland, CA 94626
Phone: 510-587-3400
    or toll free: 1-800-382-8387

2221 Martin Luther King Jr Way
Oakland, CA 94612
Phone: 510-267-7800
    or toll free: 1-800-382-8387

250 W Citrus Grove Ave, Ste 150
Oxnard, CA 93030
Phone: 805-983-6384

41-865 Boardwalk, Ste 103
Palm Desert, CA 92211
Phone: 760-341-5570

351 Hartnell Ave
Redding, CA 96002
Phone: 530-226-7555
    or toll free: 1-800-382-8387

Mental Health Clinic at Mather
10633 Grissom Rd
Sacramento, CA 95655
Phone: 916-366-5420
    or toll free: 1-800-382-8387

McClellan Dental Clinic
5401 Arnold Ave
Sacramento, CA 95652
Phone: 916-561-7800
    or toll free: 1-800-382-8387

McClellan Outpatient Clinic
5342 Dudley Blvd
Sacramento, CA 95652
Phone: 916-561-7400
    or toll free: 1-800-382-8387

1001 Sneath Lane, Ste 300, 3rd Fl
San Bruno, CA 94066
Phone: 650-615-6000

Mission Valley
8810 Rio San Diego Dr
San Diego, CA 92108
Phone: 619-400-5000

Downtown Clinic
401 3rd St
San Francisco, CA 94107
Phone: 415-551-7300

Pasadera
420 W Las Tunas Dr
San Gabriel, CA 91776
Phone: 626-289-5973

80 Great Oaks Blvd
San Jose, CA 95119
Phone: 408-363-3011

Pacific Med Plaza
1288 Morro Street
Ste 200
San Luis Obispo, CA 93401
Phone: 805-543-1233

Bristol Medical
2740 S Bristol St, 1st Fl, # 101
Santa Ana, CA 92704
Phone: 714-825-3500

4440 Calle Real
Santa Barbara, CA 93110
Phone: 805-683-1491

10210 Orr & Day Rd
Santa Fe Springs, CA 90670
Phone: 562-864-5565

1550 E Main St
Santa Maria, CA 93454
Phone: 805-354-6000

3315 Chanate Rd
Santa Rosa, CA 95404
Phone: 707-570-3855
    or 707-570-3800

Monterey Clinic
3401 Engineering Lane
Seaside, CA 93955
Phone: 831-883-3800

197473 Greenley Rd
Sonora, CA 95370
Phone: 209-588-2600

500 W. Hospital Rd
Stockton, CA 95231
Phone: 209-946-3400

28125 Bradley Rd, Ste 130
Sun City, CA 92586
Phone: 951-672-1931

VA South Valley Clinic
1050 N Cherry St
Tulare, CA 93274
Phone: 559-684-8703

630 Kings Court
Ukiah, CA 95482
Phone: 707-468-7700

1238 E Arrow Hwy, No 100
Upland, CA 91786
Phone: 909-946-5348

Mare Island Clinic
201 Walnut Ave
Vallejo, CA 94592
Phone: 707-562-8200
    or toll free: 1-382-8387

12138 Industrial Blvd, Ste 120
Victorville, CA 92392
Phone: 760-951-2599

1840 West Dr
Vista, CA 92083
Phone: 760-643-2000

VA Regional Offices:

Federal Bldg
11000 Wilshire Blvd
Los Angeles, CA 90024
This office serves the counties of Inyo, Kern, Los Angeles, San Bernardino, San Luis Obispo, Santa Barbara, and Ventura.
Phone statewide toll free:
    1-800-827-1000

1301 Clay St, Rm 1300 North
Oakland, CA 94612
This office serves all California counties not served by the Los Angeles, San Diego, or the Reno, Nevada, VA regional offices
Phone toll free: 1-800-827-1000

8810 Rio San Diego Dr
San Diego, CA 92108
This office serves the counties of Imperial, Orange, Riverside, and San Diego.
Phone statewide toll free:
    1-800-827-1000
The counties of Alpine, Lassen, Modoc, and Mono are served by the Reno, Nevada regional office.

VA Benefits Office:

10365 Old Placerville Rd
Sacramento, CA 95827
Phone: 916-364-6500

COLORADO

VA Medical Centers:

1055 Clermont St
Denver, CO 80220
Phone: 303-399-8020
or toll free: 1-888-336-8262

2121 North Ave
Grand Junction, CO 81501
Phone: 970-242-0731
or toll free: 1-866-206-6415

Health Administration Center:

3773 Cherry Creek N Dr
Denver, CO 80209
Phone: 303-331-7500

VA Clinics:

San Luis Valley Clinic/
Sierra Blanca Med Ctr
622 Del Sol Dr
Alamosa, CO 81101
Phone: 719-587-6800
or toll free: 1-866-659-0930

13001 E 17th Pl
Bldg 500, 2nd Fl, West Wing
Aurora, CO 80045
Phone: 303-724-0190

1177 Rose Ave
Burlington, CO 80807
Phone: 719-346-5239

25 N Spruce St
Colorado Springs, CO 80905
Phone: 719-327-5660
or toll free: 1-800-278-3883

551 Tucker St
Craig, CO 81625
Phone: 970-824-9721
or 970-242-0731

400 S Camino Del Rio
Durango, CO 81301
Phone: 970-247-2214

1100 Poudre River Dr
Ft Collins, CO 80524
Phone: 970-224-1550

2020 16th St
Greeley, CO 80631
Phone: 970-313-0027

1100 Carson Ave, Ste 104
La Junta, CO 81050
Phone: 719-383-5195

155 Van Gordon St, Ste 395
Lakewood, CO 80225
Phone: 303-914-2680

High Plains Community Health Ctr
201 Kendall Dr
Lamar, CO 81052
Phone: 719-336-5972

4 Hillcrest Plaza Way
Montrose, CO 81401
Phone: 970-249-7791
or 970-242-0731

4112 Outlook Blvd
Pueblo, CO 81008
Phone: 719-553-1000
or toll free: 1-800-369-6748

VA Regional Office:

Denver Regional Office
155 Van Gordon St
Lakewood, CO 80228
Mailing address:
PO Box 25126
Lakewood, CO 80228
Phone statewide toll free:
    1-800-827-1000

CONNECTICUT

VA Medical Centers:

555 Willard Ave
Newington, CT 06111
Phone: 860-666-6951

950 Campbell Ave
West Haven, CT 06516
Phone: 203-932-5711

VA Clinics:

7 Germantown Rd, Ste 2B
Danbury, CT 06810
Phone: 203-798-8422

Shaw's Cove Four
New London, CT 06320
Phone: 860-437-3611

1275 Summer St, Ste 102
Stamford, CT 06905
Phone: 203-325-0649

95 Scovill St
Waterbury, CT 06706
Phone: 203-465-5292

Windham Hospital
96 Mansfield St
Windham, CT 06226
Phone: 860-450-7583

Winsted Health Ctr
115 Spencer St
Winsted, CT 06908
Phone: 860-738-6985

VA Regional Office:

Hartford Regional Office
Building 2E, Rm 5137
555 Willard Ave.
Newington, CT 06111
Phone statewide toll free:
    1-800-827-1000

DELAWARE

VA Medical Center:

1601 Kirkwood Hwy
Wilmington, DE 19805
Phone: 302-994-2511
    or toll free: 1-800-461-8262

VA Clinics:

214 W DuPont Hwy
Millsboro, DE 19966
Phone: 302-934-0195

121 S Front St
Seaford, DE 19973
Phone: 302-628-8324

VA Regional Office:

1601 Kirkwood Hwy
Wilmington, DE 19805
Phone: 302-994-2511

DISTRICT OF COLUMBIA

VA Medical Center:

50 Irving St, NW
Washington, DC 20422
Phone: 202-745-8000
    or toll free: 1-888-553-0242

VA Clinic:

820 Chesapeake St, SE
Washington, DC 20032
Phone: 202-745-8685

VA Regional Office:

1722 I St, NW
Washington, DC 20421
Phone toll free:
    1-800-827-1000

FLORIDA

VA Medical Centers:

10000 Bay Pines Blvd
Bay Pines, FL 33744
Mailing address:
PO Box 5005
Bay Pines, FL 33744
Phone: 727-398-6661
    or toll free: 1-888-820-0230

1601 SW Archer Rd
Gainesville, FL 32608
Phone: 352-376-1611
    or toll free: 1-800-324-8387

619 S Marion Ave
Lake City, FL 32025
Phone: 386-755-3016
    or toll free: 1-800-308-8387

1201 NW 16th St
Miami, FL 33125
Phone: 305-575-7000
    or toll free: 1-888-276-1785

5201 Raymond St
Orlando, FL 32803
Phone: 407-629-1599
    or toll free: 1-800-922-7521

13000 Bruce B Downs Blvd
Tampa, FL 33612
Phone: 813-972-2000
    or toll free: 1-888-716-7787

7305 N Military Trail
West Palm Beach, FL 33410
Phone: 561-422-8262
    or toll free: 1-800-972-8262

VA Clinics:

901 Meadows Rd
Boca Raton, FL 33433
Phone: 561-416-8995

14540 Cortez Blvd, Ste 200
Brooksville, FL 34613
Phone: 352-597-8287

9900 W Sample Rd, Ste 100
Coral Springs, FL 33065
Phone: 954-575-4940

551 National Healthcare Dr
Daytona Beach, FL 32114
Phone: 386-323-7500

2100 SW 10th St
Deerfield Beach, FL 33442
Phone: 954-570-5572

4800 Linton Blvd
Building E, Ste 300
Delray Beach, FL 33445
Phone: 561-495-1973

1721 Main St
Dunedin, FL 34698
Phone: 727-734-5276

4333 US Hwy 301 N
Ellenton, FL 34222
Phone: 941-721-0649

3033 Winkler Extension
Ft Myers, FL 33916
Phone: 239-939-3939

727 N US 1
Ft Pierce, FL 34950
Phone: 772-595-5150

3702 Washington St, Ste 201
Hollywood, FL 33021
Phone: 954-986-1811

Pembroke Pines
7369 W Sheridan St, Ste 102
Hollywood, FL 33024
Phone: 954-894-1668

950 Krome Ave, Ste 401
Homestead, FL 33030
Phone: 305-248-0874

1833 Blvd
Jacksonville, FL 32206
Phone: 904-232-2751

105662 Overseas Hwy
Key Largo, FL 33037
Phone: 305-451-0164

1300 Douglas Cir, Bldg L-15
Key West, FL 33040
Phone: 305-293-4609

2285 N Central Ave
Kissimmee, FL 34741
Phone: 407-518-5004

3240 S Florida Ave
Lakeland, FL 33803
Phone: 863-701-2470

2804 W Marc Knighton Court, Ste A
Lecanto, FL 34461
Phone: 352-746-8000

711 W Main St
Leesburg, FL 34748
Phone: 352-435-4000

Healthcare for Homeless Vets
1492 W Flagler St
Miami, FL 33135
Phone: 305-541-5864

Substance Abuse Clinic
1492 W Flagler St, #101
Miami, FL 33135
Phone: 305-541-8435

2685 Horseshoe Dr, Ste 101
Naples, FL 34104
Phone: 239-659-9188

9912 Little Rd
New Port Richey, FL 34654
Phone: 727-869-4100

Fort Lauderdale
5599 N Dixie Hwy
Oakland Park, FL 33334
Phone: 954-771-2101

1515 Silver Springs Blvd
Ocala, FL 34470
Phone: 352-369-3320

1201 N Parrot Ave
Okeechobee, FL 34972
Phone: 863-824-3232

6703 W Hwy 98
Panama City Beach, FL 32407
Phone: 850-636-7000

Naval Support Activity-
    Panama City
101 Vernon Ave, #387
Panama City Beach, FL 32407
Phone: 850-636-7000

312 Kenmore Rd
Pensacola, FL 32503
Phone: 850-476-1100

4161 Tamiami Trail Unit 4
Port Charlotte, FL 33952
Phone: 941-235-2710

1403 Med Plaza Dr, Ste 109
Sanford, FL 32771
Phone: 407-323-5999

5682 Bee Ridge Rd, Ste 100
Sarasota, FL 34233
Phone: 941-371-3349

3760 US Hwy 27 S
Sebring, FL 33870
Phone: 863-471-6227
Mental health phone: 863-314-0325

1955 US 1 S, Ste 200
St Augustine, FL 32086
Phone: 904-829-0814
    or toll free: 1-866-401-8387

3420 8th Ave South
St Petersburg, FL 33711
Phone: 727-322-1304

3501 SE Willoughby Blvd
Stuart, FL 34997
Phone: 772-288-0304

1607 St James Court
Tallahassee, FL 32308
Phone: 850-878-0191

Laurel Lake Professional Park
1950 Laurel Manor Dr, Bldg 240
The Villages, FL 32162
Phone: 352-205-8900

372 17th St
Vero Beach, FL 32960
Phone: 772-299-4623

2900 Veterans Way
Viera, FL 32940
Phone: 321-637-3788

6937 Medical View Lane
Zephyrhills, FL 33541
Phone: 813-780-2550

VA Regional Office:

9500 Bay Pines Blvd
St Petersburg, FL 33708
Mailing address:
PO Box 1437
St Petersburg, FL 33731
Phone statewide toll free:
    1-800-827-1000

VA Benefits Offices:

Vocational Rehabilitation
    and Employment (VR&E)
299 E Broward Blvd, Rm 324
Fort Lauderdale, FL 33301
Phone toll free: 1-800-827-1000

Vocational Rehabilitation and
    Employment (VR&E)
7825 Baymeadows Way, Ste 120-B
Jacksonville, FL 32256
Phone toll free: 1-800-827-1000

1000 Legion Pl
VRE-Ste 1500
C&P-Ste 1550
Orlando, FL 32801
Phone toll free: 1-800-827-1000

C&P
312 Kenmore Rd, Rm 1G250
Pensacola, FL 32503
Phone toll free: 1-800-827-1000

C&P
7305 N Military Trail, Ste 1A-167
West Palm Beach, FL 33410
Phone toll free: 1-800-827-1000

GEORGIA

VA Medical Centers:

1 Freedom Way
Augusta, FL 30904
Phone: 706-733-0188
    or toll free: 1-800-836-5561

1670 Clairmont Rd
Decatur, FL 30033
Phone: 404-321-6111
    or toll free: 1-800-944-9726

1826 Veterans Blvd
Dublin, FL 31021
Phone: 478-272-1210
    or toll free: 1-800-595-5229

VA Clinics:

951 Millbrook Rd
Aiken, FL 29803
Phone: 803-643-9016

417 4th Ave
Albany, FL 31701
Phone: 229-446-9000

9249 Hwy 29
Athens, FL 30601
Phone: 706-227-4534

1310 13 St
Columbus, FL 31906
Phone: 706-257-7200

755 Commerce Dr, 2nd Fl
Decatur, FL 30030
Phone: 404-417-5200

1513 Cleveland Ave
East Point, FL 30344
Phone: 404-321-6111, Ext 2600

1970 Riverside Pkwy
Lawrenceville, FL 30043
Phone: 404-417-1750

5398 Thomaston Rd, Ste B
Macon, FL 31220
Phone: 478-476-8868

3931 Munday Mill Rd
Oakwood, FL 30566
Phone: 404-728-8212

30 Chateau Dr, SE
Rome, FL 30161
Phone: 706-235-6581

325 W Montgomery Crossroads
Savannah, FL 31406
Phone: 912-920-0214

562 Concord Rd
Smyrna, FL 30082
Phone: 404-417-1760

2841 N Patterson St
Valdosta, FL 31602
Phone: 229-293-0132

Regional Office:

1700 Clairmont Rd
Decatur, FL 30033
Phone statewide toll free:
    1-800-827-1000

GUAM

VA Clinic:

U.S. Naval Hospital
Bldg 1, E-200
Box 7608
Agana Heights, GU 96919
Phone: 671-344-9200

VA Benefits Office:

Reflection Ctr, #201
222 Chalan Santo Papa St
Hagatna, GU 96910
Phone: 671-472-7161

HAWAII

VA Medical Center:

459 Patterson Rd, E Wing
Honolulu, HI 96819
Phone toll free from Hawaii,
Guam, Saipan, Rota, and Tinian:
    1-800-827-1000;
toll free from American Samoa:
    1-877-899-4400

VA Clinics:

Hilo CBOC
1285 Wainuenue Ave, Ste 211
Hilo, HI 96720
Phone: 808-935-3781

National Ctr for PTSD
3375 Koapaka St, Ste I-560
Honolulu, HI 96819
Phone: 808-566-1546

Kauai CBOC
3-3367 Kuhio Hwy, Ste 200
Lihue, HI 96766
Phone: 808-246-0497

Kailua-Kona CBOC
75-377 Hualalai Rd
Kailua-Kona, HI 96740
Phone: 808-329-0774

Maui CBOC
203 Ho'ohana St, Ste 303
Kahului, HI 96732
Phone: 808-871-2454

Regional Office:

459 Patterson Rd, E Wing
Honolulu, HI 96819
Mailing address:
PO Box 29020
Honolulu, HI 96820
Phone toll free from Hawaii, Guam,
Saipan Saipan, Rota, and Tinian:
    1-800-827-1000;
toll free from American Samoa:
    1-877-899-4400

IDAHO

VA Medical Center:

500 W Fort St
Boise, ID 83702
Phone: 208-422-1000

VA Clinics:

120 E Pine St
Caldwell, ID 83605
Phone: 208-454-4820

444 Hospital Way, Ste 801
Pocatello, ID 83201
Phone: 208-232-6214

111 Lillian St, # 203
Salmon, ID 83467
Phone: 208-756-8515

260 2nd Ave, E
Twin Falls, ID 83301
Phone: 208-732-0947

VA Regional Office:

805 W Franklin St
Boise, ID 83702
Phone statewide toll free:
    1-800-827-1000

ILLINOIS

VA Medical Centers:

820 S Damen Ave
Chicago, IL 60612
Phone: 312-569-8387

1900 E Main St
Danville, IL 61832
Phone: 217-554-3000
    or toll free: 1-800-320-8387

Fifth and Roosevelt Rd
PO Box 5000
Hines, IL 60141
Phone: 708-202-8387

2401 W Main
Marion, IL 62959
Phone: 618-997-5311

3001 Green Bay Rd
North Chicago, IL 60064
Phone 847-688-1900
    or toll free: 1-800-393-0865

VA Clinics:

1700 N Landmark Rd
Aurora, IL 60506
Phone: 630-859-2504

6500 W Main St
Belleville, IL 62223
Phone: 314-286-6988

7731 S Halsted St
Chicago, IL 60620
Phone: 773-962-3700

Lakeside
333 E Huron St
Chicago, IL 60611
Phone: 312-569-8387

30 E 15th St, Ste 207
Chicago Heights, IL 60411
Phone: 708-756-5454

3035 E Mound Rd
Decatur, IL 62526
Phone: 217-875-2670

1901 S 4th St, Ste 21
Effingham, IL 62401
Phone: 217-347-7600

450 W Dundee Rd
Elgin, IL 60123
Phone: 847-742-5920

107-109 Clyde St
Evanston, IL 60202
Phone: 847-869-6315

1301 Kiwanis Dr
Freeport, IL 61032
Phone: 815-235-4881

387 E Grove
Galesburg, IL 61401
Phone: 309-343-0311

2000 Glenwood Ave
Joliet, IL 60435
Phone: 815-744-0492

2970 Chartres St
La Salle, IL 61301
Phone: 815-223-9678

Illinois Veterans Home
One Veterans Dr
Manteno, IL 60950
Phone: 815-468-1027

620 S Route 31
McHenry, IL 60050
Phone: 815-759-2306

1 Doctors Park Rd
Mt. Vernon, IL 62864
Phone: 618-246-2910

4700 W 95th St
Oak Lawn, IL 60453
Phone: 708-499-3675

149 S Oak Park Ave
Oak Park, IL 60302
Phone: 708-386-3008

411 Dr Martin Luther King Jr Dr
Peoria, IL 61605
Phone: 309-497-0790

721 Broadway St
Quincy, IL 62301
Phone: 217-224-3366

4940 E State St
Rockford, IL 61108
Phone: 815-227-0081

700 N 7th St, Ste C
Springfield, IL 62702
Phone: 217-522-9730

VA Regional Office:

2122 W Taylor St
Chicago, IL 60612
Phone statewide toll free:
    1-800-827-1000

INDIANA

VA Medical Centers:

2121 Lake Ave
Fort Wayne, IN 46805
Phone: 260-426-5431
    or toll free: 1-800-360-8387

1481 W 10th St
Indianapolis, IN 46202
Phone: 317-554-0000
    or toll free: 1-888-878-6889

1700 E 38th St
Marion, IN 46953
Phone: 765-674-3321
    or toll free: 1-800-360-8387

VA Clinics:

455 S Landmark Ave
Bloomington, IN 47403
Phone: 812-336-5723
    or toll free: 1-877-683-0865

9330 S Broadway
Crown Point, IN 46307
Phone: 219-662-5000

500 E Walnut St
Evansville, IN 47713
Phone: 812-465-6202

1600 Flossie Dr
Greendale, IN 47025
Phone: 812-539-2313

3500 W Purdue Ave
Muncie, IN 47304
Phone: 765-284-6822

811 Northgate Blvd
New Albany, IN 47150
Phone: 502-287-4100

4351 South A St
Richmond, IN 47374
Phone: 765-973-6915

5735 S Ironwood Rd
South Bend, IN 46614
Phone: 574-299-4847

110 W Honey Creek Pkwy
Terre Haute, IN 47802
Phone: 812-232-2890

3851 N River Rd
West Lafayette, IN 47906
Phone: 765-464-2280

VA Regional Office:

575 N Pennsylvania St
Indianapolis, IN 46204
Phone statewide toll free:
    1-800-827-1000

IOWA

VA Medical Centers:

3600 30th St
Des Moines, IA 50310
Phone: 515-699-5999
    or toll free: 1-800-294-8387

601 Hwy 6 W
Iowa City, IA 52246
Phone: 319-338-0581
    or toll free: 1-800-637-0128

1515 W Pleasant St
Knoxville, IA 50138
Phone: 641-842-3101
    or toll free: 1-800-816-8878

VA Clinics:

2979 Victoria St
Bettendorf, IA 52722
Phone: 563-332-8528

Mercy Health Ctr
250 Mercy Dr
Dubuque, IA 52001
Phone: 563-589-8899

2419 2nd Ave N
Fort Dodge, IA 50501
Phone: 515-576-2235

520 S Pierce, Ste 150
Mason City, IA 50401
Phone: 641-421-8077

1551 Indian Hills Dr, Ste 206
Sioux City, IA 51104
Phone: 712-258-4700

1310 Lake St
Spirit Lake, IA 51360
Phone: 712-336-6400

1015 S Hackett Rd
Waterloo, IA 50701
Phone: 319-235-1230

VA Regional Office:

210 Walnut St, Rm 1063
Des Moines, IA 50309
Phone statewide toll free:
    1-800-827-1000

KANSAS

VA Medical Centers:

4101 S 4th St
Leavenworth, KS 66048
Phone: 913-682-2000
    or toll free: 1-800-952-8387

2200 SW, Gage Blvd
Topeka, KS 66622
Phone: 785-350-3111
    or toll free: 1-800-574-8387

5500 E Kellogg Dr
Wichita, KS 67218
Phone: 316-685-2221
    or toll free: 1-888-878-6881

VA Clinics:

510 NE 10th St
Abilene, KS 67410
Phone: 785-263-2100, Ext 161

Neosho Memorial Med Ctr
629 S Plummer
Chanute, KS 66720
Phone: 620-431-4000, Ext 1553

Newman Hospital
919 W 12th Ave, Ste D
Emporia, KS 66801
Phone: 620-342-7432

300 Custer
Fort Dodge, KS 67801
Phone toll free: 1-888-878-681,
    Ext 41040

Newman Young Clinic
902 Horton St
Fort Scott, KS 66701
Phone: 620-223-8400, Ext 8655

Anderson County Hospital
421 S Maple St
Garnett, KS 66032
Phone: 785-448-3131, Ext 309

Hays Clinic
207-B E Seventh St
Hays, KS 67601
Phone toll free: 1-888-878-6881,
    Ext 41000

Holton Community Hospital
1110 Columbine Dr
Holton, KS 66436
Phone: 785-364-2116,
    Ext 115 or 154

715 Southwind Dr
Junction City, KS 66441
Phone toll free:
    1-800-574-8387, Ext 54670

21 N 12th St
Bethany Med Bldg # 110
Kansas City, KS 66102
Phone toll free:
    1-800-952-8387, Ext 56990

2200 Harvard Rd
Lawrence, KS 66049
Phone toll free:
    1-800-574-8387, Ext 54650

Liberal Clinic
2 Rock Island Rd, Ste 200
Liberal, KS 67901
Phone: 620-626-5574

510 S Hospital Dr
Paola, KS 66071
Phone: 816-922-2160

1401 N Main St
Parsons, KS 67357
Phone toll free:
    1-888-878-6881, Ext 41060

Regional Hospital Med Arts Bldg
200 S. Main St
Russell, KS 67665
Phone: 785-483-3131, Ext 155

1410 E Iron, Ste 1
Salina, KS 67401
Phone toll free:
    1-888-878-6881, Ext 41020

Nemaha Valley Hospital
1600 Community Dr
Seneca, KS 66538
Phone: 785-336-6181, Ext. 162

VA Regional Office:

Robert J Dole Regional Office
5500 E Kellogg Ave
Wichita, KS 67218
Phone toll free: 1-800-827-1000

KENTUCKY

VA Medical Centers:

Cooper Division
1101 Veterans Dr
Lexington, KY 40502
Phone: 859-233-4511
    or toll free: 1-888-824-3577

Leestown Div
2250 Leestown Rd
Lexington, KY, 40511
Phone: 859-233-4511
    or toll free: 1-888-824-3577

800 Zorn Ave
Louisville, KY 40206
Phone: 502-287-4000
    or toll free: 1-800-376-8387

VA Clinics:

103 Landmark Dr
Bellevue, KY 41073
Phone: 859-392-3840

Hartland Med Plaza
1110 Wilkinson Trace Cir
Bowling Green, KY 42103
Phone: 270-796-3590

7711 Ewing
Florence, KY 41042
Phone: 859-282-4480

Desert Storm Ave, Bldg 39
Fort Campbell, KY 42223
Phone: 270-798-4118

851 Ireland Loop
Fort Knox, KY 40121
Phone: 502-624-9396

926 Veterans Dr
Hanson, KY 42413
Phone: 270-322-8019

4010 Dupont Cir
Louisville, KY 40207
Phone: 502-287-6986

VA Healthcare Ctr, Newburg
3430 Newburg Rd
Louisville, KY 40218
Phone: 502-287-6223

VA Healthcare Ctr, Shively
3934 N Dixie Hwy, Ste 210
Louisville, KY 40216
Phone: 502-287-6000

VA Healthcare Ctr, Standiford Field
Air National Guard Complex
1101 Grade Lane
Louisville, KY 40213
Phone 502-413-4635

2620 Perkins Creek Dr
Paducah, KY 42001
Phone: 270-444-8465

Highlands Regional Med Ctr
5000 KY Route 321
PO Box 668
Prestonsburg, KY 41653
Phone: 606-886-1970

104 Hardin Lane
Somerset, KY 42503
Phone: 606-676-0786

VA Regional Office:

321 W Main St, Ste 390
Louisville, KY 40202
Phone statewide toll free:
    1-800-827-1000

LOUISIANA

VA Medical Centers:

PO Box 69004
Alexandria, LA 71306
Phone: 318-473-0010
    or toll free: 1-800-375-8387

510 E Stoner Ave
Shreveport, LA 71101
Phone: 318-221-8411
    or toll free: 1-800-863-7441

VA Clinics:

7968 Essen Park Ave
Baton Rouge, LA 70809
Phone: 225-761-3400

1131 S. Morrison Ave
Hammond, LA 70403
Phone: 985-902-5026

1750 Martin Luther King Jr Blvd,
    Ste 107
Houma, LA 70360
Phone: 985-851-0188

1907 Johnson St
Jennings, LA 70546
Phone: 337-824-1000

2100 Jefferson St
Lafayette, LA 70501
Phone: 337-261-0734

501 Rue De Sante, Ste 10
LaPlace, LA 70068
Phone: 504-565-4705

250 De Siard Plaza Dr
Monroe, LA 71203
Phone: 318-343-6100

1601 Perdido St
New Orleans, LA 70161
Mailing address:
PO Box 61011
New Orleans, LA 70161
Phone: 504-412-3700
    or toll free 1-800-935-8387

340 Gateway Dr
Slidell, LA 70461
Phone toll free: 1-800-935-8387

VA Regional Office:

671A Whitney Ave
Gretna, LA 70056
Phone statewide toll free:
    1-800-827-1000

MAINE

VA Medical Center:

1 VA Ctr
Augusta, ME 04330
Phone: 207-623-8411
    or toll free: 1-877-421-8263

VA Clinics:

304 Hancock St, Ste 3B
Bangor, ME 04401
Phone: 207-561-3600

50 Union St
Calais, ME 04619
Phone: 207-904-3700

163 Van Buren Dr, Ste 6
Caribou, ME 04736
Phone: 207-493-3800

99 River Rd
Lincoln, ME 04457
Phone: 207-403-2000

431 Franklin St
Rumford, ME 04726
Phone: 207-369-3200

655 Main St
Sacco, ME 04072
Phone: 207-294-3100

MARYLAND

VA Medical Centers:

10 N Greene St
Baltimore, MD 21201
Phone: 410-605-7000
    or toll free: 1-800-463-6295

Perry Point, MD 21902
Phone: 410-642-2411
    or toll free: 1-800-949-1003

VA Clinics:

Loch Raven VA Outpatient Clinic
3901 the Alameda
Baltimore, MD 21218
Phone: 410-605-7651

830 Chesapeake Dr
Cambridge, MD 21613
Phone: 410-228-6243
    or toll free: 1-877-864-9611

State Veterans Home
29431 Charlotte Hall Rd
Charlotte Hall, MD 20622
Phone: 301-884-7102

200 Glenn St
Cumberland, MD 21502
Phone: 301-724-0061

9600 N Point Rd
Fort Howard, MD 21052
Phone: 410-477-1800
    or toll free: 1-800-531-8387

808 Landmark Dr, Ste 128
Glen Bernie, MD 21061
Phone: 410-590-4140

7525 Greenway Ctr Dr
Professional Ctr, # T-4
Greenbelt, MD 20770
Phone: 301-345-2463

Hub Plaza Bldg
1101 Opal Court
Hagerstown MD 21742
Phone: 301-665-1462

101B Market St
Pocomoke, MD 21851
Phone: 410-957-6718

VA Regional Office:

31 Hopkins Plaza Federal Bldg
Baltimore, MD 21201
Phone toll free: 1-800-827-1000

MASSACHUSETTS

VA Medical Centers:

200 Springs Rd
Bedford, MA 01730
Phone: 781-687-2000
    or toll free: 1-800-422-1617

940 Belmont St
Brockton, MA 02301
Phone: 508-583-4500

150 S Huntington Ave
Jamaica Plain, MA 02130
Phone: 617-232-9500

Northampton VA
421 N Main St
Leeds, MA 01053
Phone: 413-584-4040
    or toll free: 1-800-893-1522

1400 VFW Pkwy
West Roxbury, MA 02132
Phone: 617-323-7700

VA Clinics:

251 Causeway St
Boston, MA 02114
Phone: 617-248-1000

895 Blue Hill Ave
Dorchester, MA 02121
Phone: 617-822-7146

Burbank Hospital
275 Nichols Rd
Fitchburg, MA 01420
Phone: 978-342-9781

61 Lincoln St, Ste 112
Framingham, MA 01702
Phone: 508-628-0205

Addison Gilbert Hospital
298 Washington St
Gloucester, MA 01930
Phone: 978-282-0676, Ext 1782

143 Munson St
Greenfield, MA 01301
Phone: 413-773-8428

108 Merrimack St
Haverhill, MA 01830
Phone: 978-372-5207

145 Falmouth Rd
Hyannis, MA 02601
Phone: 508-771-3190

130 Marshall Rd
Lowell, MA 01852
Phone: 978-671-9000

225 Boston Rd, Ste 107
Lynn, MA 01904
Phone: 781-595-9818

Hospital Rd
Martha's Vineyard, MA 02557
Phone: 508-693-0410

Nantucket Cottage Hospital
57 Prospect St
Nantucket, MA 02554
Phone: 508-825-8387

174 Elm St
New Bedford, MA 02740
Phone: 508-994-0217

73 Eagle St
Pittsfield, MA 01201
Phone: 413-443-4857

Quincy Med Ctr, 2nd Fl
114 Whitwell St
Quincy, MA 02169
Phone: 617-376-2010

25 Bond St
Springfield, MA 01104
Phone: 413-731-6000

605 Lincoln St
Worchester, MA 01605
Phone: 508-856-0104

VA Regional Office:

JFK Federal Bldg
Rm 1265, Government Ctr
Boston, MA 02203
Phone statewide toll free:
    1-800-827-1000

The towns of Fall River and New Bedford and the counties of Barnstable, Dukes, Nantucket, Bristol, and part of Plymouth are served by the Providence, Rhode Island, VA regional office.

MICHIGAN

VA Medical Centers:
2215 Fuller Rd
Ann Arbor, MI 48105
Phone: 734-769-7100
    or toll free: 1-800-361-8387

5500 Armstrong Rd
Battle Creek, MI 49015
Phone: 269-966-5600
    or toll free: 1-888-214-1247

4646 John R St
Detroit, MI 48201
Phone: 313-576-1000
    or toll free: 1-800-511-8056

325 E H St
Iron Mountain, MI 49801
Phone: 906-774-3303
or toll free: 1-800-215-8262

1500 Weiss St
Saginaw, MI 48602
Phone: 989-497-2500
or toll free: 1-800-406-5143

VA Clinics:

115 Main St
Benton Harbor, MI 49022
Phone: 269-934-9123

G-3267 Beecher Rd
Flint, MI 48532
Phone: 810-720-2913

806 S Otsego Ave
Gaylord, MI 49735
Phone: 989-732-7525

3019 Coit St, NE
Grand Rapids, MI 49505
Phone: 616-365-9575

787 Market St
Quincy Ctr Ste 9
Hancock, MI 49930
Phone: 906-482-7762

629 W Cloverland Dr, Ste 1
Ironwood, MI 49938
Phone: 906-932-0032

Townsend Family Med
400 Hinckley Blvd, Ste 300
Jackson, MI 49203
Phone: 517-782-7436

Sault Ste Marie Clinic
16523 S Watertower Dr, #1
Kincheloe, MI 49788
Phone: 906-495-3030

2025 S Washington Ave
Lansing, MI 48910
Phone: 517-267-3925

425 Fisher St
Marquette, MI 49855
Phone: 906-226-4618

1101 10th St, Ste 101
Menominee, MI 49858
Phone: 906-863-1286

165 E Apple Ave, Ste 201
Muskegon, MI 49442
Phone: 231-725-4105

5671 Skeel Ave, Ste 4
Oscoda, MI 48750
Phone: 989-747-0026

1701 Baldwin Ave, Ste 101
Pontiac, MI 48340
Phone: 248-409-0585

3271 Racquet Club Dr
Traverse City, MI 49684
Phone: 231-932-9720

7470 Brockway Dr
Yale, MI 48097
Phone: 810-387-3211

VA Regional Office:

Patrick V McNamara Federal Bldg
477 Michigan Ave, Rm 1400
Detroit, MI 48226
Phone toll free: 1-800-827-1000

MINNESOTA

VA Medical Centers:

One Veterans Dr
Minneapolis, MN 55417
Phone: 612-725-2000
      or toll free: 1-866-414-5058

4801 Veterans Dr
St. Cloud, MN 56303
Phone: 320-252-1670
      or toll free: 1-800-247-1739

VA Clinics:

705 5th St
Bemidji, MN 56601
Phone: 218-755-6360

11800 State Hwy 18
Brainerd, MN 56401
Phone: 218-855-1115

Veterans Home
1821 N Park St
Fergus Falls, MN 56537
Phone: 218-739-1400

1101 E 37th St, Ste 220
Hibbing, MN 55746
Phone: 218-263-9698

2785 White Bear Ave, Ste 210
Maplewood, MN 55109
Phone: 651-290-3040

1025 N 13th St
Montevideo, MN 56265
Phone: 320-269-2222

1617 Skyline Dr
Rochester, MN 55902
Phone: 507-252-0885

1101 Moultin and Parsons Dr
St. James, MN 56081
Phone: 507-375-3391

VA Regional Office:

Bishop Henry Whipple
      Federal Bldg
1 Federal Dr
St Paul, MN 55111
Phone toll free: 1-800-827-1000

The counties of Becker, Beltrami, Clay, Clearwater, Kittson, Lake of the Woods, Mahnomen, Marshall, Norman, Otter Tail, Pennington, Polk, Red Lake, Roseau, and Wilkin are served by the Fargo, North Dakota, VA Regional Office

MISSISSIPPI

VA Medical Centers:

400 Veterans Ave
Biloxi, MS 39531
Phone: 228-523-5000
      or toll free: 1-800-296-8872

1500 E Woodrow Wilson Dr
Jackson, MS 39216
Phone: 601-362-4471
      or statewide toll free:
      1-800-949-1099

VA Clinics:

12 E Brunswick St
Byhalia, MS 38611
Phone: 662-838-2163

824 Alabama St
Columbus, MS 39702
Phone: 662-244-0391

1502 S Colorado St
Greenville, MS 38703
Phone: 662-332-9872

231 Methodist Blvd
Hattiesburg, MS 39401
Phone: 601-296-3530

106 Walker St
Houlka, MS 38850
Phone: 662-568-3316

332 Hwy 12 W
Kosciusko, MS 39090
Phone: 662-289-1800

595 Main St E
Meadville, MS 39653
Phone: 601-394-3650

13th St
Meridian, MS 39301
Phone: 601-482-7154

46 Sgt. Prentice Dr, Ste 16
Natchez, MS 39120
Phone: 601-442-7141

VA Regional Office:

1600 E Woodrow Wilson Ave
Jackson City, MS 39216
Phone statewide toll free:
    1-800-827-1000

MISSOURI

VA Medical Centers:

800 Hospital Dr
Columbia, MO 65201
Phone: 573-814-6000
    or toll free: 1-800-349-8262

4801 Linwood Blvd
Kansas City, MO 64128
Phone: 816-861-4700
    or toll free: 1-800-525-1483

1500 N Westwood Blvd
Poplar Bluff, MO 63901
Phone: 573-686-4151

Jefferson Barracks Div
1 Jefferson Barracks Dr
St. Louis, MO 63125
Phone: 314-652-4100
    or toll free: 1-800-228-5459

John Cochran Division
915 N Grand Blvd
St Louis, MO 63106
Phone: 314-652-4100
    or toll free: 1-800-228 -5459

VA Clinics:

17140 Bel-Ray Pl
Belton, MO 64012
Phone: 816-922-2161

Land of the Ozarks Clinic
246 E Hwy 54
Camdenton, MO 65020
Phone: 573-317-1150

1111 Euclid Dr
Cameron, MO 64429
Phone: 816-922-2500, Ext 54251

2420 Veterans Memorial Dr
Cape Girardeau, MO 63701
Phone: 573-339-0909

1580 W Columbia St
Farmington, MO 63640
Phone: 573-760-1365

126 Missouri Ave, Box 1239
Fort Leonard Wood, MO 65473
Phone: 573-329-8305

1108 E Patterson, Ste 9
Kirksville, MO 63501
Phone: 660-627-8387

Missouri Veterans Home
1 Veterans Dr
Mexico, MO 65265
Phone: 573-581-9630

600 N Main
Mount Vernon, MO 65712
Phone: 417-466-0118

322 S Prewitt
Nevada, MO 64772
Phone: 417-448-8905

Hwy 72 N
Salem, MO 65560
Phone: 573-729-6626
    or toll free: 1-888-557-1860

7 Jason Court
St Charles, MO 63304
Phone: 314-286-6988

Missouri Veterans Home
620 N Jefferson St
St. James, MO 65559
Phone: 573-265-0448

1314 N 36 St, Ste A
St. Joseph, MO 64506
Phone toll free:
    1-800-952-8387, Ext 56925

10600 Lewis and Clark Blvd
St Louis, MO 63136
Phone: 314-286-6988

1300 Veterans Dr
Warrensburg, MO 64093
Phone: 816-922-2500, Ext 54281

1211 Missouri Ave
West Plains, MO 65775
Phone: 417-257-2454

VA Regional Office:

400 S 18th St
St Louis, MO 63103
Phone statewide toll free:
    1-800-827-1000

VA Benefits Office:

4801 Linwood Blvd
Kansas City, MO 64128
Phone: 816-922-2660
    or toll free: 1-800-525-1483,
    Ext 52660

MONTANA

VA Medical Centers:

3687 Veterans Dr
PO Box 1500
Fort Harrison, MT 59636
Phone: 406-442-6410

VA Clinics:

118 E 7th St
Anaconda, MT 59711
Phone: 406-563-6090

2345 King Ave W
Billings, MT 59102
Phone: 406-651-5670

Glacier Community Health
519 E Main St
Cut Bank, MT 59427
Phone: 406-873-5670

300 N Wilson, Ste 703G
Bozeman, MT 59715
Phone: 406-522-8923

621 3rd St S, Ste 107
Glasgow, MT 59230
Phone: 406-228-3554

2000 Montana Ave
Glendive, MT 59330
Phone: 406-488-2307

1417-9th St, S, Ste 200
Great Falls, MT 59405
Phone: 877-468-8387, option three

31 Three Mile Dr, Ste 102
Kalispell, MT 59901
Phone: 406-751-5980

Clinic/Nursing Home
210 S Winchester
Miles City, MT 59301
Phone: 406-874-5600

2687 Palmer St, Ste C
Missoula, MT 59808
Phone toll free: 1-877-468-8387

VA Regional Office:

3633 Veterans Dr
PO Box 1500
Fort Harrison, MT 59636
Phone toll free: 1-800-827-1000

NEBRASKA

VA Medical Centers:

2201 N Broadwell Ave
Grand Island, NE 68803
Phone: 308-382-3660
    or toll free: 1-866-580-1810

600 S 70th St
Lincoln, NE 68510
Phone: 402-489-3802
    or toll free: 1-866-851-6052

4101 Woolworth Ave
Omaha, NE 68105
Phone: 402-346-8800
    or toll free: 1-800-451-5796

VA Clinics:

524 Box Butte Ave
Alliance, NE 69301
Phone: 605-745-2000, Ext 2474

301 N 27th St, Ste #1
Norfolk, NE 68701
Phone: 402-844-8000

600 E Francis, Ste 3
North Plate, NE 69101
Phone: 308-532-6906

300 E 8th St
Rushville/Gordon, NE 69343
Phone: 605-745-2000, Ext 2474

1720 E Portal Pl
Scottsbluff, NE 69361
Phone: 308-220-3930

1116 10th Ave
Sidney, NE 69162
Phone: 308-254-5575

VA Regional Office:

5631 S 48th St
Lincoln, NE 68516
Phone statewide toll free:
    1-800-827-1000

NEVADA

VA Medical Centers:

901 Rancho Lane
Las Vegas, NV 89106
Mailing address:
PO Box 360001
North Las Vegas, NV 89036
Phone: 702-636-3000
    or toll free: 1-888-633-7554

1000 Locust St
Reno, NV 89502
Phone: 775-786-7200
    or toll free: 1-888-838-6256

VA Clinics:

William B Ririe Hospital
6 Steptoe Cir
Ely, NV 89301
Phone: 775-289-3612

Lahontan Valley Outpatient Clinic
345 West A St
Fallon, NV 89406
Phone: 775-428-6161

2920 N Greenvalley Pkwy, Ste 215
Henderson, NV 89014
Phone: 702-636-6363

Center for Homeless Veterans
916 W Owens Ave
Las Vegas, NV 89106
Phone: 702-636-6380

Carson Valley Clinic
925 Ironwood Dr, #2102
Minden, NV 89423
Phone toll free:
    1-888-838-6256, Ext 4000

2100 E Calvada Blvd
Pahrump, NV 89048
Phone: 775-727-7535

VA Regional Office:

5460 Reno Corporate Dr
Reno, NV 89520
Phone statewide toll free:
    1-800-827-1000

VA Benefits Office:

4800 Alpine Pl, Ste 12
Las Vegas, NV 89107
Phone toll free: 1-800-827-1000

NEW HAMPSHIRE

VA Medical Center:

718 Smyth Rd
Manchester, NH 03104
Phone: 636-624-4366
    or toll free: 1-800-892-8384

VA Clinics:

7 Greenwood Ave
Conway, NH 03818
Phone: 603-047-3500, Ext 11

Littleton Regional Hospital
600 St Johnsbury Rd
Littleton, NH 03561
Phone: 603-444-9328

Pease Intl
Tradeport 302 Newmarket St
Portsmouth, NH 03803
Phone: 603-624-4366, Ext 5500

200 Routes 108
Somersworth, NH 03878
Phone: 603-624-4366, Ext 5700

NH Veterans Home
139 Winter St
Tilton, NH 03276
Phone: 603-624-4366, Ext 5600

VA Regional Office:

Norris Cotton Federal Bldg
275 Chestnut St
Manchester, NH 03101
Phone toll free: 1-800-827-1000

NEW JERSEY

VA Medical Centers:

385 Tremont Ave
East Orange, NJ 07018
Phone: 973-676-1000

151 Knollcroft Rd
Lyons, NJ 07939
Phone: 908-647-0180

VA Clinics:

970 Route 70
Brick, NJ 08724
Phone: 732-206-8900

1 Monroe Ave
Cape May, NJ 08204
Phone: 609-898-8700

654 E Jersey St, Ste 2A
Elizabeth, NJ 07206
Phone: 908-994-0120

Patterson Army Health Clinic
Bldg 1075, Stevenson Ave
Fort Monmouth, NJ 07703
Phone: 732-532-4500

Marshall Hall
8th and Alabama
Fort Dix, NJ 08640
Phone: 609-562-2999

385 Prospect Ave
Hackensack, NJ 07601
Phone: 201-487-1390

115 Christopher Columbus Dr
Jersey City, NJ 07302
Phone 201-435-3055
     or 201-425-3305

340 W Hanover Ave
Morristown, NJ 07960
Phone: 973-539-9791
     or 973-539-9794

317 George St
New Brunswick, NJ 08901
Phone: 732-729-0646
     or 732-729-9555

20 Washington Pl
Newark, NJ 07102
Phone: 973-645-1441

St. Joseph Hospital and Med Ctr
275 Getty Ave
Paterson, NJ 07503
Phone: 973-247-1666

211 County House Rd
Sewell, NJ 08080
Phone: 856-401-7665

171 Jersey St, Bldg 36
Trenton, NJ 08611
Phone: 609-989-2355

6601 Ventnor Ave, Ste 406
Ventnor, NJ 08406
Phone: 609-823-3122

Veterans Memorial Hall
Northwest Blvd
Vineland, NJ 08360
Phone: 856-692-1588

1051 W Sherman Ave
Vineland, NJ 08360
Phone: 856-692-2881

VA Regional Office:

20 Washington Pl
Newark, NJ 07102
Phone statewide toll free:
    1-800-827-1000

The Philadelphia, Pennsylvania, regional office serves the counties of Atlantic, Burlington, Camden, Cape May, Cumberland, Gloucester, and Salem.

NEW MEXICO

VA Medical Center:

1501 San Pedro Dr, SE
Albuquerque, NM 87108
Phone: 505-265-1711
    or toll free: 1-800-465-8262

VA Clinics:

1410 Aspen
Alamogordo, NM 88310
Phone: 505-437-7000

1700 W Main St
Artesia, NM 88210
Phone: 505-746-3531

91 E Llano Estacado
Clovis, NM 88101
Phone: 505-763-4335

620 Coronado St, Ste B
Espanola, NM 87532
Phone: 505-753-7395

1001 W Broadway, Ste B
Farmington, NM 87401
Phone: 505-326-4383

320 Hwy 564
Gallup, NM 87301
Phone: 505-722-7234

1601 N Turner, 4th Fl
Hobbs, NM 88340
Phone: 505-391-0354

1635 Don Roser
Las Cruces, NM 88001
Phone: 505-522-1241

1235 8th St
Las Vegas, NM 87701
Phone 505-425-6788

1275 S 2nd St
Raton, NM 87440
Phone: 505-445-2391

2213 Brothers Rd, Ste 600
Santa Fe, NM 87505
Phone: 505-986-8645

1302 32nd St
Silver City, NM 88601
Phone: 505-538-2921

1960 N Date St
Truth or Consequences, NM 87901
Phone: 505-894-7662

VA Regional Office:

Dennis Chavez Federal Bldg
500 Gold Ave, SW
Albuquerque, NM 87102
Phone statewide toll free:
　　1-800-827-1000

NEW YORK

VA Medical Centers:

113 Holland Ave
Albany, NY 12208
Phone: 518-626-5000

222 Richmond Ave
Batavia, NY 14020
Phone: 585-297-1000
　　or toll free: 1-888-798-2302

76 Veterans Ave
Bath, NY 14810
Phone 607-664-4000
　　or toll free: 1-877-845-3247

130 W Kingsbridge Rd
Bronx, NY 10468
Phone: 718-584-9000
　　or toll free: 1-800-877-6976

800 Poly Pl
Brooklyn, NY 11209
Phone: 718-836-6600

3495 Bailey Ave
Buffalo, NY 14215
Phone: 716-834-9200
　　or toll free: 1-800-532-8387

400 Fort Hill Ave
Canandaigua, NY 14424
Phone: 585-394-2000

Route 9D
Castle Point, NY 12511
Phone: 845-831-2000
　　or toll free: 1-800-269-8749

2094 Albany Post Rd
Route 9A,
PO Box 100
Montrose, NY 10548
Phone: 914-737-4400, Ext 2400
　　or toll free: 1-800-269-8749

423 E 23rd St
New York, NY 10010
Phone: 212-686-7500

79 Middleville Rd
Northport, NY 11768
Phone: 631-261-4400
　　or toll free: 1-800-551-3996

800 Irving Ave
Syracuse, NY 13210
Phone: 315-425-4400
　　or toll free: 1-800-792-4334

VA Clinics:

17 Lansing St
Auburn, NY 13021
Phone: 315-255-7002

109 N Main St
Bainbridge, NY 13733
Phone: 607-967-8590

Garvin Bldg
425 Robinson St
Binghamton, NY 13901
Phone: 607-772-9100

953 Southern Blvd
Bronx, NY 10459
Phone: 718-741-4900

40 Flatbush Ave Extension, 8th Fl
Brooklyn, NY 11201
Phone: 718-439-4300

Warwick Savings Bank, 2nd Fl
1875 Route 6
Carmel, NY 10512
Phone: 845-228-5291

3 Bridge St
Carthage, NY 13619
Phone: 315-493-4180

Columbia Greene Med Arts Bldg
Ste A102, 159 Jefferson Heights
Catskill, NY 12414
Phone: 518-943-7515

1673 Route 9
Clifton Park, NY 12065
Phone: 518-383-8506

1104 Commons Ave
Cortland, NY 13045
Phone: 607-662-1517

166 E 4th St
Dunkirk, NY 14048
Phone toll free: 1-800-310-5001

PO Box 2
77 Park St
Elizabethtown, NY 12932
Phone: 518-873-3295

200 Madison Ave, Ste 2E
Elmira, NY 14901
Phone toll free: 1-877-845-3247

2623 State Hwy 30A
Fonda, NY 12068
Phone: 518-853-1247

84 Broad St
Glens Falls, NY 12801
Phone: 518-798-6066

30 Hatfield Lane, Ste 204
Goshen, NY 10924
Phone: 845-294-6927

10 Arrowwood Dr
Ithaca, NY 14850
Phone: 607-274-4680

The Resource Ctr
896 E 2nd St
Jamestown, NY 14701
Phone: 716-661-1447

63 Hurley Ave
Kingston, NY 12401
Phone: 845-331-8322

OLV Family Care Ctr
227 Ridge Rd
Lackawanna, NY 14218
Phone: 716 822-5944

Ambulatory Care Ctr
5875 S Transit Rd
Lockport, NY 14094
Phone: 716-433-2025

183 Park St
Malone, NY 12953
Phone: 518-481-2545

Memorial Hospital
1 Hospital Dr
Massena, NY 13662
Phone: 315-769-4253

60 Jefferson St
Unit 3 Lower Parking Lot
Monticello, NY 12701
Phone: 845-791-4936

20 Squadron Blvd
New City, NY 10970
Phone: 845-634-8942

55 W 125th St
New York, NY 10027
Phone: 212-828-5265

Opiate Substitution Program
437 W 16th St
New York, NY 10011
Phone: 212-462-4461

2201 Pine Ave
Niagara Falls, NY 14301
Phone toll free:
    1-800-223-4810, Ext 65295

465 N Union St
Olean, NY 14760
Phone: 716-373-7709

105 County Route 45A, Ste 400
Oswego, NY 13126
Phone: 315-343-0925

4 Phyllis Dr
Patchogue, NY 11772
Phone: 631-475-6610

2881 Church St
Route 199
Pine Plains, NY 12567
Phone: 518-398-9240

1425 Old Country Rd
Plainview, NY 11803
Phone: 516-572-8567

80 Sharron Ave
Plattsburgh, NY 12901
Phone: 518-561-6247

150 Pike St
Port Jervis, NY 12771
Phone: 845-856-5396

Route 55
488 Freedom Plains Rd, Ste 120
Poughkeepsie, NY 12603
Phone: 845-452-5151

465 Westfall Rd
Rochester, NY 14620
Phone: 585-463-2600

125 Brookley Rd, Bldg 510
Rome, NY 13441
Phone: 315-334-7100

1322 Gerling St
Sheridan Plaza
Schenectady, NY 12308
Phone: 518-346-3334

1150 S Ave
3rd Fl, Ste 301
Staten Island, NY 10314
Phone: 718-761-2973

41-03 Queens Blvd
Sunnyside, NY 11104
Phone: 718-741-4800

295 River St
Troy, NY 12180
Phone: 518-274-7707

Wyoming County Community
Hospital
400 N Main St
Warsaw, NY 14569
Phone: 585-786-2233

3458 Riverside Dr, Route 19
Wellsville, NY 14895
Phone toll free: 1-877-845-3247

Community Air Base
150 Old Riverhead Rd
Westhampton, NY 11978
Phone: 631-898-0599

23 S Broadway
White Plains, NY 10601
Phone: 914-421-1951

124 New Main St
Yonkers, NY 10705
Phone: 914-375-8055

VA Regional Offices:

Niagara Center
130 S Elmwood Ave
Buffalo, NY 14202
Phone toll free: 1-800-827-1000
This office serves counties not served by the New York City VA Regional Office.

245 W Houston St
New York City, NY 10014
Phone statewide toll free:
    1-800-827-1000
This office serves the counties of Albany, Bronx, Clinton, Columbia, Delaware, Dutchess, Essex, Franklin, Fulton, Green, Hamilton, Kings, Montgomery, Nassau, New York, Orange, Otsego, Putnam, Queens, Rensselaer, Richmond, Rockland, Saratoga, Schenectady, Schoharie, Suffolk Sullivan, Ulster, Warren, Washington, and Westchester.

VA Benefits Offices:

113 Holland Ave
Albany, NY 12208
Phone toll free: 1-800-827-1000

465 Westfall Rd
Rochester, NY 14620
Phone toll free: 1-800-827-1000

344 West Genesee St
Syracuse, NY 13202
Phone toll free: 1-800-827-1000

NORTH CAROLINA

VA Medical Centers:

1100 Tunnel Rd
Asheville, NC 28805
Phone: 828-298-7911
    or toll free: 1-800-932-6408

508 Fulton St
Durham, NC 27705
Phone: 919-286-0411

2300 Ramsey St
Fayetteville, NC 28301
Phone: 910-488-2120
    or toll free: 1-800 771-6106

1601 Brenner Ave
Salisbury, NC 28144
Phone: 704-638-9000
    or toll free: 1-800-469-8262

VA Clinics:

Presbyterian Plaza
8401 Med Ctr Dr, #350
Charlotte, NC 28262
Phone: 704-547-0020

1824 Hillendale Rd
Durham, NC 27705
Phone: 919-383-6107

800 Moye Blvd
Greensville, NC 27858
Phone: 252-830-2149

1021 Hargett St
Jacksonville, NC 28540
Phone: 910-219-1339

5420 Hwy 70
Morehead City, NC 28557
Phone: 252-240-2349

3305 Sungate Blvd
Raleigh, NC 27610
Phone: 919-212-0129

1606 Physicians Dr, Ste 104
Wilmington, NC 28401
Phone: 910-362-8811

190 Kimel Park Dr
Winston-Salem, NC 27103
Phone: 336-768-3296

VA Regional Office:

Federal Bldg, 251 N Main St
Winston-Salem, NC 27155
Phone statewide toll free:
1-800-827-1000

NORTH DAKOTA

VA Medical Center:

2101 Elm St
Fargo, ND 58102
Phone: 701-232-3241
or toll free: 1-800-410-9723

VA Clinics:

2700 State St
Bismarck, ND 58503
Phone: 701-221-9152

33 9th St
Dickinson, ND 58601
Phone: 701-483-6017

Developmental Ctr Health Bldg
W 6th St
Grafton, NC 58237
Phone: 701-352-4059

419 5th St NE
Jamestown, ND 58401
Phone: 701-952-4787

10 Missile Ave
Minot, ND 58705
Phone: 701-727-9800

3 4th St E, Ste 104
Williston, ND 58801
Phone: 701-577-9838

VA Regional Office:

2101 Elm St
Fargo, ND 58102
Phone statewide toll free:
1-800-827-1000

OHIO

VA Medical Centers:

10000 Brecksville Rd
Brecksville, OH 44141
Phone: 440-526-3030

17273 State Route 104
Chillicothe, OH 45601
Phone: 740-773-1141
    or toll free: 1-800-358-8262

3200 Vine St
Cincinnati, OH 45220
Phone: 513-861-3100

10701 East Blvd
Cleveland, OH 44106
Phone: 216-791-3800

543 Taylor Ave
Columbus, OH 43203
Phone: 614-257-5200
    or toll free: 1-888-615-9448

4100 W 3rd St
Dayton, OH 45428
Phone: 937-268-6511
    or toll free: 1-800-368-8262

VA Clinics:

55 W Waterloo
Akron, OH 44319
Phone: 330-724-7715

1230 Lake Ave
Ashtabula, OH 44004
Phone: 440-964-6454

510 W Union St
Athens, OH 45701
Phone: 740-593-7314

2146 Southgate Pkwy
Cambridge, OH 43727
Phone: 740-432-1963

733 Market Ave S
Canton, OH 44702
Phone: 330-489-4600

4355 Ferguson Dr, Ste 270
Cincinnati, OH 45245
Phone: 513-943-3680

4242 Loraine Ave
Cleveland, OH 44113
Phone: 216-939-0699

15655 State Route 170
E Liverpool, OH 43920
Phone: 330-386-4303

1955 Ohio Ave
Grove City, OH 43123
Phone: 614-257-5800

1755-C S Erie Hwy
Hamilton, OH 45011
Phone: 937-378-3413

1550 Sheridan Dr, Ste 100
Lancaster, OH 43130
Phone: 740-653-6145

1303 Bellefontaine Ave
Lima, OH 45804
Phone: 419-222-5788

205 W 20th St
Lorain, OH 44052
Phone: 440-244-3833

1456 Park Ave W
Mansfield, OH 44906
Phone: 419-529-4602

418 Colgate Dr
Marietta, OH 45750
Phone: 740-568-0412

1203 Delaware Ave
Corporate Ctr #2
Marion, OH 43302
Phone: 740-223-8089

675 N University Blvd
Middletown, OH 45042
Phone: 513-423-8387

1260 Monroe Ave, Ste 1A
New Philadelphia, OH 44663
Phone: 330-602-5339

Tamarck Rd
Newark, OH 43055
Phone: 740-788-8328

7 W Jackson St
Painesville, OH 44077
Phone: 440-357-6740

621 Broadway St
Portsmouth, OH 45622
Phone: 740-353-3236

6751 N Chestnut St
Ravenna, OH 44266
Phone: 330-296-3641

3416 Columbus Ave
Sandusky, OH 44870
Phone: 419-625-7350

512 S Burnett Rd
Springfield, OH 45505
Phone: 937-328-3385

107 Plaza Dr
St Clairsville, OH 43950
Phone: 740-695-9321

3333 Glendale Ave
Toledo, OH 43614
Phone: 419-259-2000

1400 Tod Ave
Warren, OH 44485
Phone: 330-392-0311

2031 Belmont Ave
Youngstown, OH 44505
Phone: 330-740-9200

840 Bethesda Dr, Bldg 3A
Zanesville, OH 43701
Phone: 740-453-7725

VA Regional Office:

Anthony J Celebrezze Federal Bldg
1240 E 9th St
Cleveland, OH 44199
Phone toll free: 1-800-827-1000

VA Benefits Offices:

36 E Seventh St, Ste 210
Cincinnati, OH 45202
Phone toll free: 1-800-827-1000

Federal Bldg, Rm 309
200 N High St
Columbus, OH 43215
Phone toll free:
    1-800-827-1000

OKLAHOMA

VA Medical Centers:

1011 Honor Heights Dr
Muskogee, OK 74401
Phone: 918-577-3000
    or toll free: 1-888-397-8387

21 N E 13th St
Oklahoma City, OK 73104
Phone: 405-270-0501
    or toll free: 1-866-835-5273

VA Clinics:

1015 S. Commerce
Ardmore, OK 73401
Phone: 580-223-2266

4303 Pittman and Thomas Bldg
Ft Sill, OK 73503
Phone: 580-353-1131

527 W 3rd St
PO Box 358
Konawa, OK 74849
Phone: 580-925-3286

9322 E 41st St
Tulsa, OK 74145
Phone: 918-628-2500

215 N 3rd St
Ponca City, OK 74601
Phone: 580-762-1777

VA Regional Office:

Federal Bldg
125 S Main St
Compensation & Pension
Muskogee, OK 74401
Phone toll free: 1-800-827-1000

VA Benefits Office:

Federal Campus
301 N W 6th St, Ste 113
Oklahoma City, OK 73102
Phone toll free: 1-800-827-1000

OREGON

VA Medical Centers:

3710 SW US Veterans Hospital Rd
Portland, OR 97239
Phone: 503-220-8262
      or toll free outside Portland
      area: 1-800-949-1004

913 NW Garden Valley Blvd
Roseburg, OR 97470
Phone: 541-440-1000
      or toll free: 1-800-549-8387

VA Clinics:

1010 1st St, SE, Ste 100
Bandon, OR 97411
Phone: 541-347-4736

2115 NE Wyatt Ct, Ste 201
Bend, OR 97701
Phone: 503-220-8262
      or toll free outside Portland
      area: 1- 800-949-1004,
      Ext 51494

555 5th St
Brookings, OR 97415
Phone: 541-412-1152

100 River Ave
Eugene, OR 97404
Phone: 541-607-0897

2819 Dahlia St
Klamath Falls, OR 97601
Phone: 541-273-6206

20 SW 3rd St
Ontario, OR 97914
Phone: 208-422-1303

10535 NE Glison St.
Gateway Med Bldg, 2nd fl
Portland, OR 97220
Phone: 503-220-8262
    or toll free outside Portland
    area: 1-800-949-1004

1660 Oak St SE
Salem, OR 97301
Phone: 503-220-8262
    or toll free outside Portland
    area: 1-800-949-1004

91400 Rilea Neacoxie St, Bldg 7315
Warrenton, OR 97146
Phone: 503-220-8262
    or toll free outside Portland
    area: 1-800-949-1004

VA Regional Office:

Edith Green/Wendell Wyatt
    Federal Bldg
1220 SW 3rd Ave
Portland, OR 97204
Phone toll free: 1-800-827-1000

PENNSYLVANIA

VA Medical Centers:

2907 Pleasant Valley Blvd
Latona, PA 16602
Phone: 814-943-8164

325 New Castle Rd
Butler, PA 16001
Phone: 724-287-4781
    or toll free: 1-800-362-8262

1400 Black Horse Hill Rd
Coatesville, PA 19320
Phone: 610-384-7711

135 E 38th St
Erie, PA 16504
Phone: 814-868-8661
    or toll free: 1-800-274-8387

1700 S Lincoln Ave
Lebanon, PA 17042
Phone: 717-272-6621
    or toll free: 1-800-409-8771

University and Woodland Aves
Philadelphia, PA 19104
Phone: 215-823-5800
    or toll free: 1-800-949-1001

Delafield Rd
Pittsburgh, PA 15260
Phone: 412-688-6000
    or toll free: 1-866-482-7488

Highland Dr Div
7180 Highland Dr
Pittsburgh, PA 15206
Phone: 412-365-4900
    or toll free: 1-866-482-7488

University Dr Div
University Dr
Pittsburgh, PA 15240
Phone toll free: 1-866-482-7488

1111 E End Blvd
Wilkes-Barre, PA 18711
Phone: 570-824-3521
    or toll free: 1-877-928-2621

VA Clinics:

3110 Hamilton Blvd
Allentown, PA 18103
Phone: 610-776-4304

701 Slate Belt Blvd
Bangor, PA 18013
Phone: 610-599-0127

301 W 3rd St
Berwick, PA 18603
Phone: 570-759-0351

25 N 32nd St
Camp Hill, PA 17011
Phone: 717-730-9782

190 W Park Ave, Ste 8
Dubois, PA 15801
Phone: 814-375-6817

Elwood City Hospital
Med Arts Bldg, #201, 304 Evans Dr
Elwood City, PA 16117
Phone: 724-285-2203

ACV Med Ctr
855 Route 58, Ste 1
Foxburg, PA 16036
Phone: 724-659-5601

10 E Spruce St
Frackville, PA 17931
Phone: 570-621-4904

Hempfield Plaza, Route 30
Greensburg, PA 15601
Phone: 724-837-5200

295 N Kerrwood Dr, Ste 110
Hermitage, PA 16148
Phone: 724-346-1569

433 Caredean Dr
Horsham, PA 19044
Phone: 215-823-6050

1425 Scalp Ave, Ste 29
Johnstown, PA 15904
Phone: 814-266-8696

Armstrong Memorial Hospital
1 Nolte Dr
Kittanning, PA 16201
Phone: 724-543-8711

1861 Charter Lane
Green Field Corporation Ctr, #118
Lancaster, PA 17605
Phone: 717-290-6900

18955 Park Ave, Plaza
Meadville, PA 16335
Phone: 814-337-0170

90 Wagner Rd
Monaca, PA 15061
Phone: 724-216-0326

Jameson Hospital
1000 S Mercer St
New Castle, PA 16101
Phone: 724-285-2203

174 Bissell Ave
Oil City, PA 16301
Phone: 814-678-2631

Venango County Clinic
UPMC Northwest,
    174 E Bissell Ave
Oil City, PA 16301
Phone: 814-677-7591
    or toll free: 1-800-274-8387

214 N 40th St
Philadelphia, PA 19106
Phone: 215-923-2600

Good Samaritan Med Mall
700 Schuylkill Manor Rd, #6
Pottsville, PA 17901
Phone: 570-621-4115

St Joseph's Community Ctr
145 N 6th St
Reading, PA 19601
Phone: 610-208-4717

1537 Elmira St
Sayre, PA 18840
Phone: 570-888-6803

6 S Greenview Rd
Schuylkill, PA 17972
Phone: 570-621-4115

406 Franklin St
Smethport, PA 16749
Phone: 814-887-5655

11 Independence Dr
Springs City, PA 19475
Phone: 610-948-0981

Crozier Keystone Healthplex
194 W Sproul Rd, #105
Springfield, PA 19064
Phone: 610-543-3246

3048 Enterprise Dr
State College, PA 16801
Phone: 814-867-5415

Tobyhanna Army Depot Bldg 220
Tobyhanna, PA 18466
Phone: 570-895-8341

404 W Main St
Uniontown, PA 15401
Phone: 724-439-4990

3 Farm Colony Dr
Warren, PA 16365
Phone: 814-723-9763

100 Ridge Ave
Washington, PA 15301
Phone: 724-250-7790

1111 E End Blvd
Wilkes-Barre, PA 18711
Phone: 570-924-3521

1705 Warren Ave
Warner Bldg, 3rd Fl, # 304
Williamsport, PA 17701
Phone: 570-322-4791

1797 3rd Ave
York, PA 17402
Phone: 717-854-2481
   or 717-854-2322

VA Regional Offices:

Regional Office and Insurance Ctr
PO Box 8079
5000 Wissahickon Ave
Philadelphia, PA 19101
Phone toll free: 1-800-827-1000
This office serves the counties of Adams, Bradford, Berks, Cameron, Carbon, Chester, Clinton, Columbia, Dauphin, Delaware, Franklin, Juniata, Lackawanna, Lancaster, Lebanon, Lehigh, Luzerne, Mifflin, Monroe, Montgomery, Montour, Northampton, Northumberland, Perry, Philadelphia, Pike, Potter, Schuylkill, Snyder, Sullivan, Susquehanna, Tioga, Union, Wayne, Wyoming, and York.

1000 Liberty Ave
Pittsburgh, PA 15222
Phone statewide toll free:
   1-800-827-1000
This office serves the remaining counties of Pennsylvania

VA Benefits Office:

1123 E End Blvd, Bldg 35, Ste
11Wilkes-Barre, PA 18702
Phone toll free: 1-800-827-1000

RHODE ISLAND

VA Medical Center:

830 Chalkstone Ave
Providence, RI 02908
Phone: 401-273-7100
     or toll free: 1-866-592-2976

VA Clinic:

1 Corporate Pl
Middletown, RI 02842
Phone: 401-847-6239

VA Regional Office:

380 Westminster St
Providence, RI 02903
Phone statewide toll free:
     1-800-827-1000

SOUTH CAROLINA

VA Medical Centers:

109 Bee St
Charleston, SC 29401
Phone: 843-577-5011
     or toll free: 1-888-878-6884

6439 Garners Ferry Rd
Columbia, SC 29209
Phone: 803-776-4000

VA Clinics:

1702 E Greenville St
Anderson, SC 29621
Phone: 864-T-2 4-5450

Pickney Rd
Beaufort, SC 29902
Phone: 843-770-0444

514-H Dargan St
Florence, SC 29505
Phone: 843-292-8383

3510 Augusta Rd
Greenville, SC 29605
Phone: 864-299-1600

3381 Phyllis Blvd
Myrtle Beach, SC 29577
Phone: 843-477-0177

9237 University Blvd
North Charleston, SC 29406
Phone: 843-789-6400

1767 Villagepark Dr
Orangeburg, SC 29118
Phone: 803-533-1335

205 Piedmont Blvd
Rock Hill, SC 29730
Phone: 803-366-4848

407 N Salem Ave
Sumter, SC 29150
Phone: 803-938-9901

VA Regional Office:

1801 Assembly St
Columbia, SC 29201
Phone statewide toll free:
     1-800-827-1000

SOUTH DAKOTA

VA Medical Centers:

113 Comanche Rd
Fort Meade, SD 57741
Phone: 605-347-2511
or toll free: 1-800-743-1070

500 N 5th St
Hot Springs, SD 57747
Phone: 605-745-2000
or toll free: 1-800-764-5370

2501 W 22nd St
PO Box 5046
Sioux Falls, SD 57117
Phone: 605-336-3230
or toll free: 1-800-316-8387

VA Clinics:

10 15 Ave Northwest
Aberdeen, SD 57401
Phone: 605-622-2640

15 Main St
Eagle Butte, SD 57625
Phone: 605-964-8000

153 Main St
Mission, SD 57555
Phone: 605-856-2295

1601 N Harrison St, Ste 6
Pierre, SD 57501
Phone: 605-945-1710

Pine Ridge VA Clinic
next to Dialysis Bldg
across from IHS Hospital
Pine Ridge, SD 57770
Phone: 605-745-2000, Ext 2474

3525 5th St
Rapid City, SD 57701
Phone: 605-718-1095

1436 E 10th St
Winner, SD 57580
Phone: 605-842-2443

VA Regional Office:

PO Box 5046
2501 W 22nd St
Sioux Falls, SD 57117
Phone statewide toll free:
1-800-827-1000

TENNESSEE

VA Medical Centers:

1030 Jefferson Ave
Memphis, TN 38104
Phone: 901-523-8990
or toll free: 1-800-636-8262

Corner of Lamont & Sydney Sts
PO Box 4000
Mountain Home, TN 37684
Phone: 423-926-1171
or toll free: 1- 877-573-3529

3400 Lebanon Pike
Murfreesboro, TN 37129
Phone: 615-867-6000
or toll free: 1-800-876-7093

1310 24th Ave S
Nashville, TN 37212
Phone: 615-327-4751
or toll free: 1-800-228-4973

VA Clinics:

225 First St
Arnold Air Force Base, TN 37389
Phone: 931-454-6134

150 Debra Rd
Ste 5200, Bldg 6200
Chattanooga, TN 37411
Phone: 423-893-6500

1731 Memorial St, Ste 110
Clarksville, TN 37043
Phone: 931-221-2171

851 S Willow Ave, Ste 108
Cookeville, TN 38501
Phone: 931-284-4060

1021 Spring St
Dover, TN 37204
Phone: 931-232-5329

601 Benton Ave
Nashville, TN 37204
Phone: 615-292-9770

9031 Cross Park Dr
Knoxville, TN 37923
Phone: 865-545-4592

765-A Florence Rd
Savannah, TN 38372
Phone: 731-925-2300

VA Regional Office:

110 9th Ave, South
Nashville, TN 37203
Phone statewide toll free:
    1-800-827-1000

TEXAS

VA Medical Centers:

6010 Amarillo Blvd W
Amarillo, TX 79106
Phone: 806-355-9703
    or toll free: 1- 800-687-8262

300 Veterans Blvd.
Big Spring, TX 79720
Phone: 432-263-7361
    or toll free: 1-800-472-1365

1201 E 9th St
Bonham, TX 75418
Phone: 903-583-2111
    or toll free: 1-800-924-8387

4500 S Lancaster Rd
Dallas, TX 75216
Phone: 214-742-8387
    or toll free: 1-800-849-3597

5001 N Piedras St
El Paso, TX 79930
Phone: 915-564-6100
    or toll free: 1-800-672-3782

South Texas VA Health Care Ctr
2106 Treasure Hills Blvd
Harlingen, TX 78550
Phone: 956-366-4500

2002 Holcombe Blvd
Houston, TX 77030
Phone: 713-791-1414
    or toll free: 1-800-553-2278

3600 Memorial Blvd
Kerrville, TX 78028
Phone: 830-896-2020

7400 Merton Minter Blvd
San Antonio, TX 78229
Phone: 210-617-5300
    or toll free: 1-888-686-6350

1901 Veterans Memorial Dr
Temple, TX 76504
Phone: 254-778-4811
    or toll free: 1-800-423-2111

4800 Memorial Dr
Waco, TX 76711
Phone: 254-752-6581
    or toll free: 1- 800-423-2111

VA Clinics:

4225 Woods Pl
Abilene, TX 79602
Phone: 325-695-3252

2901 Montopolis Dr
Austin, TX 78741
Phone: 512-389-1010

3420 Veterans Cir
Beaumont, TX 77707
Phone: 409-981-8550
    or toll free: 1-800-833-7734

302 S Hillside Dr
Beeville, TX 78102
Phone: 361-358-9912

808 Woodrow Wilson Ray Cir
Bridgeport, TX 76426
Phone: 940-683-2297

2600 Memorial Park Dr
Brownwood, TX 76801
Phone: 325-641-0568

701 Whitestone Blvd
Cedar Park, TX 78613
Phone: 512-260-1368

1001 Highway 83 N
Childress, TX 79201
Phone: 940-937-3636

1605 Rock Prairie Rd, Ste 212
College Station, TX 77845
Phone: 979-680-0361

800 Riverwood Court, Ste 100
Conroe, TX 77304
Phone: 936-522-4000

5283 Old Brownsville Rd
Corpus Christi, TX 78405
Phone: 361-806-5600

2223 Colorado Blvd
Denton, TX 76205
Phone: 940-213-4100

300 W Rosedale St
Fort Worth, TX 76104
Phone: 817-335-2205
    or toll free: 1-800-443-9672

855 Montgomery St.
Fort Worth, TX 76107
Phone: 817-735-2228

501 N Main
Fort Stockton, TX 79735
Phone: 432-336-0700

6115 Ave L
Galveston, TX 77551
Phone: 409-741-0256
    or toll free: 1-800-310-5001

2006 Fall Creek Hwy
Granbury, TX 76049
Phone: 816-326-3440

4311 Wesley St
Greenville, TX 75407
Phone: 903-455-5958

1629 Treasure Hills Blvd, Ste 5-B
Harlingen, TX 78550
Phone: 956-366-4500

6551 Star Court
Laredo, TX 78041
Phone: 956-523-7850
    or toll free: 1-800-209-7377

1205 E Marshall Ave
Longview, TX 75601
Phone: 903-247-8262
    or toll free: 1-800-957-8262

6104 Ave Q South Dr
Lubbock, TX 79412
Phone: 806-472-3400

1301 Frank Ave
Lufkin, TX 75901
Phone: 936-637-1342
    or toll free: 1-800-209-3120

2101 S Col. Rowe Blvd
McAllen, TX 78501
Phone: 956-618-7100
    or toll free: 1-866-622-5536

189 E Austin Rd, Ste 106
New Braunfels, TX 78130
Phone: 830-629-3614

4241 N Tanglewood Rd., Ste 201
Odessa, TX 79762
Phone: 432-550-0149

2000 S Loop 256, Ste 201
Palestine, TX 75801
Phone: 903-723-9006

625 Stone Ave
Paris, TX 75462
Phone 903-785-9900

Frank M Tejeda OPC
5788 Eckhert Rd
San Antonio, TX 78240
Phone: 210-699-2100

San Antonio Dental Clinic
8410 Data Point
San Antonio, TX 78299
Phone: 210-949-8900

2018 Pulliam St
San Angelo, TX 76905
Phone: 325-658-6138

1831 S General McMullen
San Antonio, TX 78226
Phone: 210-434-1400

2455 N East Loop 410, Ste 100
San Antonio Greenway, TX 78217
Phone: 210-599-6000

14100 Nacogdoches, Ste 116
San Antonio Northern Hills,
    TX 78217
Phone: 210-653-8989

4243 E Southcross, Ste 205
San Antonio Pecan Valley,
    TX 78222
Phone: 210-304-3500

2612 N Loy Lake, Ste 300
Sherman, TX 75090
Phone: 903-891-8317

Box 911, Hwy 6 E
Stamford, TX 79553
Phone: 325-773-2710

1220 Pernell Dr
PO Box 1107
Stratford, TX 79084
Phone: 806-396-2852

9300 Emmett F Lowry Expressway,
Ste 206
Texas City, TX 77591
Phone: 409-986-1129
    or toll free: 1-800-310-5001

3414 Golden Rd
Tyler, TX 75701
Phone: 903-593-6064

1502 E Airline Dr, Ste 40
Victoria, TX 77901
Phone: 361-382-7700
    or toll free: 1-800-209-7377

1800 7th St
Wichita Falls, TX 76301
Phone: 940-723-2373

VA Regional Offices:

6900 Almeda Rd
Houston, TX 77030
Phone statewide toll free:
    1-800-827-1000
*This office serves the counties of
Angelina, Aransas, Atacosa, Austin,
Bandera, Bee, Bexar, Blanco,
Brazoria, Brewster, Brooks, Caldwell,
Calhoun, Cameron, Chambers,
Colorado, Comal, Crockett, DeWitt,
Dimitt, Duval, Edwards, Fort Bend,
Frio, Galveston, Gillespie, Goliad,
Gonzales, Grimes, Guadeloupe,
Hardin, Harris, Hays, Hidalgo,
Houston, Jackson, Jasper, Jefferson,
Jim Hogg, Jim Wells, Karnes,
Kendall, Kerr, Kimble, Kinney,
Kleberg, La Salle, Lavaca, Liberty,
Live Oak, McCulloch, McMullen,
Mason, Matagorda, Maverick,
Medina, Menard, Montgomery,
Nacogdoches, Newton, Nueces,*

*Orange, Pecos, Polk, Real, Refugio,
Sabine, San Augustine, San Jacinto,
San Patricio, Schleicher, Shelby,
Starr, Sutton, Terrell, Trinity,
Tyler, Uvalde, Val Verde, Victoria,
Walker, Waller, Washington, Webb,
Wharton, Willacy, Wilson, Zapata,
and Zavala.*

One Veterans Plaza
701 Clay St
Waco, TX 76799
Phone statewide toll free:
    1-800-827-1000
This office serves the rest of the state.

*In Bowie County, the city of
Texarkana is served by the Little
Rock, Arkansas, VA regional office.*

VA Benefits Offices:

Taylor County Plaza Bldg
Ste 103, 400 Oak St
Abilene, TX 79602
Phone toll free: 1-800-827-1000

6010 Amarillo Blvd W
Amarillo, TX 79106
Phone toll free: 1-800-827-1000

2901 Montopolis Dr, Rm 108
Austin, TX 78741
Phone toll free: 1-800-827-1000

4646 Corona Dr, Ste 150
Corpus Christi, TX 78405
Phone toll free: 1-800-827-1000

4500 S. Lancaster Rd
Dallas, TX 75216
Phone toll free: 1-800-827-1000

5000 1 Piedras Dr
El Paso, TX 79930
Phone toll free: 1-800-827-1000

300 W Rosedale St
Fort Worth, TX 76104
Phone toll free: 1-800-827-1000

6104 Ave Q S Dr, Rm 132
Lubbock, TX 79410
Phone toll free: 1-800-827-1000

109 Toronto Ave
McAllen, TX 78503
Phone toll free: 1-800-827-1000

5788 Eckert Rd
San Antonio, TX 78240
Phone toll free: 1-800-827-1000

1901 Veterans Memorial Dr
Rome 538 (BRB)
Temple, TX 76504
Phone toll free: 1-800-827-1000

1700 S S E Loop 323, Ste 310
Tyler, TX 75701
Phone toll free: 1-800-827-1000

UTAH

VA Medical Center:

500 Foothill Dr
Salt Lake City, UT 84148
Phone: 801-582-1565
    or toll free: 1-800-613-4012

VA Clinics:

300 W 300 S
Fountain Green, UT 84632
Phone: 435-623-3129

48 W 1500 N
Nephi, UT 84648
Phone: 435-623-3129

982 Chambers St
Ogden, UT 84403
Phone: 801-479-4105

740 W 800 N, Ste 440
Orem, UT 84057
Phone: 801-235-0953

210 W 300 N
Roosevelt, UT 84066
Phone: 435-725-2082

1067 E Tabernacle, Ste 7
St George, UT 84770
Phone 435-634-7608, Ext 6000

VA Regional Office:

PO Box 581900
550 Foothill Dr
Salt Lake City, UT 84158
Phone statewide toll free:
    1-800-827-1000

VERMONT

VA Medical Center:

215 N Main St
White River Junction, VT 05009
Phone: 802-295-9363
    or toll free: 1-866-687-8387

VA Clinics:

190 North St
Bennington, VT 05201
Phone: 802-447-6913

74 Hegeman Ave
Colchester, VT 05446
Phone: 802-655-1356

215 Stratton Rd
Rutland, VT 05702
Phone: 802-773-3386

VA Regional Office:

215 N Main St
White River Junction, VT 05001
Phone: 802-296-5177
    or toll free: 1-800-827-1000
    from within Vermont

VIRGINIA

VA Medical Centers:

100 Emancipation Dr
Hampton, VA 23667
Phone: 757-722-9961

1201 Broad Rock Blvd
Richmond, VA 23249
Phone: 804-675-5000
    or toll free: 1-800-784-8381

1970 Roanoke Blvd
Salem, VA 24153
Phone: 540-982-2463
    or toll free: 1-888-982-2463

VA Clinics:

6940 S Kings Hwy Ste #208
Alexandria, VA 22301
Phone: 703-313-0694

100 Vicar Pl
Danville, VA 24540
Phone: 434-836-2100

1960 Jefferson Davis Hwy, Ste 100
Fredericksburg, VA 22401
Phone: 540-370-4468

847 Cantrell Ave, Ste 100
Harrisonburg, VA 22801
Phone: 540-442-1773

315 Hospital Way, Ste 101
Martinsville, VA 24112
Phone: 276-632-5929

106 Hyde Court
Stephen City, VA 22655
Phone: 540-869-0600

308 W Main St
Saltville, VA 23470
Phone: 276-496-4433

123 Ben Bolt Ave
Tazewell, VA 24651
Phone: 276-988-2526

244 Clearfield Ave
Virginia Beach, VA 23462
Phone: 757-726-6070

VA Regional Office:

210 Franklin Rd SW
Roanoke, VA 24011
Phone statewide toll free:
    1-800-827-1000

WASHINGTON

VA Medical Centers:

1660 S Columbian Way
Seattle, WA 98108
Phone: 206-762-1010
    or toll free: 1-800-329-8387

4815 N Assembly St
Spokane, WA 99205
Phone: 509-434-7000
    or toll free: 1-800-325-7940

9600 Veterans Dr
Tacoma, WA 98493
Phone: 253-582-8440
    or toll free: 1-800-329-8387

1601 E 4th Plain Blvd
Vancouver, WA 98661
Phone: 360-696-4061
    or toll free: 1-800-949-1004

77 Wainwright Dr
Walla Walla, WA 99362
Phone: 509-525-5200
    or toll free: 1-888-687-8863

VA Clinics:

13033 Bel-Red Rd, Ste 210
Bellevue, WA 98005
Phone: 425-214-1055

925 Adele Ave
Bremerton, WA 98312
Phone: 360-782-0129

34617 11th Pl South
Federal Way, Washington 98003
Phone: 253-336-4142

946 Stevens Dr Ste C
Richland, WA 99352
Phone: 509-946-1020

12360 Lake City Way NE, Ste 200
Seattle, WA 98125
Phone 206-384-4382

2530 Chester-Kimm Rd
Wenatchee, WA 98801
Phone: 509-663-7615

717 Fruitvale Blvd
Yakima, WA 98902
Phone 509-966-0199

1111 N 1st St Ste 1
Yakima Mental Health Clinic,
    WA 98902
Phone: 509-457-2736

VA Regional Office:

Federal Bldg, 915 2nd Ave
Seattle, WA 98174
Phone statewide toll free:
    1-800-827-1000

VA Benefits Offices:

Waller Hall Rm 700
PO Box 331153
Fort Lewis, WA 98433
Phone: 253-967-7106

West Sound Pre-Separation Ctr
262 Burwell St
Bremerton, WA 98337
Phone: 360-782-9900

WEST VIRGINIA

VA Medical Centers:

200 Veterans Ave
Beckley, WV 25801
Phone: 304-255-2121
    or toll free: 1-877-902-5142

1 Med Ctr Dr
Clarksburg, WV 26301
Phone 304-623-3461
    or toll free: 1-800-733-0512

1540 Spring Valley Dr
Huntington, WV 25704
Phone: 304-429-6741
      or toll free: 1-800-827-8244

510 Butler Ave
Martinsburg, WV 25405
Phone: 304-263-0811
      or toll free: 1-800-817-3807

VA Clinics:

104 Alex Ln
Charleston, WV 25304
Phone: 304-926-6001

314 Pine St
Franklin, WV 26807
Phone 304-358-2355

513 Dingess St
Logan, WV 25601
Phone: 304-752-8355

2311 Ohio Ave, Ste A
Parkersburg, WV 26010
Phone: 304-422-5114

206 Spruce St
Parsons, WV 26287
Phone: 304-478-2219

Grant Memorial Hospital
PO Box 1019
Petersburg, WV 26847
Phone: 304-257-5817

93 Skidmore Lane
Sutton, WV 26602
Phone 304-765-3480

75 West 4th Ave
Williamson, WV 25661
Phone 304-235-2187

VA Regional Office:

640 4th Ave
Huntington, WV 25701
Phone statewide toll free:
      1-800-827-1000
*The counties of Brooke, Hancock,
Marshall, Ohio, are served by
Pittsburgh, PA, VA Regional Office.*

WISCONSIN

VA Medical Centers:

2500 Overlook Ter
Madison, WI 53705
Phone: 608-256-1901

5000 W National Ave
Milwaukee, WI 53295
Phone 414-384-2000
      or toll free: 1-888-469-6614

500 E Veterans St
Tomah, WI 54660
Phone: 608-372-3971
      or toll free: 1-800-872-8662

VA Clinics:

10 Tri-Park Way
Appleton, WI 54914
Phone: 920-831-0070

626 14th St
Baraboo, WI 53913
Phone: 608-356-9318

215 Corporate Dr
Beaver Dam, WI 53916
Phone: 920-356-9415

2501 and 2503 County Hwy I
Chippewa Falls, WI 54729
Phone: 715-720-3780

1205 North Ave
Cleveland, WI 53015
Phone: 920-693-5600

141 Siegler St
Green Bay, WI 54303
Phone: 920-497-3126

15748 County Rd B
Hayward, WI 54843
Phone: 715-934-5454

111 N Main St
Janesville, WI 53545
Phone: 608-758-9300

805 55th St
Kenosha, WI 53140
Phone: 262-653-9286

2600 State Rd
La Crosse, WI 54601
Phone 608-784-3886

141 N Main St
Loyal, WI 54446
Phone: 715-255-9799

639 W Kemp St
Rhinelander, WI 54501
Phone: 715-362-4080

2700 A College Dr
Rice Lake, WI 54843
Phone: 715-236-3355

3520 Tower Ave
Superior, WI 54880
Phone: 715-392-9711

21425 Spring St
Union Grove, WI 53182
Phone: 262-878-7000

515 S 32nd Ave
Wausau, WI 54401
Phone: 715-842-2834

710 E Grand Ave
PO Box 26
Wisconsin Rapids, WI 54494
Phone: 715-424-3844

VA Regional Office:

5400 W National Ave
Milwaukee, WI 53214
Phone toll free: 1-800-827-1000

WYOMING

VA Medical Centers:

2360 E Pershing Blvd
Cheyenne, WY 82001
Phone: 307-778-7550
    or toll free: 1-888-483-9127

1898 Fort Rd
Sheridan, WY 82801
Phone: 307-672-3473
    or toll free: 1-866-822-6714

VA Clinics:

4140 S Poplar St
Casper, WY 82601
Phone: 307-235-4143
    or toll free: 1-866-338-5168

1701 Phillips Cir
Gillette, WY 82718
Phone: 307-685-0676
    or toll free: 1-866-612-1887

1124 Washington Blvd
Newcastle, WY 57555
Phone: 605-745-2000, Ext 2474

777 Ave H
Powell, WY 82435
Phone 307-754-7257
    or toll free: 1-888-284-9308

2300 Rose Lane
Riverton, WY 82501
Phone: 307-857-1211
    or toll free: 1-866-338-2609

3000 College Dr, Ste C
Rock Springs, WY 82901
Phone: 307-362-6641
    or toll free: 1-866-381-2830

VA Benefits Office:

2360 E Pershing Blvd
Cheyenne, WY 82001
Phone statewide toll free:
    1-800-827-1000

APPENDIX 2

ADDITIONAL VA BENEFITS AND SERVICES

Veterans and their family members may also be eligible for additional VA benefits and services. These benefits and services include Aid and Attendance benefits for the spouse of a veteran receiving a service-connected disability compensation, discounted prescription medications, and replacement medals and awards.

AID AND ATTENDANCE BENEFITS FOR THE SPOUSE OF A VETERAN RECEIVING A SERVICE-CONNECTED DISABILITY COMPENSATION

A spouse of a living veteran may be entitled to Aid and Attendance benefits if the veteran receives service-connected disability compensation for a disability rating of 30 percent or greater.[1] (See "Special Circumstances" in chapter 3.) Contact a VSO for questions related to this special circumstance. If you feel this special circumstance may apply to your situation, then it may be helpful to have a basic understanding of service-connected disability compensation.

Service-connected disability compensation is a monetary benefit paid to veterans who are disabled by an injury or disease that was incurred or aggravated during active military service. Disability compensation varies with the degree of disability and the number of dependents and is paid monthly. Table A.1 shows the rate of payment related to the percentage of disability for a veteran without dependents. Typically, being approved for disability compensation is often a difficult and lengthy process for veterans because they must prove that their injuries were sustained during wartime. Their claims must be supported by medical records that may have been lost or destroyed.

Table A.1 Disability compensation rates for 2009 (Rates apply to a veteran without dependents.)[2]

Disability Rating	Monthly Rate
10 percent	$123
20 percent	$243
30 percent	$376
40 percent	$541
50 percent	$770
60 percent	$974
70 percent	$1,228
80 percent	$1,427
90 percent	$1,604
100 percent	$2,673

Note: Disability compensation rates are updated annually in December.

Veterans with disability ratings of 30 percent or greater are eligible for additional compensation for dependents, including spouses, minor children, children between the ages of eighteen and twenty-three who are attending school, children who are permanently incapable of self-support because of a disability arising before age eighteen, and dependent parents. The additional amount depends on the disability rating and the number of dependents.[3]

PHARMACY BENEFITS FOR ALL ELIGIBLE VETERANS: DISCOUNTED PRESCRIPTION MEDICATIONS

All veterans discharged under other than dishonorable conditions may be eligible for discounted pharmacy benefits; wartime service is not a requirement. Spouses of veterans are not eligible unless they are veterans themselves.

According to the 2009 financial income thresholds, veterans who have an annual income of $29,402 or less (a veteran with no dependents) or $35,284 or less (a veteran with one dependent) are eligible for pharmacy benefits.[4] *(Note: Income thresholds are updated annually in January.)* At this writing, the copayment is $8 for a thirty-day supply of medication. Even if the prescription is written for ninety days, each thirty-day-or-less supply is subject to a copayment. The copayment for a ninety-day supply would therefore be $24, or three times the thirty-day medication copayment rate. Most veterans do not pay copayments for medications dispensed during the remainder of a calendar year in which an annual cap amount has been paid. For the calendar year 2009, the cap is $960.[5]

Veterans who have never enrolled in the VA healthcare system need to complete Form 10-10EZ, Application for Health Benefits, which is available from a VSO or from the VA Web site. To be sure you have the latest version of the form,

1. Go to https://www.1010ez.med.va.gov/sec/vha/1010ez/.

2. Click on "viewing or printing the 10-10EZ" near the top of the page.

Tips for Completing Form 10-10EZ

A sample Form 10-10EZ is presented in figure 9.1 in chapter 9. Be sure to refer to it to see how to complete the form.

Section I: General Information

Box 13—Write in the name of the VA healthcare facility where you prefer to receive care. (See the list of VA facilities in appendix 1.)

Box 14—Check the "Yes" box if you want the VA to schedule a doctor's appointment for you when your application is processed. Note: Pharmacy benefits do not begin automatically; you must first have a physical with a VA physician. At your doctor's appointment, the VA physician will write your prescriptions for the VA mail-order pharmacy.

Section II: Insurance Information
Attach copies of *all health insurance cards (both sides)* to the form. If you are covered under a spouse's health insurance, be sure to include a copy of both sides of that insurance card also.

Section IV: Military Service Information
Attach a copy of your discharge record.

Be sure you sign and date the form at the bottom of page 3.

Forms should be faxed or mailed to the *eligibility department* at the VA medical center or clinic where you prefer to receive care. (See the list of VA facilities in appendix 1.) After your application has been processed, the VA will send you a letter notifying you of your eligibility, and if you checked "Yes" in box 14 in section I, you will also be informed of your doctor's appointment.

Contact a VSO for questions related to VA pharmacy benefits.

REQUESTING REPLACEMENT MEDALS, AWARDS, AND DECORATIONS

If a veteran's medals, awards, or decorations were lost or never received, the veteran or a family member may request to have them replaced or reissued. Requests for the issuance or replacement of military service medals, awards, and decorations should be directed to the specific branch of the military in which the veteran served; however, for Air Force (including Army Air Corps and Army Air Forces) and Army personnel, the National Personnel Records Center (NPRC) will verify the awards to which a veteran is entitled and forward the request with the verification to the appropriate service department for issuance of the medals. Generally, there is no charge for medal or award replacements. The length of time to receive a response or receive your medals and awards varies depending upon the branch of service.[6]

Standard Form 180 (SF 180), Request Pertaining to Military Records (discussed in chapter 7), is the recommended form for requesting medals and awards.

You can obtain Standard Form 180 in one of the following three ways:

1. Download a copy of SF 180 in PDF format from the National Archives and Records Administration (NARA) Web site. Be sure you obtain the latest version of the form:

   a. Go to http://www.archives.gov/forms/.

   b. Click on "Request Pertaining to Military Records" (which is the title of SF 180).

2. Request a copy from the National Personnel Records Center, 9700 Page Avenue, St. Louis, Missouri 63132-5100.

3. Contact a local veterans service organization and request that the form be mailed to you.

Tips for Completing Standard Form 180

A sample completed SF 180 is presented in figure A.1. Be sure to refer to it to see how to complete the form.

Section I: Information Needed to Locate Records

Boxes 1–7—Fill in as much information as possible.

Section II: Information and/or Documents Requested

Item 1—Check the "Other" box and write the following: "Please issue or reissue all medals (with certificates where appropriate), awards, and citations earned for active military service."

Item 2—Check the "Medals/Awards" box.

Section III: Return Address and Signature

Item1—Check the appropriate box.

Item 2—Print your name and address.

Item 3—Provide your signature, the date, and your phone number.

Note: Only the veteran, next of kin, or legal guardian may sign the form.

Figure A.1 Sample completed Standard Form 180 (SF180): Request Pertaining to Military Records.

Standard Form 180 (Rev. 09/08) (Page 1)
Prescribed by NARA (36 CFR 1228.168(b))

Authorized for local reproduction
Previous edition unusable

OMB No. 3095-0029 Expires 10/31/2011

REQUEST PERTAINING TO MILITARY RECORDS

* Requests from veterans or deceased veteran's next-of-kin may be submitted online by using eVetRecs at http://www.archives.gov/veterans/evetrecs/ *

(To ensure the best possible service, please thoroughly review the accompanying instructions before filling out this form. Please print clearly or type.)

SECTION I - INFORMATION NEEDED TO LOCATE RECORDS (Furnish as much as possible.)

1. NAME USED DURING SERVICE (last, first, and middle)	2. SOCIAL SECURITY NO.	3. DATE OF BIRTH	4. PLACE OF BIRTH
Brown, James Larry	555-55-5555	06-16-1924	Swisstown, PA

5. SERVICE, PAST AND PRESENT   (For an effective records search, it is important that all service be shown below.)

	BRANCH OF SERVICE	DATE ENTERED	DATE RELEASED	OFFICER	ENLISTED	SERVICE NUMBER (If unknown, write "unknown")
a. ACTIVE COMPONENT	Army Air Force	02-19-1943	10-29-1945		X	unknown
b. RESERVE COMPONENT						
c. NATIONAL GUARD						

6. IS THIS PERSON DECEASED? If "YES" enter the date of death.
[X] NO   [ ] YES

7. IS (WAS) THIS PERSON RETIRED FROM MILITARY SERVICE?
[X] NO   [ ] YES

SECTION II – INFORMATION AND/OR DOCUMENTS REQUESTED

1. CHECK THE ITEM(S) YOU WOULD LIKE TO REQUEST A COPY OF:

[ ] **DD Form 214 or equivalent.** This form contains information normally needed to verify military service. A copy may be sent to the veteran, the deceased veteran's next of kin, or other persons or organizations if authorized in Section III, below. NOTE: If more than one period of service was performed, even in the same branch, there may be more than one DD214. **Check the appropriate box below to specify a deleted or undeleted copy.** When was the DD Form(s) 214 issued? YEAR(S):

[ ] **UNDELETED:** Ordinarily required to determine eligibility for benefits. Sensitive items, such as, the character of separation, authority for separation, reason for separation, reenlistment eligibility code, separation (SPD/SPN) code, and dates of time lost are usually shown.

[ ] **DELETED:** The following items are deleted: authority for separation, reason for separation, reenlistment eligibility code, separation (SPD/SPN) code, and for separations after June 30, 1979, character of separation and dates of time lost.

[ ] **All Documents in Official Military Personnel File (OMPF)**

[ ] **Medical Records** (Includes Service Treatment Records (outpatient), inpatient and dental records.) If hospitalized, provide facility name and date for each admission:

[X] **Other** (Specify):   Please issue or reissue all medals (with certificates where appropriate), awards, and citations earned for active military service.

2. PURPOSE: (An explanation of the purpose of the request is **strictly voluntary**; however, such information may help to provide the best possible response and may result in a faster reply. Information provided will in no way be used to make a decision to deny the request.) Check appropriate box:

[ ] Benefits   [ ] Employment   [ ] VA Loan Programs   [ ] Medical   [X] Medals/Awards   [ ] Genealogy   [ ] Correction   [ ] Personal
[ ] Other, explain:

SECTION III - RETURN ADDRESS AND SIGNATURE

1. REQUESTER IS: *(Signature Required in # 3 below of veteran, next of kin, legal guardian, authorized government agent or "other" authorized representative. If "other" authorized representative, provide copy of authorization letter.)*

[X] Military service member or veteran identified in Section I, above

[ ] Next of kin of deceased veteran (Must provide proof of death).
   Show relationship:

[ ] Legal guardian (Must submit copy of court appointment.)

[ ] Other (specify)

(See item 2a on accompanying instructions.)

2. SEND INFORMATION/DOCUMENTS TO:
(Please print or type. See item 4 on accompanying instructions.)

James Larry Brown
Name

125 Rose Place
Street   Apt.

Happytown   PA   22222
City   State   Zip Code

3. AUTHORIZATION SIGNATURE REQUIRED *(See items 2a or 3a on accompanying instructions.)* I declare (or certify, verify, or state) under penalty of perjury under the laws of the United States of America that the information in this Section III is true and correct.

James Larry Brown
Signature Required - Do not print

02 -27-2009   (412) 888-0909
Date of this request   Daytime phone

Email address

*This form is available at *http://www.archives.gov/research/order/standard-form-180.pdf* on the National Archives and Records Administration (NARA) web site.*

(A blank copy of this form was obtained from the NARA Web site, http://www.archives.gov/research/order/standard-form-180.pdf.)

Send SF 180 to the appropriate address as follows:

Army	
Where to write for medals	National Personnel Records Center 9700 Page Ave St. Louis, MO 63132-5100
Where medals are mailed from	U.S. Army TACOM Clothing and Heraldry (PSID) PO Box 57997 Philadelphia, PA 19111-7997
Where to write in case of a problem or an appeal	Commander U.S. Army Human Resources Command Attn: TAPC-PDO-PA 200 Stovall St Alexandria, VA 22332-0474

Air Force (including Army Air Corps and Army Air Forces)	
Where to write for medals	National Personnel Records Center 9700 Page Ave St. Louis, MO 63132-5100
Where medals are mailed from	Headquarters Air Force Personnel Ctr AFPC/DPPPR 550 C St West, Ste 12 Randolph AFB, TX 78150-4714
Where to write in case of a problem or an appeal	Headquarters Air Force Personnel Ctr AFPC/DPPPR 550 C St West, Ste 12 Randolph AFB, TX 78150-4714

Navy

Where to write for medals	Navy Personnel Command Liaison Office Rm 5409 9700 Page Ave St. Louis, MO 63132-5100
Where medals are mailed from	Navy Personnel Command Liaison Office Rm 5409 9700 Page Ave St. Louis, MO 63132-5100
Where to write in case of a problem or an appeal	Chief of Naval Operations (OPNAV 09B33) Awards & Special Projects Washington, DC 20350-2000

Marine Corps

Where to write for medals	Navy Personnel Command Liaison Office Rm 5409 9700 Page Ave St. Louis, MO 63132-5100
Where medals are mailed from	Navy Personnel Command Liaison Office Rm 5409 9700 Page Ave St. Louis, MO 63132-5100
Where to write in case of a problem or an appeal	Commandant of the Marine Corps Military Awards Branch (MMMA) 3280 Russell Rd Quantico, VA 22134-5100

Coast Guard

Where to write for medals	Navy Personnel Command Liaison Office Rm 5409 9700 Page Ave St. Louis, MO 63132-5100
Where medals are mailed from	Navy Personnel Command Liaison Office Rm 5409 9700 Page Ave St. Louis, MO 63132-5100
Where to write in case of a problem or an appeal	Commandant U.S. Coast Guard Medals and Awards Branch (PMP-4) Washington, DC 20593-0001

NOTES

CHAPTER 1

1. All historical information in chapter 1 is from Department of Veterans Affairs, "History of the Department of Veterans Affairs," http://www1.va.gov/opa/feature/history/ (accessed January 27, 2008).

2. Department of Veterans Affairs, "FY07 Annual VA Information Pamplet (Feb 2008)," http://www1.va.gov/vetdata/docs/Pamphlet_2-1-08.pdf (accessed April 19, 2008).

CHAPTER 2

1. Department of Veterans Affairs, "Improved Disability Benefits Pension Rate Table – Effective 12/1/08," http://www.vba.va.gov/bln/21/Rates/pen01.htm (accessed December 1, 2008); and Department of Veterans Affairs, "Veterans Pension Program," http://www.vba.va.gov/bln/21/pension/vetpen.htm (accessed February 16, 2008).

2. Department of Veterans Affairs, "Improved Death Pension Benefits Rates – Effective 12/1/08," http://www.vba.va.gov/bln/21/Rates/pen02.htm (accessed December 1, 2008); Department of Veterans Affairs, "Death Pension Benefits," http://www.vba.va.gov/bln/21/pension/spousepen.htm (accessed February 16, 2008); and Code of Federal Regulations, "3.54 Marriage Dates," http://edocket.access.gpo.gov/cfr_2007/julqtr/pdf/38cfr3.54.pdf (accessed July 1, 2008).

CHAPTER 3

1. Code of Federal Regulations, "3.271 Computation of Income," http://edocket.access.gpo.gov/cfr_2007/julqtr/pdf/38cfr3.271.pdf (accessed July 1, 2008); Department of Veterans Affairs, "Veterans Pension Program"; and Department of Veterans Affairs, "Death Pension Benefits."

2. Code of Federal Regulations, "3.272 Exclusions from Income," http://edocket.access.gpo.gov/cfr_2007/julqtr/pdf/38cfr3.272.pdf (accessed July 1, 2008).

3. Ibid.

4. Code of Federal Regulations, "3.263 Corpus of Estate; Net Worth," http://edocket.access.gpo.gov/cfr_2007/julqtr/pdf/38cfr3.263.pdf (accessed July 1, 2008).

5. Department of Veterans Affairs, "Veterans Pension Program"; and Department of Veterans Affairs, "Death Pension Benefits."

6. Ibid.

7. Ibid.

8. Ibid.

9. Department of Veterans Affairs, "Periods of War for VA Benefits Eligibility," http://www.vba.va.gov/bln/21/pension/wartime.htm (accessed February 16, 2008).

10. Department of Veterans Affairs, "Special Groups of Veterans" chap 9 in *Federal Benefits for Veterans and Dependents* (Washington, DC: GPO, 2008), http://www1.va.gov/opa/vadocs/fedben_pt1.pdf (accessed February 8, 2009).

11. Ibid.

12. Ibid.

13. Department of Veterans Affairs, "Federal Benefits for Veterans and Dependents," http://www1.va.gov/opa/IS1/2.asp (accessed July 1, 2008).

14. Department of Veterans Affairs, "Veterans Pension Program."

15. Code of Federal Regulations, "3.1000 Entitlement under 38 U.S.C. 5121 to Benefits Due and Unpaid upon Death of a Beneficiary," http://edocket.access.gpo.gov/cfr_2007/julqtr/pdf/38cfr3.1000.pdf (accessed July 1, 2008).

16. Code of Federal Regulations, "3.55 Reinstatement of Benefits Eligibility Based upon Terminated Marital Relationships," http://edocket.access.gpo.gov/cfr_2007/julqtr/pdf/38cfr3.55.pdf (accessed July 1, 2008).

17. Department of Veterans Affairs, "Veterans Pension Program"; and Department of Veterans Affairs, "Death Pension Benefits."

18. Code of Federal Regulations, "3.666 Incarcerated Beneficiaries and Fugitive Felons—Pension," http://edocket.access.gpo.gov/cfr_2007/julqtr/pdf/38cfr3.666.pdf (accessed July 1, 2008).

CHAPTER 4

1. Department of Veterans Affairs, "Improved Disability Benefits Pension Rate Table."

2. Code of Federal Regulations, "3.57 Child," http://edocket.access.gpo.gov/cfr_2007/julqtr/pdf/38cfr3.57.pdf (accessed December 1, 2008).

3. Department of Veterans Affairs, "Improved Death Pension Benefits Rates."

CHAPTER 6

1. Code of Federal Regulations, "3.155 Informal Claims," http://edocket.access.gpo.gov/cfr_2007/julqtr/pdf/38cfr3.155.pdf (accessed July 1, 2008).

2. Code of Federal Regulations, "3.109 Time Limit," http://edocket.access.gpo.gov/cfr_2007/julqtr/pdf/38cfr3.109.pdf (accessed July 1, 2008).

CHAPTER 7

1. Norman Eisenberg, "20th-Century Veterans' Service Records Safe, Secure—and Available," *Prologue* 37, no. 1 (2005), http://www.archives.gov/veterans/research/prologue-spotlight-nprc.html (accessed December 11, 2008).

2. National Archives, "The 1973 Fire at the National Personnel Records Center (St. Louis, MO)," http://www.archives.gov/st-louis/military-personnel/fire-1973.html (accessed July 1, 2008).

3. Eisenberg, "20th-Century Veterans' Service Records."

4. National Archives, "How to Request Military Service Records or Prove Military Service," http://www.archives.gov/veterans/military-service-records/get-service-records.html# (accessed July 1, 2008).

5. Ibid.

6. Ibid.

7. National Archives, "eVetRecs: Request Copies of Military Personnel Records," http://www.archives.gov/veterans/evetrecs/ (accessed April 5, 2008).

8. National Archives, "How to Request Military Service Records."

9. Ibid.

10. Ibid.

CHAPTER 8

1. Department of Veterans Affairs, "Veterans Pension Program"; and Department of Veterans Affairs, "Death Pension Benefits."

2. Code of Federal Regulations, "3.57 Child."

CHAPTER 9

1. Department of Veterans Affairs, "Medical Benefits Package (Standard Benefits)," http://www.va.gov/healtheligibility/coveredservices/StandardBenefits. asp (accessed April 19, 2008); and Department of Veterans Affairs, "Special and Limited Benefits," http://www.va.gov/healtheligibility/coveredservices/ SpecialBenefits.asp#EyeEar (accessed December 6, 2008).

APPENDIX 2

1. Department of Veterans Affairs, "Federal Benefits for Veterans and Dependents."

2. Department of Veterans Affairs, "Veterans Compensation Benefits Rate Tables—Effective 12/1/08," http://www.vba.va.gov/bln/21/rates/comp01.htm (accessed December 6, 2008).

3. Department of Veterans Affairs, Federal Benefits for Veterans and Dependents (Washington, DC: GPO, 2008), 16.

4. Department of Veterans Affairs, "VA National Means Test Income Thresholds," http://www.va.gov/healtheligibility/Library/pubs/ VAIncomeThresholds/VAIncomeThresholds.pdf (accessed February 1, 2009).

5. Department of Veterans Affairs, "VA Health Care 2009 Copay Rates," http://www.va.gov/healtheligibility/Library/pubs/CopayRates/CopayRates.pdf (accessed February 1, 2009).

6. National Archives, "Military Awards and Decorations," http://www. archives.gov/veterans/military-service-records/replacement-medals.html (accessed March 4, 2008).

GLOSSARY

active duty. The status of members of the military who are serving full time in their military capacity.

activities of daily living. The self-care and physical skills people need to live independently; often seen as the acronym ADL. Examples include eating, bathing, and dressing.

ADL. Activities of daily living.

Aid and Attendance pension. A pension offered by the VA to eligible veterans and their surviving spouses who require assistance with activities of daily living.

American Legion. A veterans service organization composed of wartime service veterans. The American Legion provides assistance with obtaining veteran benefits, such as pensions.

assisted living facility. A residential care setting that combines housing, support services, and healthcare for individuals needing long-term care.

caregiver. A person who provides personal care for an individual requiring support due to a disability, mental illness, frailty, or old age.

Certification of Military Service. Equivalent to Form DD-214; used when a veteran's original discharge record has been destroyed.

certified copy. A photocopy of a filed document (such as Form DD-214) in its entirety that is sworn to be a true copy by a court clerk or veteran service officer.

claimant. A veteran or his or her surviving spouse who applies for a pension or other benefit.

countable income. Regular, irregular, or nonrecurring (one-time basis) income. For example, salary, dividends, and interest are countable income.

DAV. Disabled American Veterans.

DD-214. After January 1, 1950, the form used by the military to document discharge from military service.

Dependency and Indemnity Compensation. Compensation paid for situations where a veteran died in service or died as a result of a service-connected disability or where a veteran rated totally disabled from a service-connected disability died from a non-service-connected condition.

DIC. Dependency and Indemnity Compensation.

disability. The inability to pursue an occupation because of a mental or physical impairment.

disability compensation. Payment to veterans who are disabled by injury or disease incurred or aggravated during active military service.

Disabled American Veterans. A veterans service organization composed of disabled veterans who provide assistance to veterans in obtaining benefits, such as pensions.

discharge record. Also known as Form DD-214 or WD AGO Form 53-55, a form indicating complete separation from military service.

eVetRecs. An online military personnel record request system offered by NARA. It is the preferred method for contacting the NPRC to request discharge records.

fiduciary. An individual authorized to make legal and financial decisions for another person.

general discharge. A type of discharge from the military for service members without a sufficiently meritorious military record to deserve an honorable discharge.

honorable discharge. A type of discharge from the military for service members who meet or exceed the required standards of duty performance and personal conduct.

house physician. A physician who visits residents living in an assisted living facility or nursing home.

Housebound pension. A VA pension available for individuals who have a permanent disability and cannot leave their homes without assistance.

improved death pension. The current VA pension available to surviving spouses and surviving dependent children of wartime service veterans; also referred to as Aid and Attendance pension or Housebound pension.

improved disability pension. The current VA pension available to wartime service veterans who have a non-service-connected disability; also referred to as Aid and Attendance pension or Housebound pension.

in the line of duty. Incurred or aggravated during a period of active military service; not the result of willful misconduct.

incontinence. Individuals who have had loss of bladder and/or bowel control.

informal claim. A written communication to the VA that a claimant intends to apply for pension benefits. All subsequent filings will be considered filed as of the date of the informal claim.

long-term-care insurance. Insurance that helps provide for the cost of long-term care. Long-term care insurance covers costs generally not paid by health insurance, Medicare, or Medicaid.

MAPR. Maximum annual pension rate.

maximum annual pension rate. The maximum annual amount one can receive for a VA pension. The VA has three levels of pension ranging from basic pension at the lowest level, Housebound pension at the next level, and Aid and Attendance pension at the highest level. To be deducted, medical expenses must exceed 5 percent of the annual amount paid for the basic pension.

Medicaid. A program sponsored by the federal government and administered by states that is intended to provide healthcare and health-related services to low-income individuals.

Medicare. A federal health insurance program for people aged sixty-five and older and for individuals with disabilities.

NACVSO. National Association of County Veteran Service Officers.

NARA. National Archives and Records Administration.

National Archives and Records Administration. An independent agency of the federal government charged with preserving and documenting government and historical records.

National Association of County Veteran Service Officers. An organization composed of county veteran service officers. Officers assist veterans, their dependents and survivors with VA claims, such as pensions.

National Personnel Records Center. The repository of millions of military personnel records, including health and medical records, of discharged and deceased veterans of all branches of the military during the twentieth century. National Personnel Records Center is located in St. Louis, Missouri.

net income. Gross countable income minus eligible expenses. (A common eligible expense is an unreimbursed medical expense.)

net worth. Assets minus debts. The market value of all interest and rights in any kind of property less mortgages or other claims against the property: the value of assets minus the value of debts. Net worth does not include the house you live in or a reasonable area of land it sits on or personal items you use like one vehicle, clothing, and furniture.

nonmedical home care. Services provided by nonmedical personnel. Examples include assistance with housekeeping, shopping, meal preparation, and activities of daily living.

non-service connected. Not caused by or aggravated in the line of duty in the active military.

NPRC. National Personnel Records Center.

nursing home. A residence for individuals who need the assistance of a registered nurse and/or physical, occupational, and speech rehabilitation services following an accident or illness; also known as a skilled nursing facility.

power of attorney. A legal instrument authorizing an individual (eighteen years or older) to act as the attorney or agent of the granter.

reserve duty. The status of members of the military who perform part-time duty as opposed to full-time (active duty) soldiers.

separation. Discharge or retirement of a veteran from military service.

service-connected disability. A veteran's disability caused by an illness or combat-related injury in the line of duty in the active military.

SSI. Supplemental Security Income.

Supplemental Security Income. A program managed by the Social Security Administration that makes monthly payments to people who have low income and few resources. Eligible individuals are aged sixty-five or older, blind, or disabled.

surviving spouse. The wife or husband of a deceased wartime service veteran.

VA. Department of Veterans Affairs.

VA file number. File number assigned by the VA if the veteran files a claim.

veteran service officer. An advocate for veterans and their dependents and survivors. Officers provide benefit counseling and help with claims, such as pensions.

Veterans of Foreign Wars of the United States. A veterans service organization whose members are former members of the military and who earned an overseas campaign medal. The VFW assists veterans with VA benefits, such as pensions, and lobbies Congress for better veteran healthcare and benefits.

VFW. Veterans of Foreign Wars of the United States.

VSO. Veteran service officer.

wartime service. Inclusive dates recognized by Congress for formal periods of war in which a veteran will have been considered as eligible for non-service-related pension benefits. (See chapter 3 for dates.)

WD AGO Form 53-55. Before January 1, 1950, the form number used by the military to document discharge or separation from military service.

willful misconduct. An act involving conscious wrongdoing or known illegal action.

INDEX

A

accrued benefits, 23, 79
active duty. *See also* active military service
  defined, 201
active military service
  eligibility before 1980, 9, 10
  eligibility after 1980, 9, 10
  civilian eligibility, 19-22
  eligible wars, 18-19
activities of daily living (ADLs)
  care needs of veteran or surviving spouse,
    17, 18
  defined, 201
  spouse performing veteran's care, 23
ADL. *See* activities of daily living (ADLs)
Aid and Attendance pension. *See also* formal
  claim; Housebound pension
  care-needs qualifications, 17
  care-needs requirements
    physician documentation of need for
      care (Form 21-2680), 53
    for surviving spouse, 10
    for veteran, 8-9
  defined, 201
  discharge records for pension, 39
  eligibility criteria
    for surviving spouse, 9-10
    for veteran, 8-9
  forms for claim application, 30
    sources for obtaining, 30, 51-52
    Web site for obtaining, 52
  improved death pension rates for surviving
    spouse, 27
  improved disability pension rates for
    veteran, 26
  long-term care insurance quotes and, 28

Aid and Attendance pension (*continued*)
  nursing home resident and, 17, 23
  origin of, 2
  physician examination (Form 21-2680)
    sample of completed form, 56-57
    tips for completing form, 53-55
  special circumstances, 22-23
  state of residency, filing requirement, 31
  statement in support of claim (Form 21-
    4138)
    care provider letter for support of claim,
      60
    sample of completed form, 59
    tips for completing form, 58
  surviving spouse application for pension
    (Form 21-534)
    sample of completed form, 83-90
    tips for completing form, 79-82
  veteran's application for pension
    (Form 21-526)
    sample of completed form, 65-78
    tips for completing form, 61-64
Aid and Attendance pension recipients
  free health benefits for veterans, 99
  free prescription medications for veterans,
    99
Alabama
  American Legion, 108
  Disabled American Veterans, 116
  National Association of County Veteran
    Service Officers, 115
  VA facilities, 132-133
  VFW, 125

Alaska
  American Legion, 108
  Disabled American Veterans, 116
  National Association of County Veteran
    Service Officers, 115
  VA facilities, 133
  VFW, 125
American Legion
  defined, 201
  offices, 108-114
American Samoa, VA facilities, 133
application forms, Aid and Attendance and
  Housebound pensions
  sources for obtaining, 30, 51-52
  Web site for obtaining, 52
Arizona
  American Legion, 108
  Disabled American Veterans, 116
  National Association of County Veteran
    Service Officers, 115
  VA facilities, 133-135
  VFW, 125
Arkansas
  American Legion, 108
  Disabled American Veterans, 116
  National Association of County Veteran
    Service Officers, 115
  VA facilities, 135
  VFW, 125
assets
  examples of, 16
  net worth and, 8, 9
    spending down to threshold, 16
assisted living facility
  care needs in, 8, 9
  defined, 201
  unreimbursed cost of, 25-26

B

bank safe deposit box, discharge record in, 41
bedridden status, Aid and Attendance pension
  care-need and, 17
blindness, Aid and Attendance pension care-
  need for, 17

C

California
  American Legion, 108
  Disabled American Veterans, 116
  National Association of County Veteran
    Service Officers, 115
  VA facilities, 135-139
  VFW, 125
care provider, support of claim for pensions, 30,
  58-60

caregiver
  defined, 201
  for surviving spouse, 10
  for veteran, 9
care-needs qualifications
  for Aid and Attendance pension, 17
  for Housebound pension, 18
care-needs requirements
  for Aid and Attendance pension, 53
  for Housebound pension, 53
  for surviving spouse, 10
  for veteran, 8-9
Certification of Military Service
  defined, 201
  equivalent to discharge record, 43
certified copy
  defined, 201
  of discharge record, 39
children, dependent, 26, 62, 81
claim application process, 29-31. *See also*
  Aid and Attendance pension; Housebound
  pension
  filing requirement, state of residency, 31
  forms required for
    sources for obtaining, 30, 51-52
    Web site for obtaining, 52
  hand-delivery of application, 31
  locating discharge record, 29
  supporting documents for, 30
claimant
  for Aid and Attendance and Housebound
    pensions, 17, 18
  defined, 202
Colorado
  American Legion, 108
  Disabled American Veterans, 117
  National Association of County Veteran
    Service Officers, 115
  VA facilities, 140-141
  VFW, 126
Connecticut
  American Legion, 108
  Disabled American Veterans, 117
  National Association of County Veteran
    Service Officers, 115
  VA facilities, 141
  VFW, 126
countable income
  defined, 11, 202
  examples of, 12
  exclusions from, 12-13
  unreimbursed medical expenses and, 91
county courthouse. *See also* National
  Association of County Veteran Service
  Officers (NACVSO)
    discharge record in, 41-42

D

DAV. *See* Disabled American Veterans (DAV)
DD-214. *See also* discharge record (separation document)
    defined, 202
death of veteran or spouse, accrued benefits for, 23
death pension, 79. *See also* Aid and Attendance pension; Housebound pension
    defined, 203
    improved rates for surviving spouse, 27
Delaware
    American Legion, 109
    Disabled American Veterans, 117
    National Association of County Veteran Service Officers, 115
    VA facilities, 141
    VFW, 126
Department of Veterans Affairs (VA)
    origin of, 5
    VA facilities, 132-186
    Web site for obtaining pension claim forms, 52
dependency and indemnity compensation (DIC) (Form 21-534), 79
    defined, 202
dependent
    defined, 26
    effect on Aid and Attendance and Housebound pension rates, 26
DIC. *See* dependency and indemnity compensation (DIC)
disability
    defined, 202
    eligibility requirement for pensions
        for surviving spouse, 10
        for veteran, 8
disability compensation
    defined, 202
    service-connected
        Aid and Attendance benefits for disabled spouse, 22-23, 188-189
        rates for 2009, 188
Disabled American Veterans (DAV)
    defined, 202
    offices, 116-124
discharge, honorable or general, 9, 10
    defined, 202
discharge record request
    in case of critical or terminal illness, 45
    for certified copy from NPRC, 42-49
    checking status of, 49
    sample of completed form (Standard Form 180), 46-47

discharge record (separation document)
    certified copy of, 31, 33, 39, 42, 97
    defined, 39, 202
    for informal claim, 33
    from Korean War to present (DD-214), 39
    locating, 29, 41-49
    reconstruction of, 43
    requesting from National Personnel Records Center (NPRC), 42
    sample, 40
    storage at county courthouses, 41-42
    from World War II (WD AGO Form 53-55), 39, 40
District of Columbia
    American Legion, 109
    Disabled American Veterans, 117
    National Association of County Veteran Service Officers, 115
    VA facilities, 142
    VFW, 126
divorce
    eligibility for VA pension benefits and, 23
    ineligibility for VA pensions and, 10

E

eligibility criteria for pensions
    for surviving spouse, 9-10
    for veteran, 8-9
Europe, VFW, 126
eVetRecs
    defined, 202
    signature verification form, 44-45
    Web site for discharge record request, 44
expenses, deducted from income, 13-14

F

fiduciary (power of attorney). *See also* power of attorney (fiduciary)
    defined, 202
Florida
    American Legion, 109
    Disabled American Veterans, 117
    National Association of County Veteran Service Officers, 115
    VA facilities, 142-145
    VFW, 126
formal claim. *See also* Aid and Attendance pension; Housebound pension; informal claim
    copy of informal claim with, 34
    forms for claim application, 30
        sources for obtaining, 30, 51-52
        Web site for obtaining, 52
    informal claim vs., 29
France, American Legion Dept Svc Ofcr, 109

G

general discharge
  defined, 202
  eligibility criteria for pensions
    for surviving spouse, 10
    for veteran, 9
Georgia
  American Legion, 109
  Disabled American Veterans, 118
  National Association of County Veteran
    Service Officers, 115
  VA facilities, 145-146
  VFW, 126
Guam, VA facilities, 146

H

Hawaii
  American Legion, 109
  Disabled American Veterans, 118
  National Association of County Veteran
    Service Officers, 115
  VA facilities, 146
  VFW, 126
health benefits, free. *See also* pharmacy benefits
  eligibility for, 99
health benefits application (Form 10-10EZ)
  sample of completed form, 101-103
  tips for completing form, 100
home, discharge record in, 41
home-care services, nonmedical
  for surviving spouse, 10
  for veteran, 8
honorable discharge. *See also* general discharge
  defined, 202
house physician
  defined, 203
  physician examination (Form 21-2680), 53
Housebound pension. *See also* Aid and
  Attendance pension; formal claim
  care-needs qualifications, 18
  care-needs requirements
    physician documentation of need for
      care (Form 21-2680), 53
    for surviving spouse, 10
    for veteran, 8-9
  defined, 203
  discharge records for pension, 39
  eligibility criteria
    for surviving spouse, 9-10
    for veteran, 8-9
  forms for claim application, 30
    sources for obtaining, 30, 51-52
    Web site for obtaining, 52
  improved death pension rates for surviving
    spouse, 27

Housebound pension (*continued*)
  improved disability pension rates for
    veteran, 26
  long-term care insurance quotes and, 28
  physician examination (Form 21-2680)
    sample of completed form, 56-57
    tips for completing form, 53-55
  special circumstances, 23
  state of residency, filing requirement, 31
  surviving spouse application for pension
    (Form 21-534)
    sample of completed form, 83-90
    tips for completing form, 79-82
  transportation services
    on physician examination form, 53
    unreimbursed medical expense, 13, 91
  veteran's application for pension (Form 21-
    526)
    sample of completed form, 65-78
    tips for completing form, 61-64
Housebound pension recipients
  free health benefits for veterans, 99
  free prescription medications for veterans,
    99

I

Idaho
  American Legion, 109
  Disabled American Veterans, 118
  National Association of County Veteran
    Service Officers, 115
  VA facilities, 147
  VFW, 126
Illinois
  American Legion, 109
  Disabled American Veterans, 118
  National Association of County Veteran
    Service Officers, 115
  VA facilities, 147-148
  VFW, 126
improved death pension
  defined, 203
  rates for surviving spouse, 27
improved disability pension
  defined, 203
  rates for wartime service veteran, 26
in the line of duty, defined, 203
incarceration, pension eligibility and, 23
income. *See also* countable income
  expenses deducted from, 13-14
  reporting, 11-12
incontinence
  defined, 203
  supplies, free health benefit for veterans, 99

Indiana
American Legion, 109
Disabled American Veterans, 118
National Association of County Veteran
Service Officers, 115
VA facilities, 148-149
VFW, 127
informal claim, 29, 33-37. *See also* formal claim
appointment of VSO as claimant's
representative (Form 21-22), 37
attachment to formal claim, 34
photocopy of discharge record for, 33
defined, 203
hand-delivery of form, 33
mail delivery of form, 33, 34
payment of pension benefits, retroactive, 34
purpose of, 29
statement in support of claim (Form 21-4138)
for surviving spouse, 36
for veteran, 35
time limit on filing formal claim, 34
vs. formal application, 29
Iowa
American Legion, 109
Disabled American Veterans, 118
National Association of County Veteran
Service Officers, 115
VA facilities, 149-150
VFW, 127

K

Kansas
American Legion, 110
Disabled American Veterans, 118
National Association of County Veteran
Service Officers, 115
VA facilities, 150-151
VFW, 127
Kentucky
American Legion, 110
Disabled American Veterans, 118
National Association of County Veteran
Service Officers, 115
VA facilities, 151-152
VFW, 127
Korean War, pension eligibility and, 19

L

Latin America/Caribbean, VFW, 127
long-term-care insurance. *See also* Aid and
Attendance pension; Housebound pension
defined, 203
long-term care, pension rate for, 25
look back, and net worth eligibility for pensions,
16

Louisiana
American Legion, 110
Disabled American Veterans, 119
National Association of County Veteran
Service Officers, 115
VA facilities, 152-153
VFW, 127

M

Maine
American Legion, 110
Disabled American Veterans, 119
National Association of County Veteran
service Officers, 115
VA facilities, 153
VFW, 127
MAPR. *See* maximum annual pension rate
(MAPR)
marriage, duration for spouse's pension
eligibility, 10
Maryland
American Legion, 110
Disabled American Veterans, 119
National Association of County Veteran
Service Officers, 115
VA facilities, 153-154
VFW, 127
Massachusetts
American Legion, 110
Disabled American Veterans, 119
National Association of County Veteran
Service Officers, 115
VA facilities, 154-155
VFW, 127
maximum annual pension rate (MAPR)
defined, 203
effect on net income, 13
Medicaid
defined, 203
nursing home resident, ineligible for, 23
medical expense report (Form 21-8416)
sample of completed form, 92-93
tips for completing form, 91
medical expenses, unreimbursed, 13-14, 25-26.
See also medical expense report (Form 21-8416)
Medicare. *See also* Medicaid
defined, 203
merchant marines, pension eligibility and, 20
Mexico, American Legion, 110
Michigan
American Legion, 110
Disabled American Veterans, 119
National Association of County Veteran
Service Officers, 115
VA Medical facilities, 155-156
VFW, 127

medals, replacement of, 43, 190-195
  request form (Standard Form 180)
    addresses to send completed form,
      193-195
    sample of completed form, 192
    tips for completing form, 191
military service. *See* active military service
Minnesota
  American Legion, 110
  Disabled American Veterans, 119
  National Association of County Veteran
    Service Officers, 115
  VA facilities, 157
  VFW, 128
Mississippi
  American Legion, 110
  Disabled American Veterans, 119
  National Association of County Veteran
    Service Officers, 115
  VA facilities, 157-158
  VFW, 128
Missouri
  American Legion, 110
  Disabled American Veterans, 120
  National Association of County Veteran
    Service Officers, 115
  VA facilities, 158-159
  VFW, 128
Montana
  American Legion, 111
  Disabled American Veterans, 120
  National Association of County Veteran
    Service Officers, 115
  VA facilities, 159-160
  VFW, 128

N

NACVSO. *See* National Association of County
  Veteran Service Officers (NACVSO)
NARA. *See* National Archives and Records
  Administration (NARA)
National Archives and Records Administration
  (NARA)
  defined, 204
  Web site to obtain Standard Form 180
    for requesting discharge records, 45
    for requesting replacement medals, 191
National Association of County Veteran Service
  Officers (NACVSO), 115
  defined, 204
  Web site for locating county VSOs, 41, 115
National Personnel Records Center (NPRC)
  defined, 204
  destruction of discharge records in 1973
    fire, 43-44

National Personnel Records Center (NPRC)
  (*continued*)
  discharge record request from, 42-49
    hiring an independent researcher, 49
    using eVetRecs Web site, 44-45
    using Standard Form 180, 45-47
    by writing a letter, 48
  request for replacement of service medals,
    43, 190-195
Nebraska
  American Legion, 111
  Disabled American Veterans, 120
  National Association of County Veteran
    Service Officers, 115
  VA facilities, 160
  VFW, 128
net income, 11-15
  annual limits for pension eligibility
    for surviving spouse, 9
    for veteran, 8
  calculation of
    example for surviving spouse, 14-15
    examples for veteran, 14
  defined, 11, 204
  effect on pension rates, 13, 25, 26
net worth
  assets contributing to, examples of, 16-17
  defined, 15, 204
  eligibility criteria for pensions
    for surviving spouse, 9
    for veteran, 8
  threshold for, 15-16
Nevada
  American Legion, 111
  Disabled American Veterans, 120
  National Association of County Veteran
    Service Officers, 115
  VA facilities, 161
  VFW, 128
New Hampshire
  American Legion, 111
  Disabled American Veterans, 120
  National Association of County Veteran
    Service Officers, 115
  VA facilities, 161-162
  VFW, 128
New Jersey
  American Legion, 111
  Disabled American Veterans, 120
  National Association of County Veteran
    Service Officers, 115
  VA facilities, 162-163
  VFW, 128

New Mexico
 American Legion, 111
 Disabled American Veterans, 120
 National Association of County Veteran
  Service Officers, 115
 VA facilities, 163-164
 VFW, 128
New York
 American Legion, 111
 Disabled American Veterans, 121
 National Association of County Veteran
  Service Officers, 115
 VA facilities, 164-167
 VFW, 129
nonmedical home care
 defined, 204
 as medical expense, 13, 25-26
non-service-connected. *See also* non-service-
 connected disability of veteran
 defined, 204
non-service-connected disability of veteran
 eligibility criteria for pensions
  for surviving spouse, 10
  for veteran, 8
North Carolina
 American Legion, 111
 Disabled American Veterans, 121
 National Association of County Veteran
  Service Officers, 115
 VA facilities, 167-168
 VFW, 129
North Dakota
 American Legion, 111
 Disabled American Veterans, 121
 National Association of County Veteran
  Service Officers, 115
 VA facilities, 168
 VFW, 129
NPRC. *See* National Personnel Records Center
 (NPRC)
nursing home. *See also* nursing home resident
 defined, 204
nursing home resident
 Aid and Attendance pension eligibility and,
  17, 23

O

Ohio
 American Legion, 112
 Disabled American Veterans, 121
 National Association of County Veteran
  Service Officers, 115
 VA facilities, 169-170
 VFW, 129

Oklahoma
 American Legion, 112
 Disabled American Veterans, 121
 National Association of County Veteran
  Service Officers, 115
 VA facilities, 170-171
 VFW, 129
Oregon
 American Legion, 112
 Disabled American Veterans, 121
 National Association of County Veteran
  Service Officers, 115
 VA facilities, 171-172
 VFW, 129

P

Pacific Areas, VFW, 129
Pennsylvania
 American Legion, 112
 Disabled American Veterans, 122
 National Association of County Veteran
  Service Officers, 115
 VA facilities, 172-175
 VFW, 130
pension application forms
 sources for obtaining, 30, 51-52
 Web site for obtaining, 52
pension rates. *See also* Aid and Attendance
 pension; Housebound pension
 improved, for surviving spouses, 27
 improved, for veterans, 26
 net income basis for, 13
 Web site for obtaining, 27
pensions. *See* Aid and Attendance pension;
 Housebound pension
pensions and benefits
 historical background on, 1-5
Persian Gulf War, pension eligibility and, 19
pharmacy benefits
 application form (Form 10-10EZ)
  sample of completed form, 101-103
  tips for completing form for discounted
   prescriptions, 189-190
  tips for completing form for free
   prescriptions, 100
 eligibility for
  discounted prescriptions, 189
  free prescriptions, 99
 Web site for obtaining application forms
  for discounted prescription
   medications, 189
  for free prescription medications, 99
Philippines, American Legion, 112
physician, documentation of need for caregiver
 services. *See* eligibility criteria for pensions

physician examination (Form 21-2680)
  for Aid and Attendance and Housebound
    pensions, 53-57
  sample of completed form, 56-57
  tips for completing form, 53-55
power of attorney (fiduciary)
  attachment to pension application, 97
  defined, 204
  investigation of, 53
prescription medications. *See* pharmacy benefits
prison, pension eligibility and, 23
Puerto Rico
  American Legion, 113
  Disabled American Veterans, 122
  VFW, 130

R

reserve duty
  defined, 204
  proof of, 97
Rhode Island
  American Legion, 113
  Disabled American Veterans, 122
  National Association of County Veteran
    Service Officers, 115
  VA facilities, 175
  VFW, 130

S

Separation. *See also* discharge record (separation
  documents)
  defined, 204
service medals, awards, and decorations,
  replacement of. *See* medals, replacement of
service-connected disability. *See also* service-
  connected disability compensation
  defined, 205
service-connected disability compensation
  Aid and Attendance benefits for disabled
    spouse, 22-23, 188
  compensation rates for 2009, 188
signature verification form. *See* eVetRecs
South Carolina
  American Legion, 113
  Disabled American Veterans, 122
  National Association of County Veteran
    Service Officers, 115
  VA facilities, 175
  VFW, 130
South Dakota
  American Legion, 113
  Disabled American Veterans, 122
  National Association of County Veteran
    Service Officers, 115
  VA facilities, 176
  VFW, 130

spouse. *See* surviving spouse
SSI. *See* Supplemental Security Income (SSI)
Standard Form 180 (SF 180). *See* National
  Archives and Records Administration
  (NARA)
state of residency, for pension claim. *See* Aid
  and Attendance pension; Housebound
  pension
Statement in Support of Claim (Form 21-4138)
  for formal claim
    sample completed form, 59
  for informal claim
    sample completed form for surviving
      spouse, 36
    sample completed form for veteran, 35
Supplemental Security Income (SSI)
  defined, 205
  exclusion from countable income, 12
surviving spouse. *See also* Aid and Attendance
  pension; Housebound pension
  defined, 205

T

Tennessee
  American Legion, 113
  Disabled American Veterans, 122
  National Association of County Veteran
    Service Officers, 115
  VA facilities, 176-177
  VFW, 130
Texas
  American Legion, 113
  Disabled American Veterans, 123
  National Association of County Veteran
    Service Officers, 115
  VA facilities, 177-181
  VFW, 131
threshold, for net worth, 15-16
transportation services. *See* Housebound
  pension

U

unreimbursed medical expenses. *See* medical
  expenses, unreimbursed
Utah
  American Legion, 113
  Disabled American Veterans, 123
  National Association of County Veteran
    Service Officers, 115
  VA facilities, 181
  VFW, 131

V

VA. *See* Department of Veterans Affairs (VA)
VA file number
  defined, 205
  on pension application forms
    for surviving spouse, 79, 95
    for veteran, 61, 95
VA facilities, 132-186
Vermont
  American Legion, 113
  Disabled American Veterans, 123
  National Association of County Veteran
    Service Officers, 115
  VA facilities, 181-182
  VFW, 131
veteran application for pensions (Form 21-526).
  See Aid and Attendance pension; Housebound
  pension
veteran service officer (VSO)
  answering claimant's questions
    for completing claim forms, 51
    for health and pharmacy benefits, 100
    for informal claim, 34
    for special circumstances, 22-23
  appointment as claimant's representative to
    VA (Form 21-22)
    sample of completed form, formal
      claim, 96
    sample of completed form, informal
      claim, 37
    tips for completing form, 95
  assistance with pension claim, checking
    forms for errors, 31
  authorization to represent and assist you,
    30, 33-34
  defined, 205
  locating, at a veterans service organization
    American Legion, 108-114
    county (NACVSO), 115
    DAV, 116-124
    VFW, 125-131
  representation of claimant to VA, 30, 37
  selection of, 94
Veterans Administration. *See* Department of
  Veterans Affairs (VA)
Veterans of Foreign Wars of the United States
  (VFW),
  defined, 205
  offices, 125-131
veterans service organization, 94
VFW. *See* Veterans of Foreign Wars of the
  United States (VFW)
Vietnam War, pension eligibility and, 19

Virginia
  American Legion, 113
  Disabled American Veterans, 123
  National Association of County Veteran
    Service Officers, 115
  VA facilities, 182
  VFW, 131
vision loss. *See* blindness
VSO. *See* veteran service officer (VSO)

W

WAAC. *See* Women's Army Auxiliary Corps
  (WAAC)
wartime service. *See also* active military service
  defined, 205
wartime service veteran. *See* veteran
Washington
  American Legion, 113
  Disabled American Veterans, 123
  National Association of County Veteran
    Service Officers, 115
  VA facilities, 182-183
  VFW, 131
WASPS. *See* Women's Air Force Service Pilots
  (WASPS)
WD AGO Form 53-55. *See also* discharge record
  (separation document)
  defined, 205
Web sites
  eVetRecs, for requesting discharge record,
    44
  NACVSO, for locating county veteran
    service officers, 41, 115
  NARA, for obtaining Standard Form 180
    to request discharge records, 45
    to request replacement medals, 191
  for obtaining pension forms, 52
  for pension rates, 27
  prescription medications, for obtaining
    application form
    for free medications, 99
    for discounted medications, 189
West Virginia
  American Legion, 114
  Disabled American Veterans, 123
  National Association of County Veteran
    Service Officers, 115
  VA facilities, 183-184
  VFW, 131
willful misconduct
  defined, 205
  ineligibility for pensions
    for surviving spouse, 10
    for veteran, 9

Wisconsin
    American Legion, 114
    Disabled American Veterans, 123
    National Association of County Veteran
      Service Officers, 115
    VA facilities, 184-185
    VFW, 131
Women's Air Force Service Pilots (WASPS),
    pension eligibility and, 19
Women's Army Auxiliary Corps (WAAC),
    pension eligibility and, 19
World War I service
    bonus march of 1932, 3
    pension eligibility and, 18-19

World War II service
    pension eligibility and, 19
    WD AGO Form 53-55, discharge record,
      39, 40
Wyoming
    American Legion, 114
    Disabled American Veterans, 124
    National Association of County Veteran
      Service Officers, 115
    VA facilities, 185-186
    VFW, 131

ABOUT THE AUTHOR

Joseph Scott McCarthy is a veteran advocate with more than eight years' experience working with Aid and Attendance and Housebound pensions. With the help of veteran service officers at the American Legion, county veteran service officers, and VA personnel, he has educated and guided thousands of veterans and their surviving spouses through the VA pension process. Joe has given numerous presentations explaining VA pension benefits to veterans' organizations, assisted living and skilled nursing facilities, hospital staff, social workers' organizations, and lawyers who work with veterans. In 2005, he earned the Western Pennsylvania American Legion annual award for "selfless service" to veterans.

He has been a healthcare professional for twenty-nine years in Pennsylvania. Eleven of those years have been in long-term care marketing and administration for national and regional assisted living, independent living, and skilled nursing facilities. Joe is a registered respiratory therapist and for sixteen years, he was the director of cardiopulmonary services at the University of Pittsburgh Medical Center. Joe is the president of McCarthy LTC Consulting, LLC.

He is a graduate of the University of Pittsburgh with a bachelor of science degree in biology and a master of business administration degree. He received his respiratory therapy education at Northwestern University Medical School.

ORDER INFORMATION

CHECKS *for* VETS

Web orders:

www.checksforvets.com.

Inquiries for bulk order discounts:

E-mail address:

orders@checksforvets.com

Phone toll free:

877-CHX-VETS (877-249-8387)

Mailing address:

Jourda Publishing

511 Towne Square Way

Pittsburgh, PA 15227

Note: The author or the publisher cannot accept phone calls or mail for any questions about completing application forms for Aid and Attendance pensions or Housebound pensions. Consult your local veterans service officer or VA office for questions related to pension application forms.

CPSIA information can be obtained at www.ICGtesting.com
Printed in the USA
BVOW060058170312

285392BV00002B/1/P

9 780982 035122